Between Pets and People

Between

The Importance of

Pets and

Animal Companionship

People

Alan Beck &
Aaron Katcher

Purdue University Press / West Lafayette, Indiana

∞ The paper used in this book meets the minimum requirements of
American National Standard for Information Sciences—Permanence of
Paper for Printed Library Materials, ANSI Z39.48-1992.

Cover Photo by Mary Bloom
Design by Chiquita Babb
Printed in the United States of America

Library of Congress Cataloging-in-Publication Data

Beck, Alan M.
    Between pets and people : the importance of animal companionship /
Alan Beck and Aaron Katcher. — Rev. ed.
        p.   cm.
    Includes bibliographical references and index.
    ISBN 1-55753-077-7 (paper : alk paper)
    1. Pets—Therapeutic use. 2. Pets—Social aspects. I. Katcher,
Aaron Honori. II. Title.
RM931.A65B43 1996
615.8'515—dc20   96-6044
                                                          CIP

This book is dedicated by Alan Beck to Gail Beck, wife and best friend; to Andrea and Gillian, great children; and to Howard and Tom, new family; and by Aaron Katcher to Anne Menard, and to Ananda, Scott, Paul, Jonathan, and Ariana.

Contents

Foreword

Humans have been domesticating animals for thousands of years, and the domestication of animals marks one of the great milestones in the development of human civilization. Although animals were first kept for purely utilitarian purposes—to provide food and clothing—this has led to the astonishing popularity of the household pet.

Each year Americans spend billions of dollars on their pets, providing them with everything from rhinestone collars to catnip mice and dog biscuits. Why are we willing to spend such sums on living beings that have little or no utilitarian value and bring us little or no status? This difficult question has many answers, all explored in this splendid and fascinating book.

Surely the most important role our pets play in our lives is that they love us. No person is too old or ugly or poor or disabled to win the love of a pet—they love us uncritically and without reserve. Such love has actually been shown to have a physical benefit to our species, in that many of the illnesses that are exacerbated by loneliness, illnesses such as heart disease and certain kinds of cancer, can be mitigated by the love of an animal, just as they can be mitigated by human love. A now famous study conducted some years ago by one of the authors of this book revealed the astonishing fact that the mortality rate of heart patients with pets was one-third that of patients without pets.

Not surprisingly, many of us admit our pets into the most intimate areas of our lives. We are not in the least embarrassed when a dog sees us in the shower or overhears an argument. In this, a companion animal provides an intimacy that exceeds any we may experience with virtually any other human being, including our spouses and children; the intimacy is on a par with that of mother and newborn infant, or of our own skins. A dear friend once expressed this feeling beautifully. She had been resting on her couch with her dog, and as she looked into his eyes, it seemed to her that she and he could give each other transfusions if necessary, that their very blood must be compatible.

Paradoxically, our society often does not permit us to acknowledge this intimacy. In the United States, at least, animals are defined as objects. Seen as hazardous to health, they must be crated to ride on public transportation and are never allowed in restaurants (whereas in Europe, dogs are not only allowed on trains and subways but also into certain restaurants, where they are often preferred above children and may be served special meals). When a beloved companion animal dies, we are not expected to mourn for it (yet we might be encouraged to buy a plot in a pet cemetery). What's more, this intimacy can be terminated at any moment at the will of the owner. Why the schizophrenic gap?

Most people that I encounter on my book tours throughout the country are fully as sensitive to their pets as their pets must be to them. Even so, many, if not most, people are under the impression that their affection for their pets is somehow shameful, or that the strength of their feeling is shameful. Many discussions of a pet begin with a disclaimer or an apology—"I know you'll think I'm crazy," or "I know I shouldn't say this." But I believe that the people who approach me with stories of their pets are excellent observers who know as much that is important about animals as anyone, including many scientists, may ever know, especially if the scientists insist on treating animals as mere objects. Birds and mammals obviously think, and they also feel emotions.

This above all makes pets interesting and makes the human-pet relationship satisfying. They mirror us and we mirror them. As they benefit our physical and emotional health, so we benefit theirs. And if we do things in the presence of our pets that we would not do in the presence of other people, so they do things in our presence that they would not do in the presence of other members of their species. A dog of ours, for instance, eats avidly when alone with us but sparingly or not at all when with her colleagues, probably because in our household she is Dog Four and must demonstrate that she fully understands her lowly status when in the company of her social superiors, Dogs One, Two, and Three.

All this allows us to enter the innermost lives of our pets and companion animals as they enter ours. No act can be more pleasurable or rewarding, and in terms of our future health and happiness, no subject could be a more important one for study. Here then is a book that explores the cross-species relationship in all its ramifications. No longer are pets seen as one kind of thing and people as another, and no longer are pets studied in a vastly different way than people are studied. We belong together, our species and theirs. We should be viewed together. And in this fine book, we are.

—*Elizabeth Marshall Thomas*

Preface

We know the cost of our pets. Americans own more than 500 million pet creatures—dogs, cats, birds, horses, small mammals, reptiles, and fish. They spend more than $14 billion a year to feed and care for this menagerie and another $5 billion on accessories such as leashes, collars, and cages. Yet we are just beginning to realize the benefits of being with pets and the nature of the relationship between people and their pets.

Our interest in this subject grew out of a study of patients with severe coronary artery disease (discussed in chapter 1). Patients with pets had a significantly greater survival rate during the first year after their discharge from the hospital. At that time it seemed almost impossible that an activity as ordinary as keeping a pet could influence the course of a deadly disease. It was only later, when the investigators knew more about the ways in which pets change their owners' lives, that the life-preserving effect of pets became believable.

This study was followed by many others, which were summarized in the first edition of this book. Since then, our work has stimulated an explosive growth of the literature on how people interact with animals and the health benefits of that interaction. This new edition of *Between Pets and People* incorporates the insights of more than ten years of new information. Now we can conclude that to be healthy, it is necessary to make contact with other kinds of living things. If human beings are going to reach their full potential for health, they must not limit their companions to their own kind. If people are to come to terms with their own animal nature, they must feel the rest of the living world around them. We do mean this metaphorically, saying that living close to nature is in some aesthetic or moral way good. It is also a statement of fact established by solid research that has demonstrated that an activity as simple as keeping pets can protect our health from threats such as heart disease and hypertension, can increase our life expectancy, can help protect us from those physical and mental disorders that loneliness and isolation bring in their wake. Touching the fur of a dog or cat can undo the stress of competitive living and thereby lower blood pressure. Watching the undulant colors of fish swimming in a tank is as effective a way of relaxing as the most mannered Eastern meditative technique. The intimacy that people feel as they stroke a pet while talking to it and to themselves is a protective armor against much of the pain of living. Few human beings can give this kind of protection with such unvarying constancy.

The information that will be presented in this book was derived from a concerted study of how people and companion animals interact that was carried out by the authors and their colleagues at the Veterinary School of the University of Pennsylvania. They brought together scholars from many disciplines within the university to examine the meaning of animal companionship. At that time, there were no controlled observational studies of people interacting with pets or any reports of the impact of pets on objective measures of health. (Of course, there were many studies of pets as a source of disease, but hardly any information suggesting they could be a source of health.)

The interest in pets and health at that time was largely a result of the work of three scientists—Boris Levinson and Samuel and Elizabeth Corson. Levinson was a child psychologist who used his own pet dog, Jingles, as a cotherapist. Over the years he wrote a series of clinical papers and books exploring the value of pets in treatment and in normal human development. Samuel Corson is an experimental psychologist whose animal laboratory was located on the grounds of a mental hospital. He noted the patients' interest in his dogs, and with his wife, Elizabeth, conducted the first clinical trial using pets as part of psychiatric treatment. In contrast to this therapeutic interest, our research focused on what pets did for ordinary people or what actually happened when normal people and normal cats and dogs shared the same home.

Using the research techniques developed by ethologists to study animals in the wild, we observed people and pets in parks, homes, and clinic waiting rooms. Behavioral observation was combined with physiological measurement of heart rate and blood pressure, with epidemiological techniques for studying health and disease, and with the methods of anthropology and psychiatry. This work created a new field of scientific inquiry. Previously biologists and psychologists had separated people and animals in research, studying animals in one kind of laboratory and people in another. Ethologists had studied wild species, and anthropologists had studied totem animals in primitive tribes. Psychiatrists —even though Freud was a great lover of dogs—concentrated on animal phobias and animals in dreams, but not on animals in their patients' homes. With our students we focused on the ordinary and mundane events that occur between people and pets right here in American homes. What followed from these investigations was a burst of new knowledge about both people and animals. In six years there were more than thirty publications from the University of Pennsylvania describing this new field.

Ideas are never captives of any one person or institution, and what was taking place at the University of Pennsylvania was also occurring at other universities in the United States and at several research centers in Europe. In 1981 the University of Pennsylvania hosted an international conference on the human/companion animal bond at which fifty-four new research papers on companion animals were presented. This body of information, which was edited by the authors of this book under the title *New Perspectives on Our Lives with*

Companion Animals, is the largest collection of scientific information in this field. These research data made a great contribution to the first edition of this book. However, in the thirteen years since the first publication of *Between Pets and People,* there have been eight annual conferences sponsored by the Delta Society and five international conferences on people and animals. The rich body of research presented at these meetings and reported in scientific journals has added greatly to our knowledge and necessitated revision of our earlier work.

The scope of studies on companion animals, ecology, and public health is so broad that much of our education has come from interacting with other professionals in these fields. There are many individuals who aided us in writing this book, though some did not consciously know it. Their continued friendship contributed to ideas that we developed over the years. They listened, instructed, suggested, and criticized because they share, with Dr. Beck, the notion that trying to understand our world is great fun. Specifically, these people are Drs. Edwin Gould, Richard Vogl, and Charles Southwick, who contributed to Beck's basic knowledge in the sciences and to his career. Hildy Rubin, Dooley Worth, Honey Loring, Michael Fox, Peter Borchelt, and Jill Bressler all worked with Beck on projects that developed data used in this book and were important friends. Alan Ternes has also been a particularly effective gadfly to Beck's thought processes, for which he is grateful. Caroline Stevens suggested many specific ideas for this book, and we have truly benefited from her important insights. In recent years Dr. Katcher has had the privilege of working with Kathleen Dunn and James Serpell and has always profited from the enlightened leadership that Andrew Rowan has given this field.

Among the rewards of working in a new but rapidly expanding field of knowledge are the friendships and sense of common purpose that develop within a group that is still small enough to meet in the living room of a Philadelphia town house. We owe a great deal to our colleagues, who have contributed so much—this book is as much theirs as our own. We were privileged to express some of that indebtedness when we presented an award to Levinson and Samuel and Elizabeth Corson at a 1981 conference. These three wise and gentle scholars have drawn serious attention to the therapeutic potential of animals. Two other friends—Leo Bustad, dean of the College of Veterinary Medicine, Washington State University; and Dr. Michael McCulloch, a psychiatrist in Portland, Oregon—have tirelessly and skillfully worked within the veterinary profession to create a climate that will encourage the study of human-animal relationships and find it a place within the veterinary-school curriculum. They were also instrumental in founding the Delta Society, a scholarly organization that has cemented relationships among scientists of many disciplines who are studying pets and people.

Beck and Katcher were brought together through the activity of two remarkable groups of people. Katcher would not have thought of studying the impact of pets on health were it not for his association with Dr. James Lynch, professor of psychiatry at the University of Maryland School of Medicine. Their decision to study the impact of social conditions on heart disease brought Erika Friedmann, then a graduate student of biology at the University of Pennsylvania, to Baltimore to conduct that research for her doctoral dissertation. On finding that pets do help people survive heart disease, Katcher went to the Veterinary School at the University of Pennsylvania to talk about research. There, Dean Robert Marshak and Dr. Leon Weiss, chairman of the Department of Animal Biology, persuasively urged Katcher to apply for a grant from the National Institutes of Health to pursue studies of companion animals. Marshak and Weiss were also the moving forces who brought Beck to the University of Pennsylvania to continue his own research in human-animal relationships. Friedmann and Lynch have always provided intellectual stimulation and friendly support throughout all of the years that we worked in this field.

In 1990, Beck left the University of Pennsylvania to become the Dorothy N. McAllister Professor of Animal Ecology and to head the Center for Applied Ethology and Human-Animal Interaction at the School of Veterinary Medicine of Purdue University. There he directs an extensive curriculum on the social significance of animals and actively pursues his research on interactions between people and animals. Beck's later studies have benefited from the collaboration and insights of Larry and Nita Glickman, Gary Patronek, Gail Melson, Jack Albright, Lilly-Marlene Russow, Peter Waser, and Erich Klinghammer at Purdue University. The administrative support and skills of Dean Hugh Lewis, Alan Rebar, and Ralph Richardson greatly facilitated his accomplishments at Purdue. Activities were initially supported by the generosity of Dorothy N. McAllister and Henry Sakowitz.

Katcher continues some work at the University of Pennsylvania Veterinary School, but most of his time is spent with research into the value of animal-assisted therapy with severely disturbed children in residential treatment at the Devereux Foundation. His research reflects the commitment of the Devereux Foundation to animal-assisted therapy and would not have been possible without the active support of Leonard Green and the close collaboration of Gregory Wilkins. His work has also profited from the long experience of Sam Ross at Green Chimneys and the encouragement of Susan Cohen of the Animal Medical Center.

Last, we owe a great debt to the thousands of pet owners and their animals who were willing to talk to us and put up with being photographed and measured.*

---

*Fictitious names and place locations are used throughout this book to protect the privacy of our patients, clients, and subjects.

Between Pets and People

One

Pets, Life, and Health

Is it possible that a dog leaping and barking as you return from work or a cat cushioned in your lap can alter the course of heart disease? And if the animals we live with can have such an effect on our health, how could the medical profession have ignored the value of animal companions for so long? The two phenomena—pets and heart disease—seem too far apart to be related. One is part of the pleasant trivia of human existence, like fireplaces, sunsets, slippers, the evening newspaper, a good movie, an evening out with friends; the other is part of the reality of life and death, part of the drama of existence. Yet as we found out, pets have a definite, positive effect on human health. This was first demonstrated in a study of heart disease carried out at the University of Maryland from 1977 to 1979.

THE HEART DISEASE STUDY

It is certainly hard to ask a physician to believe that a heart patient's pet may be critical for his recovery from the heart attack that nearly resulted in his death. However, until recently doctors did not believe that loneliness could be lethal. Yet the evidence about the significance of marriage and other forms of social support for longevity and health has been around for a century. Between the ages of thirty-five and fifty, the years in which premature death from heart disease becomes too common in men, divorced men have a death rate more than twice that of married men. For hypertension, the death rate is almost three times greater among divorced men in the fourth and fifth decades of life. There is a similar but slightly smaller increase in vulnerability to heart disease in divorced, single, and widowed women.

A similarly high death rate among single, widowed, and divorced men and women is found in the statistics for another great killer—cancer. For causes of death that are related to behavior, such as alcoholism, accidental death, suicide, and homicide, the death rate among single people may be up to ten times greater than that of married people.

Much of this epidemiological evidence linking loneliness to disease and death can be found in James Lynch's book *The Broken Heart: The Medical Consequences of Loneliness*, which was published when Aaron Katcher, James Lynch, and Erika Friedmann were planning the heart disease study. Friedmann had worked with Katcher since she (and her sheep dog, Kerri) had sat in on his freshman seminar on emotions and health. She was going to study social conditions and heart disease at the University of Maryland, where Lynch was studying the emotional responses of patients in the coronary-care unit. Because of the statistics suggesting the importance of marriage to health and longevity, we expected to find marriage playing a large role in determining survival after a heart attack. Other social factors related to companionship were expected to play lesser but supporting roles.

Our study was designed very thoroughly. We planned to look at every social variable known to be associated with mortality from heart disease: income (more money equals better health); the kind of neighborhood the patients lived in; and social encounters (the number of friends and relatives who were accessible to the patient). We accumulated data on where our patients were born, where they spent their lives (people born in rural areas or who stay put have a greater life expectancy than people who are born in the city or who move about frequently), and how frequently there were changes in critical areas of life and work (high frequency of change is associated with greater probability of illness). Last, we included a measure of mood, because depression is associated with increased vulnerability to illness.

The study began in 1977, and Friedmann worked in wards where sudden death and resurrection were commonplace events. She interviewed patients and recorded answers. There was extensive follow-up. Patients were given preaddressed postcards to write to us at monthly intervals, telling us what they were doing, where they were going, whom they were seeing, and generally how they were feeling. Patients who did not write were called and interviewed. We kept track of the patients' charts and recorded physician visits and, inevitably, deaths.

Of the ninety-two patients, fourteen died within one year. At the end of the year, when the data on every patient were recorded, we tabulated the differences between those who lived and those who died. Some answers about the importance of human contact emerged, as we had predicted; but quite unexpectedly, we determined that man's best friend was the dog—as well as the cat, the chicken, the horse, and the iguana. The data were displayed in a simple table.

	Pets	No Pets	Total
Living	50	28	78
Dead	3	11	14
Total	53	39	92

The mortality rate among people with pets seemed to be one-third that of patients without pets. We greeted this evidence with disbelief. "What, you have severe chest pain? Pat your dog three times and call me in the morning!" The finding was a joke come true, and we began an immediate attack, checking for clerical errors in preparing the data and for mistakes in the computer analysis.

When no mistakes were found, we looked for other explanations that could alter the interpretation of the data. Perhaps we were looking at an effect of exercise on coronary-artery disease. The protective effect of pets might have been a result of the extra exercise gained by walking dogs. We tabulated the results again but this time excluded patients with dogs from the study.

	Pets (no dogs)	No Pets	Total
Living	10	28	38
Dead	0	11	11
Total	10	39	49

The results were the same. The cats, gerbils, parakeets, chickens, iguanas, fish, rabbits, and all the other animals had the same effect as dogs.

The next question was more difficult to answer. Perhaps, we speculated, pets were only a *marker* of good health, their presence indicating that the patient had had less severe heart disease before this recent episode of illness. These people would be the ones most likely to have the energy and the inclination to keep pets. To answer this question, we had to measure the severity of the patients' coronary-artery disease at the start of the study. If only the healthier patients had pets at that time, we would have to conclude that both the ability to keep pets and survival were related to better health; or in other words, the likelihood of keeping pets was an effect, not a cause, of better health.

Using medical data from the patients' files, Friedmann constructed an index of the severity of their heart disease. A computer program combined this index with data about pet ownership to estimate how much influence pets had on survival when the severity of the illness was taken into account. The analysis determined that having a pet did indeed improve a patient's chances of surviving and did in some way help the patient to be healthier. Pets were cause, not effect. The analysis also told us how much influence a pet could have on a patient's chances of survival. For the patients in this study, having a high score on the severity-of-heart-disease index (severe heart disease) increased the probability of dying by 20 percent. Having a pet could *decrease* the probability of dying by about 3 percent. Three percent might seem to be a small amount of protection, but with this type of statistical analysis (known technically as multivariate analysis), most social factors that influence health have this same level of predictive strength. In reality, if pets had a stronger statistical effect, we would have been more rather than less suspicious.

After all, pets are not a "miracle" drug like penicillin, chicken soup, Prozac, vitamin C, or garlic. Like any other healthy component of our lifestyles, they make a small but significant contribution to our health. Keeping a pet will not completely reverse the effect of thirty or forty years of too much eating and smoking and too little exercise and relaxation. All the little things we do to keep ourselves healthier— eating in moderation, keeping our family together, relaxing effectively, staying away from tobacco, drinking in moderation, and resisting the cultural impetus to constant change —have small positive influences that help, but they fall far short of a cure. Abstemious joggers who are loved by their families drop dead on occasion, while obese, frequently divorced libertines live on.

Even if pets cannot actually ward off heart disease in the way that garlic was once thought to ward off vampires, their effect may be greater than the 3-percent figure might suggest. There are more than a million people who die of heart disease each year. A 3-percent effect could, in any one year, result in a savings of thirty thousand lives—not a bad record for a public-health measure that almost half the country adopts voluntarily with no thought of the health benefit.

Satisfied at last that having pets did improve our patients' survival chances, we then examined the importance of marriage to the health of these patients. Was the pet simply a solace for those who were single? In our study, most pet owners were married. This is understandable, since it is easier to raise a pet if you have some help. However, the protective effect of the presence of a pet was just as strong among married patients as among single patients, and in this subject group the married did not survive any more frequently than the single. The data suggested that pets do not just substitute for human relationships; they complement and add to them, giving a special and unique dimension to human life.

With this observation that pets could have a strong influence on the course of serious disease, we had fallen into an area where people's common sense and scientific medicine were worlds apart. In 1980 people knew that friends, family, community, religion, the pleasures of a country walk, pets, gardens, and time spent in contemplation or meditation were good for you. Medicine, however, was still invested in technology, drugs, heroic surgery, and blitzkrieg treatment that may have prolonged life but did not respect the quality of life. Since that time, medicine has recognized that technology is not always the answer. Many hospitals help patients die with dignity and with concern for the quality of the last days instead of the number of days. Some of the same institutions have relaxed visiting hours, letting family, children, and even pets visit more liberally. Hospitalized premature infants now gain weight faster because they are being held by their mothers instead of lying in plastic isolettes. The *Journal of the American Medical Association* has reported that people who live alone or lack a confidant die earlier than patients with social support. The National Institutes of Health issued guidelines to physicians suggesting that meditation and relaxation may be as effective as drugs in treating early hypertension.

At the same time that traditional medicine was beginning to acknowledge the importance of the mind and the environment in health and disease, we and our colleagues were able to extend our knowledge about the importance of animals and other living things for our health and emotional balance. After the initial heart disease study, more and more evidence began to surface.

Almost everybody with a pet talks to it as if it were a person, and the way people talk to cats, dogs, and birds resembles the way we talk to infants.

While talking to people usually raises blood pressure, sometimes to very high levels, the touch-talk dialogue we establish with pets reduces stress and lowers blood pressure.

Just having a pet in a room makes people feel safer and reduces blood pressure.

Looking at an aquarium can be as effective as hypnosis in reducing the anxiety and discomfort of patients undergoing dental surgery.

Even the sight of a park and trees through a hospital window can be good medicine, decreasing pain and leading to earlier recovery.

People with pets make fewer doctor visits.

Pets can coax smiles and words out of socially withdrawn institutionalized patients of all ages.

Pets can make psychotherapy progress faster. In children, carefully controlled studies have shown that contact with pets and nature can reduce the symptoms of attention deficit hyperactivity disorder.

All of these findings were important and demonstrated that pets had the power to influence health, but for us the most important research has been published within the past five years. In 1992 an Australian cardiologist published a report on five thousand relatively healthy people who were seen at a clinic designed to help people reduce their risk of contracting heart disease. This rigorous study found that people with pets had lower blood fat levels (lower cholesterol and lower triglycerides) and lower blood pressure than people without pets. Importantly, there were no differences in their health habits, including fat in the diet, exercise, or smoking. There were some differences in the results between men and women and between older and younger subjects, and fractional differences in blood pressure and blood fat levels were not large, ranging between 2 percent and 12 percent. Considering that 60 percent of Australians own pets, the public-health implications of these findings were highly significant. Then in 1995 we had the pleasure of hearing Friedmann describe how she had confirmed the results of the original heart disease study with a new group of patients. In this most recent research, she drew her subjects from a national study of patients who had recovered from a myocardial infarction (heart attack) but had irregular heartbeats originating from the damaged ventricle. Because of this kind of dangerous arrhythmia, these patients were worse off than the subjects of the original study. Nevertheless, the data on one-year survival showed that fewer than 1 percent of the patients with pets died, but almost 7 percent of patients without pets died. The statistical analysis demonstrated that both the presence of a pet and human social support increased the longevity of heart disease patients. With these two critical studies, we could be quite certain that pets could have a beneficial effect on the health of people with a condition as severe as coronary artery disease.

The rest of this book is an exploration of how our pets keep us in emotional balance and help to sustain our health. We will also explore the problems created by pets, for both individual people and society—there is no medicine that doesn't have some side effects—and last, we will describe how we can learn from our pets and become better companions to our friends and family members.

Two

Pets Can Be Good Companions

IN THE PRECEDING chapter we described the way pets prolong the life of patients with heart disease. That study was undertaken because of the evidence indicating that human companionship has a profound effect on human health and longevity. The importance of friends and family on health was summarized in a 1988 paper in *Science* in which James House, Karl Landis, and Debra Umberson reviewed the many epidemiological studies of social support and health and concluded:

> The evidence on social relationships is probably stronger, especially in terms of prospective studies, than the evidence which led to the certification of the Type A behavior pattern as a risk factor for coronary disease. The evidence regarding social relationships and health increasingly approximates the evidence in the 1964 Surgeon General's report that established cigarette smoking as a cause or risk factor for

mortality and morbidity from a range of disease. The age-adjusted relative risk ratios are stronger than the relative risks [for all causes of] mortality reported for cigarette smoking.

Other researchers found that social support could even extend the life of patients with terminal cancer.

It is possible that pet animals can protect our health and sustain our emotional balance because we treat them like people. Our family and friends and the quality of our social life have a profound influence on our health. To the extent that animals can act like family and friends, they also protect our health.

The choice to treat an animal like a person is ours, not the animal's. Only human beings can make an animal into a kind of person, just as children make persons out of stuffed toys. It may seem unnecessary to describe the ways in which animals are treated like people, because in some sense everyone knows that pets are sometimes people. Nonetheless, most people feel a little uncomfortable admitting this. We may like to kiss our dogs but would not like people to comment on it. It's all right for children to love their animals, sleep with them, talk to them on the telephone, write letters to them from camp, bake birthday cakes for them, and mourn them when they die, yet some are uneasy with this kind of sentimentality in adults. When adults are shown treating a pet as a person, the portrait is usually humorous or satirical, such as overdressed women talking baby talk to poodles decorated with rhinestone collars, painted toenails, and little bows. Films frequently use a love of cats to mark a man as gay or villainous or both.

People become uncomfortable when someone they suspect might not share their affection for animals draws attention to it. Loving animals is thought to be a little bit childish, like crying at movies. It feels good as long as no one brings up the house lights too quickly. Because of this discomfort in watching ourselves with our animals, it is useful to review the ways in which animals are treated as if they were people and family.

NAME-GIVING

Having a name is the essence of being an individual and being a person. If our name were taken away from us, we would feel that we were no longer a person. Naming an animal affirms its individuality, as demonstrated in this list of pet names supplied by the clients we interviewed in our veterinary-school clinic:

Tenny White, Taffy, Sadie, Sonny, Alex, Charlotte, Shanon, Pepe, Frisky, Jampas Snow Poppy, Tonka, Wendy, Scamper, Angie, Sheba, Bristol, Molly, Cassidy, Rebel, Mr. Beau Jangles, Tiger, Shane, Scot, Chinook, Now Now, Hassa, Tiva, Sam, Rosi, Charo, Brandy, Mugsey, Kelly, Meatball, Chief, Snoopy, Charcoal, Bandit, Prissy, Nazz, Kibbi, Patches, Kiddles, Nicole, Heather, Baron, Huddle, Simmie, and Miro.

The same diversity and idiosyncrasy can be seen in a list of pet names one of our clients gave us. This young woman's pets included four Great Danes, a basset hound, a part-German shepherd mutt, eight Afghans, ten horses, many cats, two goats, bantam roosters, and two canaries. The names of these animals were:

Falcon, Naphu, Clio, Brutus, Longfellow, Raja, Dudley, Butterball, Guinevere, Pagan, Becket, Sundance, Weird Harold, Princess, Daydream, Patty, Virgil, Alice Fatface, Thunder Nobody, Nervous, Tom, Bug Eyes I, Bug Eyes II, Ivan, Ballou, Iolanthe, Bambi, Sylvia, Sembu, Peach, and Emily.

In these and other examples, about half the names are first and last human names, nicknames, or titles. The rest come from almost anywhere—colors, events, places, epithets, activities, and objects. People tend to name a pet after other people or some thing they consider important. Although some names in the list are common—Snoopy, Sheba, Baron, and Chief—the variety indicates how inventive we can be with animal names, a freedom we rarely enjoy in naming children. A glance at the first names of the students in almost any class reveals how stereotyped we are with human names, which must link children to their family and their segment of society. Animal names need only reflect the individuality and personality of the pet and are free of the family and cultural rules that limit the variety of human names. One subject, age thirteen, said, "Naming my little brother was a big hassle. Mom and Dad didn't agree for a long time and everybody was worried what Grandma would think. Naming the dog [Mr. Beetles] was fun. Everyone thought up funny names, and I got to name him because he was supposed to be my dog and I like the Beatles." Another subject brought in a huge black male Doberman called Sue and explained simply, "It's fun—being called Sue doesn't embarrass the dog and it doesn't mean people will pick on him either."

The pet's name goes beyond the individuality provided by the breed and the association, even by a family name, to some word or symbol that links the animal and person. The flavor of the reasoning behind the choice of name can again be simply described in the words of our clients at the veterinary school. Some explanations were brief and obvious. Mon Petite Cocotte and Fifi were poodles. Von Richtofen and Liebchen were German shepherds. Chinook was a malamute, and Shannon was an Irish setter, and the one English bloodhound in the group was called Dame Agatha Christie. On the other hand, Mac's master was a Scot, and Rachel's mistress wanted a Jewish name. Other explanations were more complex but reflected the need to identify the animals with the specifics of their owners' lives.

Name	Reason
Blue	After Ray Charles's "I'll Sing the Blues."
Bunni	We got her on Palm Sunday.
Nassau	My father graduated from Princeton and the tiger was Princeton's mascot. There is a hall in Princeton called Nassau Hall. My father doesn't like cats, so my mother thought Nassau would be a good name for my cat. That way my father would not get rid of her.

Name	Reason
Desi	My daughter's name was Desi, and the kitten reminded me of Desi when she was an infant.
Manny	After Manny, Moe, and Jack, the "Pep Boys."
Buffy	Was named after my mink stole.
Indy	Found in Independence Hall.
Latimer Tubbs	I live on Latimer St. and like hot tubs.

The name of the animal is linked to the owner in the same way that a snapshot is. Jay Ruby, an anthropologist who studied the logic of home photography, noted that family photographs are rarely meaningful in themselves. Instead they are used as keys to family narratives: "That was when Uncle Tom visited us just before Vera got married, and we were eating on the terrace just after coming back from the wedding rehearsal," or "That's Mother outside of the cathedral at Amiens with the hat she got at the outdoor market that morning." The pet's name and the home photograph are linked to us by specific associations, while human names are linked to us by general associations. This does not mean that there are not universal pet names—such as Snoopy, Sheba, Fluffy, and Baron. It does imply that pet names are more particularized than human names.

Pets are not the only beings that are named. Livestock is frequently named when the animal is large or expensive or raised in small numbers, but only as an option. The act of naming implies that these animals are going to be given special treatment and that individual attributes or personalities are likely to be claimed for them. They may be given more affection than unnamed animals. For example, animals raised by children in 4-H clubs for prize competition are truly pets; they are hand reared, treated with enormous affection, and always named.

Some inanimate objects—homes, ships, trains, airplanes, and trucks—are frequently given names that endow them with some personality, but it is beyond the scope of this book to discuss how the name may change our behavior toward things. Certainly inanimate objects can be given the attributes of living beings as well as some of the rights enjoyed by people. Whatever the status of named boats, paintings, or robots, the act of giving them a name is a socially significant act that alters the behavior of the name giver.

CONVERSING

We talk to our pets as if they were people. Nearly 99 percent of our clients at the University of Pennsylvania veterinary clinic said that they talked to their pets, and 80 percent said that they talked to the animal in the same way that they talked to people. One dog owner explained, "Well, when we are walking, I just talk to him about what's going on. I ask him if he saw that other dog or knew what that person was doing. You know, just talking about the ordinary things that you see on the street." Another client said, "I talk to my cats when I get home just about what happened during the day. I don't get a chance to talk to anyone else about it because it sounds too much like complaining. My cats, they don't mind." Another put it more simply: "I just talk. Just what's in my head, like I was talking to myself, only I don't feel I'm nuts, because the dog listens."

The conversation with a pet can go beyond just talk. More than 30 percent of our subject group said they confided in their pet. The importance of having a pet as a confidant is greatest for the young and the elderly. In a study of ten-year-old Scottish children, Dr. Alasdair Macdonald, a psychiatrist, discovered that 84 percent of the children talked to their pets; and, more surprisingly, 65 percent believed the pets understood the meaning of the words they were using. One-third of the subjects built substantial portions of their lives around their pets, talking to them, playing with them, caring for them, and even believing that the pet understood their moods, feelings, and words. For these children, a pet was the most significant companion.

When a child is troubled, he slams off into his room and throws himself down on the bed, curling up in tears or rage, sometimes holding a pillow or a stuffed animal. The dog follows and pokes his head into the knot, trying to find something to nuzzle or lick. The pillow is dropped and the dog is hugged and settles down next to the child, who talks, perhaps playing with the dog's fur. The dog settles with his head flat against the bed and waits or begins small activities, such as nibbling at the fur on his paws. This type of behavior demonstrates the role of true confidant that a pet may have with children.

Among adolescents who own horses, more than 70 percent confide in the animal, talking out their problems in the isolation of the barn while grooming and caring for the animal. Sometimes, if the teenager is too upset, there may be no intended contact, no grooming, and the youngster will let the horse lean or nuzzle against her, frequently with no eye contact between person and animal. The child talks, and both just look off into nowhere but feel the presence of one another. That a pet can be a confidant is not surprising; adolescents often feel alienated from parents and peers, unable to share innermost feelings with any human being for fear of invasion, correction, or ridicule.

A pet can be equally important at the other end of the life cycle. A study from Sweden found that fully 15 percent of elderly people in Göteborg considered their pet their most significant social contact, giving their life meaning. This sympathetic bond between the aged and their pets was tenderly described by Doris Lessing in her short story "An Old Woman and Her Cat," and by Albert Camus in his portrait of the old man and his dog in *The Stranger.* Both writers signaled the close social relationship between the old animal and the old person by similarity of appearance. Their closeness in a social sense is represented by closeness in a physical sense, the way emotional and physical ties are interrelated within families.

Hetty, a strong gaunt old woman wearing a scarlet wool suit she had found among her castoffs that week, a black knitted teacosy on her head, and black buttoned Edwardian boots too big for her so that she had to shuffle, invited them into her room. . . . The cat was soon a scarred warrior with fleas, a torn ear, and a ragged look to him. He was a multicolored cat and his eyes were small and yellow. He was a long way down the scale from the delicately colored, elegantly shaped pedigree cats. But he was independent, and often caught himself pigeons when he could no longer stand the tinned cat food, or the bread and packet gravy Hetty fed him, and he purred and nestled when she grabbed him to her bosom at those times she suffered loneliness. . . . She sang or chanted to the cat: "You nasty old beast, filthy old cat, nobody wants you, do they Tibby, no, you're just an alley tom, just an old stealing cat, hey Tibs, Tibs, Tibs."

As I was going up the dark staircase, I bumped into the old Salamano, my next door neighbor. He was with his dog. They have been together for eight years. The spaniel has some kind of skin disease, I think, which has caused him to lose almost all of his hair and which covers him with brown spots and scabs. For having lived with him, both alone in a little room, the old Salamano finally looks like him. He has reddish scabs on his face and sparse yellow hair. As for the dog, he has adopted his master's kind of stooped posture, putting his head forward and stretching his neck. They look as if they belong to the same race, however, they hate each other.

FEEDING

Feeding animals our own food right from our own hands or even our own lips is a deeply felt and solemn pleasure. It transforms that animal automatically into a pet and a companion. The word "companionship" is derived from the Latin *com*, meaning "together," and *panis*, or "bread"—eating together. We delight in feeding pets our own food rather than pet food, giving horses sugar cubes or apples and carrots to rabbits. Dogs are treated to all kinds of "people food," and children have the traditional right to discreetly feed pets the unliked portions of their dinners. We also allow dogs and cats to steal food and consider the theft humorous rather than serious.

Our delight in feeding pets our own food is a problem for the pet-food industry. Their advertisements must suggest that pet food is better than table scraps, while at the same time reflecting the status of the pet as a beloved companion—the rationale for the expense of purchasing their products. This dual message is conveyed by stressing both nutritional content and resemblance to human food. Some manufacturers claim their foods to be pure beef; other foods are pictured next to a red steak; some make gravy, others are moist or offer a menu including tuna, cheese, chicken, and liver. For people who are not satisfied with ordinary dog food, there are special products. A New York City store once sold frozen portions of specially prepared boeuf bourguignonne or sole meunière for dogs and cats. Health-minded owners can purchase organic pet food to protect their animals from environmental pollutants.

In France dogs are actually invited into restaurants where human children are not welcome. A guidebook for owners who want to share their vacations with their dogs describes the restaurants that prepare special meals for a pet or let you choose its meal from the regular menu at a special price. The quality of the meals for pets are rated with one, two, or three bones. Eleven of the twenty three-star restaurants listed in the *Guide Michelin* are willing to serve pets.

On a recent visit, we encountered just such a gourmet dog in a Paris restaurant, right by the Clignicourt Flea Market. We were finishing coffee and dessert when the dog climbed onto an empty stool and waited. He did not beg but just sat there, permitting himself to be petted, and listened to our conversation. Our host, knowing the game, carefully pushed a saucer with one of the unused sugar cubes toward the animal. Then and only then did he move, delicately unwrapping the sugar with his incisors and crunching the cube several times. One by one we fed him the remainder of the cubes. No one could want a more reserved dinner companion!

Children do not experience a significant encounter with an animal when they just touch it; children touch and are touched much too often and casually for it to be a meaningful act. The child and animal are truly joined by offering, and accepting, food, for in the act both pay strict attention to each other and both agree on the meaning of the encounter. The child also subordinates the animal by giving him food, for children have learned that parents always feed children but rarely allow children to feed them.

SOCIAL CELEBRATIONS

Almost 30 percent of our subjects celebrated their animal's birthday in some way. Carvel stores will make a special ice cream birthday cake in the shape of a dog. And the snapshot of the dog with a party hat sitting beside his lighted birthday cake is a familiar feature of family albums. In France a dog named Zouzou had his birthday party at the three-star restaurant Moulin des Mougins on the Riviera. The cake, complete with candles, was carried to the table by the head waiter. Birthdays are not the only family celebrations for animals—Christmas usually includes wrapped presents for the family cat or dog. Academic progress is also rewarded, and one Philadelphia obedience school has a graduation party for dogs at which the animals are forced to wear mortarboards made of paper and are presented with diplomas.

Although the Episcopal Church is uncomfortable with animals because they do not have an immortal soul, there is an annual day to bless animals. The service may have originally been for livestock but is now practiced in urban churches. And one less-orthodox minister in California has been offering to perform marriage ceremonies for pets about to be mated.

CLOTHING

In Anatole France's allegorical novel *Penguin Island*, the nearsighted, somewhat simple St. Mael baptizes a group of penguins, thinking them to be a new race of savages. His mistake is corrected in heaven when the penguins are changed into human beings. At that point the devil arrives in suitably disguised form and suggests to St. Mael that if the penguins are human, they must have clothing. The result of the clothing is to create sexual curiosity and stimulation where none existed before, an outcome desirable to the devil.

To clothe animals converts them into people. Paradoxically, animal clothing almost never conceals the genitalia, which must be concealed by human clothing. Pet clothing is only partly functional—to keep out the cold or rain. To a greater or lesser extent, it always imitates human clothing. The biker wears the same silver studding on his black leather wristband that his Doberman wears on his neck collar. The California matron puts the same rhinestones around her neck as her poodle wears around his neck. The raincoats, the plaid overcoats (your clan's plaid, of course), the hats, the boots, and the jewelry for animals are all made to be imitations of human articles. They permit adults to dress animals as people in the same way that children can transform a beagle into a baby by putting it in infant clothes and parading it around in a baby carriage. In the film *E.T.*, Elliott's sister dresses the alien as a woman, just as she would a pet.

Dressing up even extends to the animal's skin, just as humans dress their hair and skin. Animals are groomed in "boutiques" and "beauty shops," and there is a full range of pet shampoos, conditioners, dyes, perfumes, deodorants, and even nail polish.

SLEEPING TOGETHER

With the exception of horses, our pets share our rugs, chairs, and, most significantly, our beds. Dogs and cats are often sleeping partners, cuddling up under the covers, warming and sometimes paralyzing our feet and legs when they nest above the covers. Cats may even sleep on our heads, warmed by our breath. If they do not actually share the bed, they do sleep in the bedroom. Half of the urban dogs do so, and half of these are permitted on the bed. Wherever they sleep, pets are frequently allowed first rights and may even growl off human usurpers. One woman whose husband kept an overly aggressive weimaraner complained that she could not make their bed in the morning. The animal would jump on the bed after her husband went to work and would growl, snap, or even bite if she tried to displace him. She was, however, a determined housekeeper and succeeded in making the bed each morning by frightening the dog off with the sound of the vacuum cleaner. As we shall see later, the pet's privilege of sharing the master's bed elevates him above human children, who are usually banned from the parental bedroom at night.

GOING TO THE DOCTOR

On the farm, animals are treated simply to preserve their economic value, but if treatment is too expensive, the animal is "put down." When a pet is sick, however, it gets special treatment. Veterinary medicine is almost as extensive as human medicine, and its full range of procedures may be used for pets that have no economic value. Veterinarians use the latest medical drugs, including psychiatric chemicals, and our neurotic dogs pop Prozac like the rest of us. Veterinarians also have all the surgical procedures and X-ray diagnostic tools, such as the CAT scan. In a veterinary clinic that specializes in the palliative treatment of cancer, all the latest anticancer drugs, radiation, and cobalt treatments are combined with surgical procedures. In that clinic, a client was told that the new anticancer drug prescribed for her animal had not been tried in dogs but that the initial results with human beings were encouraging. The attendant was not joking.

If you shut your eyes and ignore your nose, it is not possible to differentiate ward rounds at the University of Pennsylvania Veterinary Hospital from medical rounds at the hospital for human beings a few hundred yards away. Even when people do not treat animals with terminal cancer, they are willing to spend thousands of dollars to repair broken bones or pay for repeated dialysis for dogs with terminal kidney failure. Veterinary medicine is best distinguished from human medicine by its greater flexibility in the face of terminal illness. It is possible rationally to discuss euthanasia, "the good death," with veterinarians, a privilege that many physicians are unable or unwilling to offer. Veterinarians and their clients can make rational decisions about when a pet's suffering should be terminated. In discussing the death of a pet, their owners frequently say that they wished their own death could be so gently managed.

DEATH AND BURIAL

The last tribute to the human status of pets is the manner of their burial. Most pets are not buried in cemeteries but are buried in backyards or given to veterinarians or some other agency in the belief that they will be interred in a mass grave or burned. The minimal expectation is that the animal will not be recycled in an obvious way. The relatively few pet owners who do bury their animals in the four hundred pet cemeteries in this country are practicing an ancient rite. The Egyptians embalmed their cats, and Caligula was not the only Roman who buried his pet horse in state. Yet for all the history of burying animals with the rites, artifacts, and techniques usually accorded to humans, we are exceedingly uncomfortable about the practice and often view it with satirical humor, as in the films *The Loved One* and *Heaven's Gate*. Perhaps it is the Judeo-Christian idea that animals have no immortal soul that troubles us. Without personal resurrection, why preserve the corpse? We do not mourn the calves, the cows, the lambs, and the pigs that we eat. Should we mourn the dog and the cat? Yet headstones, religious symbols like crosses and Stars of David, poetry, and pictures of the deceased adorn pet cemeteries as well as human cemeteries. And despite the position of official religions, there is a general hope expressed in the epitaphs and funeral poems that there is a "beyond" for the beast and some hope of reunion with the animal.

EATING PETS IS CANNIBALISM

In nature animals die and their bodies are eaten. They are consumed and cycled through other plants and animals until these are eaten again. Shakespeare mocks the human or unnatural state with the lines:

> *Hamlet:* A man may fish with the worm that hath eat of a king and eat of the fish that hath fed of that worm.
>
> *King:* What dost thou mean by this?
>
> *Hamlet:* Nothing but to show you how a king may go a progress through the guts of a beggar.

Human beings are not eaten, and cannibalism is a horrible crime. In most places it is criminal to let bodies fertilize the fields or feed the scavengers, and recovery of bodies has interrupted wars, from the siege of Troy to the siege of Sarajevo. Human bodies are not permitted to disappear into the general fecundity of nature.

Dogs and cats are not permitted to "go a progress through the guts" of anyone, either. Eating a dog or a cat is the next worst thing to cannibalism, and the thought horrifies most of us. The eating of dogs and cats by Chinese, Koreans, and Vietnamese is repugnant to most Westerners.

Beck became aware of this conflict of values when he was approached by a Korean import-export firm that wanted to buy dead dogs from the American Society for the Prevention of Cruelty to Animals (ASPCA) to export as a delicacy. They were willing to pay a sizable sum for the carcasses during a time when the organization dearly needed funds. They were even willing to pay for just the dog penises, which were highly valued for their purported effect on potency. In pleading their case, the Korean merchants argued that it was better than sending the dead animals to a rendering plant and that the humane society could use the income to help living animals. The plan was totally unacceptable to the ASPCA.

In the United States, few, if any, would buy dog food if it were possible that it contained the bodies of other dogs. Indeed, a Texas nutrition professor who suggested that recycled dog might be a cheap additive to dog food was the target of a vicious attack of hate mail, some of it threatening his life. In actuality, bodies of dogs and cats killed in pounds are sent to rendering plants and recycled into low-phosphate detergent and hog and chicken food. We wash our clothes in "pets" and eat them incorporated into chicken and pork, but we prefer to be unaware of the practice. In the United States, the ban on "pet cannibalism" extends to horse meat, a delicious item of table in many Western countries. Attempts to open a horse butcher shop in New Jersey resulted in such furious protests that it had to close. Dogs can be killed by the millions and buried, and horses can be killed by the millions and sent out of the country, but neither can be eaten. Pet cannibalism is one of the few moral horrors that is not a crime. There is no legal prohibition against eating dog in the United States, yet the moral prohibition is so strong that nausea is more effective than laws or police.

KILLING

Eating pets is horrifying, but Americans do eat meat in large quantities. However, city dwellers try to forget that that meat came from a living animal. There are no intact dead animals in supermarkets—all red meat is offered in small, plastic-covered packages with a towel beneath to absorb the blood. Chickens are cut into bloodless, off-white pieces or presented with no head, neck, legs, viscera, or feathers.

Shrimps come without their heads, and even fish appear as filets or table ready without scales, head, fins, or guts.

Due to our lack of experience with the realities of processing food animals into meat (urban schools do not take children on trips through slaughterhouses), it is not at all strange that people cannot think clearly about the killing of pets. As a result, animal shelters and humane societies must practice duplicity. These "shelters" were started to protect animals from cruelty. Now one of their major functions is the killing of between 4 and 8 million unwanted pets that are produced in this country each year. The humane organizations do accept responsibility for the elimination of unwanted animals; their refusal would increase the number of abandoned animals who die painfully.

To maintain the support of their clients and contributors and to make the job bearable for their personnel, all shelters run adoption programs. The existence of the adoption programs permits people who bring in animals to believe that the pet will be adopted, and they are rarely told that 60–80 percent of animals brought to shelters will be killed. Having accepted animals with the implicit promise that they are there for adoption, the shelters campaign hard to promote adoption and reduce the number of animals killed. This aggressive promotion of adoption maintains the fiction that most animals find new homes and helps people deny the consequences of handing pets over to shelters.

Because of these conflicts about killing animals, we can neither acknowledge that we kill so many pets nor refuse to continue to kill them. People cannot even think coherently about the problem. Certainly it is unthinkable to consider pets as a kind of crop that is raised for our amusement and pleasure, as chickens are raised for food. We do permit ourselves to kill a whole variety of common and exotic food animals that are probably as sentient as dogs and cats without much concern (vegetarians and animal libertarians are a small minority). Yet we even object to raising dogs like farm animals. "Puppy mill" is an inflammatory term, yet the most respectable breeders will kill puppies that do not conform to their breed standards. As a result of this refusal to permit the dog to be a "farm animal," we are forced to throw away and waste the bodies of the animals that are killed, or to pretend that we do. Even the terminology and the apparatus used to destroy animals reflect these conflicts. Animals are not "killed" or "slaughtered" like cows and sheep; they are "put to sleep," "put down," "sacrificed," or "euthanized." A firm called Animal Awareness Inc. advertised a "Euthanasia System" that is nothing more than a carbon monoxide gas chamber. Lethal chemicals for killing dogs and cats are advertised as "euthanasia agents," and one advertisement read: "Trust T-61 Euthanasia Solution."

The urban denial of animal death is part of the conceptual problem, but the major impediment to clear thought is the status of pets as people. People do not want to think about giving an animal the status of a person and then killing it "like an animal." This process of stripping animals of their human status is too close to a similar process: the act of stripping human beings of their human status before killing them. We are defined as human beings by others, even though we would like to believe that we have *inherent* human rights.

We characterize certain unspeakable acts in history as treating humans like animals. For example, the Jews could be arbitrarily slaughtered by one German government. Armenians were treated in similar fashion by a Turkish government. Vietnamese peasants were so treated by previous French and American governments, as were Cambodian children by the Pol Pot government. The process of killing people like animals continued throughout the four years of the Bosnian war. In the United States, killing a three-month-old fetus is legal, but killing an eight-month-old fetus may be a crime. At the other end of the life cycle, it is permissible to extract the organs of a living but brain dead person. Thus, at a variety of times, for a variety of reasons, humans have been willing to redefine people as animals and then kill them for various reasons, some no less trivial than the reasons that are frequently given for killing dogs. In Joseph Conrad's *Heart of Darkness*, the killing of the natives by the whites on the riverboat helps us understand how easily we can become animals in the eyes of others. In a similar vein, Jonathan Swift tried to make the English see how they were treating the Irish peasantry by writing his "Modest Proposal," which ironically suggests that Irish children be raised as an item of meat for English tables. We cannot think coherently about killing dogs that were once "like people" because we do not want to think about killing human animals that were once people.

Our treatment of pets—the acts and services we perform with and for them—clearly mirrors our treatment of people. Yet if pets were, in reality, people, then they would have all of the faults of people, and it is obvious to any pet lover that in some ways pets do not substitute for people but complement them. Pets and people are not interchangeable, and a good life may have to include both. How are pets different from people, and how may those differences make them especially good companions?

CONSTANCY

Today we believe we live in a world of constant change. Modern physics tells us that our universe is in a continuous state of evolution or involution, and every entity within it, living or inert, shares that progression. The universe began with an explosion in a primordial lump of matter and is still expanding. Individual stars can expand into novas or contract into black holes. Through biological evolution, life is a succession of more or less transient forms moving toward greater complexity and greater plasticity or ending in extinction. Our technological development has always accelerated the pace of evolution and still enlarges our capabilities at an ever increasing rate. The progress of humans is no longer limited to earth. The possibility of penetration and colonization of the universe now provides an infinitely receding target for progress. The individual, like the race, is not permitted to stand still. To be successful, life should be a series of advancements in knowledge, power, capacity, and material wealth. Those who are not advancing are required to adapt to the change in society around them. They must consume change, even though they themselves are not constructing that change.

Continual material progress, with its attendant emphasis on destruction and replacement of the past, has led to a feeling of devaluation. Nothing seems to be worth what it once was. Houses, automobiles, furniture, even electrical appliances, are not as durable or well made as they once were. Society is disorganized, and urban violence and crime are just one sign of a general loss of social control. People feel that family life is no longer what it was. Decay in the family seems to be matched by decay in the schools, and children don't seem to learn values at home or to acquire knowledge at school. These feelings of personal loss are mirrored by a more diffuse anxiety about losing all stability in general catastrophe: atomic war, economic collapse, or poisoning of the natural environment.

Against this almost cataclysmic background of rampant progress, change, and decay, the suggestion that pets offer a bulwark of stability may seem comic, childish, or stupidly insensitive. Yet they do offer us protection against change by their nature, their behavior toward us, and the feelings and actions they evoke from us. At the very least, pets protect us from the changing fortunes we experience within human society by their simple indifference to human technology, knowledge, aspirations, and achievement.

Animals are indifferent to our strivings; they do not share our changing world, and they live in their own time. The constancy of the animal is the constancy of cyclical time—life in the cycles of days, months, seasons, and lifetimes of repetition without change, like the life of the farm as it is in most places in the world and as it was in the United States until the start of this century. Plows were pulled by horses as they were for thousands of years, and the farmer's life was geared to the rising and setting of the sun, the arrival of rain and frost, the seasons for breeding and sowing, harvesting and birth. Crop after crop, animal after animal, and eventually farmer after farmer succeeded each other on the same land. This vision sees history as a wheel, with time always turned on itself, so that everyone knew where he or she was and was going to be. Pets bring a fragment of that secure vision into the lives of people who may never have walked on plowed earth. Animals are constant; they remain themselves, unaffected by human progress or failure.

The first dog in space, Laika, who was put there by the Soviet Union, could have been riding in an ox cart instead of a space capsule. She had no comprehension of space, of a rocket, or of the race between the United States and the Soviet Union. Similarly, a cat can warm herself by an open fireplace or an electric grate drawing its power from an atomic reactor. It is the warmth that matters, not how it was generated. If all technology fails, the cat will gladly wrap herself around your neck or sit on top of your head. Dogs may be shown or raced or compete in obedience trials, but the success or failure is known only to humans. The dog works for the owner. For example, in the weight-pulling contest in Jack London's *Call of the Wild*, the dog Buck pulled for love of his master. He was ignorant of the wager. In the same fashion, the grand champion of Westminster does not comprehend the honor that he wins; only his owner and other human beings know that. Success cannot spoil dogs or cats; it can only spoil their owners.

Animals are also oblivious to the status or fate of their owners. Stories about the pets of the old and the poor are secular parables about the unimportance of earthly success, of material goods, of aesthetic or technological sophistication, or even of youth and beauty. The animal loves you whether you have just won or lost your fortune in the stock market, whether you smell of perfume or soiled underwear, whether you are old and poor or young and rich, attractive or ugly. All that men and women strive for in the way of social success is irrelevant to the pet; only the owner's presence is important. An image that describes the constancy of the pet in the face of changing human fortunes is the picture of an elderly beggar sitting on a pavement with his rags of belongings, and a dog or cat curled against his side.

The ability of animals to be constant in their response to people, without taking note of the fortunes of the day, is appreciated most intensely when a pet greets its owner at the end of a workday. The time when people like their animals best is when they return home, at the threshold. A pet's greeting always has the same gestures and the same enthusiasms. It makes no demands and has no ill feelings. A pet's welcome is restorative and signals that everything is as it was when you left; everything is safe, and you have not changed, either.

Human family members, on the other hand, almost always reflect the troubles of their day and their expectations of the person returning home. Anticipation, blame, or demands color most human greetings. At the end of the Trojan War, Odysseus returned home, where his dog, Argus, wagged his tail in joy and died without betraying his master. But Odysseus had to swear his son, Telemachus, to secrecy, convince Penelope of his true identity, and prepare his revenge on the unwanted suitors.

When people face real adversity—disease, unemployment, or the disabilities of age—affection from a pet takes on new meaning. Then the pet's continuing affection is a sign that the essence of the person has not been damaged. Thus pets are important in the treatment of depressed or chronically ill patients. Pets are also used to great advantage with the institutionalized aged. In such institutions it is difficult for the staff to retain optimism when all the patients are deteriorating. Children who visit cannot help but remember what their parents or grandparents once were and be depressed by their incapacities. Animals, however, have no expectations about mental capacity. They do not worship youth. They have no memories about what the aged once were and greet them as if they were children. An old man holding a puppy can relive a childhood moment with complete accuracy. His joy and the animal's response are the same.

The pet can provide this comfort by being a child that is never expected to become an adult. We do not demand that pets progress along an axis of intellectual, moral, or social achievement. Pets stay the same, never growing up, talking, becoming independent, wearing clothes, or hiding their genitals in shame. They remain in the condition of Adam and Eve before the fall—without original sin. Being without sin, they do not need to be perfected. We do not get angry at pets the way we do with children, who are expected to perfect themselves. We accept pets as they are, and they accept us as we are, with no moral demands. To understand the bond of moral constancy between people and pets, it is worthwhile exploring the differences in our ideas about cruelty to animals and to children.

The Victorians considered punishment of children necessary for moral correction and growth. Beatings, no matter how brutal, would prevent vice, and since vice could destroy both body and soul, beating was the lesser evil. Spare the rod and spoil the child was no metaphor; it was a literal injunction to punish in order to perfect virtue. Punishment was perceived as cruel only when a child was virtuous and a parent vicious. Even then, courts and society were reluctant to intervene between parent and child. Such interference, no matter what the justification, would have set a dangerous precedent for social intrusion into the family, where parents, not social laws, were meant to rule the children.

The Victorians did assume that pets were incapable of moral growth; hence punishment of them and cruelty to them could serve no moral purpose. The first anticruelty laws were designed to protect animals. It was under such a law that for the first time a mother was prosecuted in the United States for cruelty to children, when her severely beaten child was declared to be an animal before the eyes of the court. The legal protection given to children was derived from the legal protection given to animals, thus confirming the position of the pet as an innocent, a child without original sin and without the need for moral growth. The pet is the constant child, fixed between culture and nature.

PETS AND PLAY

Pets have a special way of bringing people back to play and laughter no matter what their age. Pets engage in a kind of play that is beyond the world of competition. The games have no winners or losers. Play with an animal has the same constancy as the animal's response to us.

Human games are quite different. When parents first play with infants, the object of the game is simply to sustain the child's attention, to make it smile. Once a child is four or five years old, the games begin to include competition. They become practice for a competitive adult life. Little League baseball, football, tennis, and almost all sports set the child thinking and acting competitively. The games we teach our children are survival games that tell them how to grow up. Winning is a very serious occupation because it prepares children for the adult business of winning at life. It is hard to be loving when you are so desperately competing and when winning means so much.

Adults playing with children can find themselves in a terrible conflict. The child desperately wants to win because he or she has been taught that winning is so important. If the parent plays at full strength in order to teach the child how to lose or compete, the child often collapses in tears of frustration. If the parent tries to lose, the child feels patronized or, when he wins, engages in a kind of taunting behavior that may be difficult for some parents to tolerate. Fathers sometimes depend on winning at games in order to prove that they can still dominate their children. The film *The Great Santini*, in which a father was driven to intense competition in games with his own son in order to assert his dominant position and maintain his youthfulness, illustrates the pain of this kind of conflict.

Unlike football, chess, or space invaders, games with infants are not won or lost. The players just try to keep the game going. It's necessary to examine how we play with young children, because there is a close identity between pet and child. An infant's first games are in reality not recognized as games—they are olympic events like "drop toy." The child fingers, turns, mouths, and drools over the toy and drops it. The parent picks it up, and the process is repeated. The whole object of the game is to keep the child and adult playing together without either becoming frustrated. The adult becomes testy if toys are dropped too rapidly, and the infant whines if the adult is too slow and the infant is deprived of the toy for too long.

Another game is "smile, baby, smile," which is frequently played with the baby on its back on the changing table and the parent face-to-face above the child. The parent tickles, strokes, grimaces, laughs, and sings to make the baby smile, laugh, or make the kind of noises that seem to signal pleasure. For the game to continue, the baby must emit the signs of pleasure with reasonable frequency and not scream. The parent must be inventive enough to keep the baby interested. Later "smile, baby, smile" turns into "peekaboo," "patty-cake," "chase me around," and "exchange toy."

These same sustaining games are played with pets, and to maintain interest, the roles of the players continually reverse. The pet and the human player have to learn how to play at less than full strength. The cat or dog must learn not to bite or scratch in a way that will do too much damage, and the person must not play hard enough to hurt the animal or take the play toy too far out of reach. Typical pet games are described in some detail in chapter 8. Once they are learned, they remain the same, just as the animal does. Participation is restful and reassuring and an escape from the turmoil of the world, as restorative as the pet's untroubled greeting at the front door.

Like play, laughter is a natural restorative. As we engage pets in games or watch their own, they certainly make us laugh. The humor we see in pets is exemplified by the idea of a lion entranced by a mechanical mouse. A cat killing a mouse is not humorous, but cats chasing people, other cats, or inanimate or even imaginary objects are funny. For example, Beck's cat will run madly around the house in a frenzy, finding something to bat and pounce on as if it were a prey animal. Most of the bouts end when she bats the object under a couch or radiator. A dog chasing a squirrel is funny when the squirrel reaches the tree and scolds him from a branch or, better yet, stops at the base of the tree, making the dog put on the brakes in alarmed surprise. A dog chasing its tail and a cat in a paper bag or watching birds through a window are examples of useless action that amuses us.

Sometimes the humor is generated by the great care taken by the animal in its senseless pursuit—a dog slowly following a bug around the floor or a cat watching a goldfish for minutes at a time, waiting for one false move. These activities mock our own concern for getting things done and help us keep our own strivings in balance. The humor of pets complements their play. It is the enjoyment of going nowhere and remaining the same. There is no concern for consequences, because there are no consequences. The novelist Milos Kundera says that the ability of pets to play repetitive games with people restores us to the way we were before the fall. Pets, he says, are our last connection to paradise.

A pet's welcome after a hard day's work is one of the most
satisfying moments for a pet owner.
Photo courtesy of Pet Food Institute.

A pet can act as a
confidant for a
troubled child.
Photo by Mary Bloom.

Some elderly people consider their pets their most significant social contact. *Photo by Mary Bloom.*

Whether we are just relaxing or engaged in specific activities, our pets' presence is soothing and meaningful.
Photos courtesy of Pet Food Institute.

Only human beings can make an animal into a kind of person. *Photo courtesy of Pet Food Institute.*

Whether it is the famous Checkers Nixon or just the mutt next door, the burial of our pets reflects their human status. *Photo by Alan Beck.*

When people face real adversity, affection from a pet takes on new meaning.
Photo by Mary Bloom.

Not just dogs but also birds, fish, and other animals have a beneficial effect on our health. *Photo by Mary Bloom.*

Pets engage in a kind of play that is beyond the world of competition. *Photo by Mary Bloom.*

Three

Pets Are Family

Do our family members have to be human? A geneticist would say yes, but most pet owners would answer with an unequivocal no. In this chapter we will explore how we treat our pets as family and why it might benefit our health and well-being to do so.

One of the first news films following the Mount St. Helens volcanic eruption in May 1980 showed a gnarled old woodsman in checkered shirt and suspenders being rescued by helicopter. His first act was to place his dog carefully on the seat of the helicopter; then, and only then, did he enter the aircraft. It was clear that he would not leave without the dog, in spite of the exploding volcano, because the dog was family.

In less dramatic ways, clients in the veterinary clinic demonstrate again and again that their pets are family. Owners keeping a dog who has destroyed thousands of dollars' worth of rugs and furniture or a cat that had not used the litter box in three years would say, "We can't get rid of him. He's a member of the family." More than 70 percent of our subjects considered the animal to be a family member. Dr. Ann Cain, a nurse and family therapist, found that 87 percent of her subjects placed the animal within the family. Barbara Jones, who studies adolescent pony-club members, found that more than 80 percent considered the horse to be a family member. Thus the feeling that pets are kin is not dependent upon the animal living in the house.

Someone living with a pet is living with a family. A pet owner is greeted at the door when she returns at night; she has someone to sit on the couch with and share the television. There is someone she must shop for, feed, and care for and who thus gives to her own life the paced, circular rhythm of family life.

Family members are devoted to each other, and even when the family member is a pet, there is a strong feeling that family members should stick together. We rescue our dogs, and we believe that our dogs are capable of rescuing us. Franklin Roosevelt was accused of sending a destroyer to the Aleutian Islands to rescue his family pet, Fala. There is no doubt in anyone's mind that Richard Nixon's family pet, Checkers, saved his campaign for the vice presidency. Both men are remembered for speeches in which the image of their family pets was used to enhance their own image. The scene of a dog waking the sleeping members of a family as smoke fills the house, drawing an unconscious person from the flames, or bringing the fire fighters to an unconscious master hidden beneath rubble are constant elements of dog stories, real and invented. Animals are family, and the family sticks together.

Pets are usually not just any member of the family, however. They are children, a designation partly reflecting the realities of our treatment of pets. Like children, the animal must be continually cared for: fed and watered, kept from eating dangerous foods and objects, bathed, groomed, protected against the elements, clothed when necessary, brought to the doctor, and spoken for at the doctor's. Like children, pets are petted, stroked, and touched at the will of the owner. The pet's range of motion is curtailed to protect it from harm, and its sexual expression is controlled and limited. However, the act that critically defines a pet as a child is our willingness to put up with the excrement of cats and dogs— to handle it, to permit it in the house, to accept it in the streets.

Dogs are the quintessential pet because, more than any other animal, they have been shaped genetically to look and behave like juveniles. The cat is much more adult in form and behavior, and domestic cats closely resemble the wild forms. In contrast, think of the difference between a wolf and a basset hound or a Chihuahua. Even horses, with their massive size and power, are only a partial exception. Although most riders think of their mounts as children, adolescents frequently think of their horses as brothers or sisters.

Most pets are members of families that also have human children. Yet pets are treated like children, even when human children are around, because they provide continual access to the kind of uncomplicated affection that parents exchange with young children. As soon as children grow into independent beings, they are not available for affection on demand. Love becomes complex, and affection must be meted out according to the child's behavior. The child, sensing the relationship between affection and subordination, begins to refuse his mother's and father's kisses and hugs in search of his or her own independence.

But pets are constant. They do not grow up the way children do. A mother of a high-school junior, distraught at the death of her dog, said of her son, "He's a big boy now and I'm proud of him, but he just grabs breakfast and is out the door with a quick good-bye, hardly ever a hug. But Tibbs [the dog] was always there for *me* in the morning. He stayed on the couch with me while I took my coffee, the cup in one hand and the other around his neck."

Touching an animal, as this woman did, is part of the way we treat it like a young child. In touching and talking to animals, people achieve a kind of intimate dialogue, even if they have just met the animal. Their contact resembles the most intimate exchanges between a parent and an infant or between lovers who know and trust each other. When petting animals, a person's face changes: the lines of tension smooth out; the smile becomes less forced, more relaxed and open; and the voice becomes softer, slower, and slightly higher in pitch than normal, with prolongation of vowels and ending consonants. Much of the speech consists of questions framed for the animal. Said one cat owner, "What's a mattah? Are you all right? All right? What are you doing there? Yes! Yes! What are you doing there? What d'yah see? Nice cat! What d'yah see there?" Between each question the speaker looked at her cat as if waiting for a reply, petting the animal to draw its attention. Sometimes the owner will take the animal's head in hand to force direct eye contact or solicit a kiss or both. Such dialogues parallel the talk and touch between mothers and infants. The childlike position of animals brings forth a loving intimacy that is appropriate to children. The dialogue between owner and pet confirms the family role of the pet.

Smiles and strokes are not the only vocabulary used to express the childlike position of pets, and dogs in particular. Dogs are disciplined and restrained with physical force. It is possible to hit them when they disobey or jerk them about with their leash. In turn, dogs are permitted to bite other family members. Only very young children are restrained and disciplined in this way and permitted to strike back in return. In this respect, too, pets are more privileged than children, and few children over the age of two would be permitted to assault adults the way some pets do.

To gain an impression of the dimensions of their feelings toward their pets, we asked our subjects, "What about your animal gives you the most satisfaction?"

They're the *best* friends any time and all the time!

He is pleasant, self-sufficient, friendly, independent, and has his own relationship with people and other animals.

He is the greatest thing to love. I take care of my André like I take care of my children. We all love him very much.

Her personality being geared toward people. Her love of children. Her friendliness. Her companionship. Her cute behavior.

The obvious love and affection shown in return. The fun of enjoying her company. Knowing she enjoys us and is content in an adopted home. (She was six years old when we got her from the SPCA.)

His presence seems to contribute to a complete home.

My five children are fairly grown. Three are not living at home, and the activity that pets provide is appreciated—noise, interaction of cat and dog, plus the physical care of animals. I like to see the cat and dog play or sleep together while I work. It's rewarding to feed them and walk with them.

She is so loving, affectionate, adorable, is tiny, so I can take her with me anywhere practically.

His love all day and night.

He is a cat. I love cats. He is always around. He's interesting. He's cute. He responds. He needs me. He purrs. He plays. He loves me. When I come home from work, he is always at the door, and he meows and is happy to see me.

There were many other long answers and many more of only one or two words. The common words, repeated again and again, were "love," "affection," "companionship," "trust," "loyalty," "need," and "care." These words seem to be at the core of almost all descriptions of the bond between people and pets and are also central to any intimate family relationship. Play, activity, obedience, and control were mentioned only slightly less frequently. These sentiments are also central to our life with children. We found, then, that our subjects' perception of their most important feelings about their pets can best be expressed with the metaphor of the pet as a family member.

Family members can be close or distant, and it is possible to get people to describe how close they are to their pets within the family circle. There is a very simple but effective technique for obtaining this information. You simply draw a large empty circle on a sheet of paper and designate it as "the family circle." You then ask the person to draw herself within the circle, to place the other family members in the circle as well, and then to mark the position of her pet or pets. When people do this, they almost always draw their pet closer to themselves than other family members. Pets are not only family members, they may be preferred family members, the ones we feel closest to.

People who do not intuitively feel that pets are family tend to view them as only substitute children for those who are childless. They are in part correct. When Katcher's barber, who is happily and militantly gay, heard of his interest in pets, the comment was, "We can't have children, so we teach school or have pets. Teaching school, you only have children for a year, but pets you have for a long time. They're the closest thing to children we can have." The barber shop was guarded by an obese ten-pound mongrel dog called Wolf, who had huge liquid eyes and approached each customer with lowered head and wagging tail, begging to be petted. When she was petted, she would collapse, belly up, waving her paws in pleasure, while the owner would call out with delighted irony, "That's right, Wolf! Kill, girl! Kill!"

Most pets, however, are members of families that also have human children. Among our sample of veterinary-school clients, only 15 percent of pet owners lived alone, and the number of these who considered their pet a member of the family was no higher than in homes with children: seven out of ten. A survey by the American Veterinary Medical Association found that 72.4 percent of households with children also have a pet, compared with 54.4 percent of couples with no children having pets. The high percentage of pets found in families is partly because they are said to be good for children and partly because a family has more resources for raising a pet and is more likely to live in the kind of housing where pets are permitted.

One of the roles that an animal can play within the family is that of a bridge between people. Two people within the family who have difficulty talking to each other can sometimes interact through or around a pet. Katcher interviewed a young wildlife photographer who was accompanied by her dog, Need. "I named her that," the woman explained, "because I needed her and she needed me." She had found the animal at the scene of an accident in which both its front paws had been severely damaged, with fragmented bone and extensive tissue injury. No one could find the dog's owner, so the driver of the car that was responsible took both the dog and the photographer to the hospital. He offered to pay part of the costs of the animal's extensive surgery. The woman tried in vain to locate an owner. Instead, at the site of the accident, she found several witnesses who were willing to contribute toward the animal's care. During the months of repetitive operations and recovery, she maintained contact with this network of people who were connected to her through the dog. On the afternoon that Katcher interviewed her, they were having a small party at her apartment to celebrate the final removal of the casts. The party was her first in the new apartment where she now lived with Need and four other stray animals. Need had brought all these people together.

This same woman described her own family, in which pets were the only bridge to her father. As a child she could approach him only when he was with his dog and only by starting to pet and play with the dog. Her father would join in the play and begin to talk. At other times he was at best taciturn and frequently would not talk at all. Now, because he no longer has an animal, she always takes Need or another pet along when she visits. As it was in the past, their dialogue is always through the animal.

Parents frequently attempt to engineer this kind of bridging when they obtain animals for their children. For example, a family moves to a distant suburb and buys a horse for one of their children. The process of keeping the horse and teaching the child to ride and even to compete in shows becomes a family occupation in which large amounts of resources are pooled. In less dramatic fashion, buying a dog for a child is one way that some parents hope to establish a renewed bond of activities with children. It is not surprising that while 30 percent of all families own dogs, 56 percent of families with children under thirteen have at least one dog.

This effort at bridging the generations is not always successful, and difficulties arise when the child rejects the parents' attempts. A parent, usually the mother, ends up assuming the entire burden of the animal's care, while the child treats the animal quite casually, like a toy, playing with it intermittently at most. The animal may become the focus of family conflict and, instead of bringing parents and children together, push them further apart. There are two possible solutions to this standoff. The parent may get rid of the pet, taking it to a shelter. The "pet incident" then becomes another failure recorded in the child's family history or for the child may become the memory of another arbitrary parental crime—"giving away my dog." Alternatively, the mother may keep the animal as a substitute child, enjoying with the dog the kind of closeness and intimacy that is no longer possible with the child. Many mothers who complain that pet care devolves to them actually welcome the perpetuation of care and intimacy that the animal brings.

At the other extreme, children can close themselves off from the world of adults with an animal. We have already described Alasdair Macdonald's study of Scottish children who regarded their animals as their most significant social contact. When Katcher was growing up, he was very small for his age, two grades ahead of his peers in school, and somewhat uncoordinated to boot. After-school games and sports offered him only pain, failure, ridicule, and isolation. He filled the time with reading unless his mother drove him out of the house. Then he would take his dog, Wags, to the park, avoiding schoolyards and corners where his classmates played. Once he was deep in the park, he could begin a constant dialogue with the animal. They were in a safe world of their own.

In a study done at the University of Minnesota, Michael Robin, a social worker, investigated pet ownership among high-school students who stayed out of trouble with the law and those who had a police record. He found that delinquent youth had pets just as frequently as the other high-school children. This result alone was important because there are wide-eyed animal lovers who believe that pets are the answer for most of the world's ills. One overly credulous veterinarian we encountered was sure that pets could protect against delinquency, venereal disease, and teenage pregnancy. When Robin investigated the relationship between child and pet, however, there were significant differences between the two groups. The children who had no difficulties with the law considered their animals to be companions and members of the family. The delinquents, however, considered their pets to be personal friends, a bulwark *against* the family and the world.

"Trixie was very special to me," said one delinquent. "We went on walks together, went to the park and played. She even slept on the edge of my bed. When I was sad, I could cuddle up to her and she wouldn't hold anything against me. She just sat there and loved me." Said another, "My favorite pet was my dog Bell. I loved her very much. I took care of her all the time and never mistreated her. Sometimes she was the only person I could talk to." Or again, "My kitty was the joy of my life. She never hurt me or made me upset like my parents. She always came to me when she wanted affection." The anger behind the delinquent's defensive love of animals was revealed by another child. "Pets are important especially for kids without brothers and sisters. They can get close to this animal and they both can grow up to love one another. Men have killed for loved animals."

Unfortunately for these delinquent children, their families did not protect their pets. At the time of the study, half of the untroubled children still had their special pet, but fewer than 30 percent of the delinquent children had theirs. More strikingly, more than a third of the delinquent children's special pets had been deliberately killed by family or others. The rate of such loss among the other children was only 12 percent. This kind of violent loss characterizes the family life of many delinquent and disturbed children, and both child and pet suffer. In an English study that looked at the characteristics of families who were reported for animal abuse, there was a close association between disturbed family life, maltreatment of children, and abuse of animals.

Pets can also isolate people from each other. In the film *Le Chat*, Simone Signoret and Jean Gabin play a husband and wife bound together by dependency and hatred. The husband's cat was the only object of his affection, the center of his emotional life, his friend, affectionate partner, and constant companion in the house. The wife, finally overwhelmed by the contrast between her state and the cat's, shoots the animal. Love for the pet became magnified into hate for another family member.

The same sentiment is captured in an Honoré Daumier etching from *Humors of Married Life*. An elderly couple is shown sitting at a table, the woman knitting, with a cat on her shoulder, and the man hand-feeding the dog, who sits on the table. The caption reads, "She has her animal. He has his own, and the four get on like cats and dogs."

Pets can also cause problems in the bedroom, most frequently when the pet's owner introduces a new sleeping partner. In one case a graduate student became engaged to a young woman who had lived alone with her cat for two years. She was now quite attached to her pet. Her new fiancé was the first friend to sleep overnight in her apartment. When he began a sexual relationship with her, the cat was disturbed by the "new" activity. He had never seen male genitalia and attempted on several occasions to bat at these strange objects with his paws. Although the graduate student avoided contact or injury, he became frightened and began to lose his erection when the cat was present. The young woman did not wish to ban the cat from the bedroom, insisting that the cat's howling and scratching when it was put out spoiled the experience of lovemaking for her. The conflict was resolved simply by having the graduate student reassure his friend that he liked and accepted her cat, while she was able to agree that it would not be harmful for the cat to learn to spend a little time outside her bedroom. Obviously the initial responses of both parties indicated other problems, and managing the pet did not remove the male client's castration anxiety or resolve the young woman's ambivalence about an adult sexual role. It did, however, permit them and the cat to continue life together.

Some sexual conflicts that involve a pet cannot be so easily resolved, and animals can be among the mechanisms that people use to avoid sexual encounters. One couple was seen in consultation at the veterinary school because they were having difficulty agreeing to put down their terminally ill pet. The dog had severe arthritis and was incontinent. Over the past five years, he had been a major source of friction in the marriage. The husband felt sexually inhibited and turned off when the animal was in the bed, yet his wife would not otherwise have intercourse. "The dog would feel punished," she said, "if he were not permitted to sleep in his usual place." The dog never took any notice of sexual activity when it did occur but simply curled up at the foot of the bed. The husband felt particularly humiliated because he was forced to lift the dog when the animal's arthritis prevented it from jumping into bed. The battle over sex and the dog was only one of a number of chronic quarrels between them, and the animal was used by the wife to subordinate her husband's needs to her own.

In similar fashion, pets can be used to express a variety of quarrels between family members. A mother can complain loudly to her cat about the way in which other people are treating her. Our ability to talk to animals permits us to express feelings about other people that we cannot express directly. We can do this either by talking to the animal in private or by going through the charade of talking to the pet when others in the family are around to hear. This is safer than complaining directly, because if the words bring conflict, it is possible to retreat by saying, "I was only talking to the cat."

Sometimes animals are used in more direct combat. At her animal-behavior clinic, Victoria Voith received a call from a terrified wife who complained that she lived in constant fear of her husband's German shepherd, which would growl and threaten her whenever she came into the same room as the dog. During the day she would have to sneak about the house, peering around corners to avoid the animal. Her husband refused to discipline his pet and delighted in the animal's "fighting spirit." The wife was bitten and twice required emergency-room treatment. Each time the husband blamed the wife, not the dog. The woman called Voith when her husband was away and said that she was too frightened to talk to him about treatment for the animal. She was encouraged to come in and talk and was given an appointment, which she did not keep. When a social worker called her, she refused to talk to him and asked that he not call again.

Sometimes it is possible to make a therapeutic mistake by recommending that the wrong kind of family take a pet. Michael McCulloch was treating a woman who became depressed when she was disappointed by a lifelong dream not being fulfilled: she had always wanted a close and loving marriage but had married a man who was addicted to work. She then soothed herself with the belief that after his retirement they would enjoy the close, affectionate marriage she wanted. But her husband kept putting off retirement, and she became depressed. McCulloch suggested that she and her husband get a pet, which could act as a kind of a bridge between them. With characteristic enthusiasm, the husband bought a large Doberman, which terrified his wife. The dog, not the wife, became the center of his life and his wife's live-in rival.

Another case had a happier ending. The family beagle, Postman, did not like the father. He would run and hide when the father returned home, and if the father approached, Postman would cower, leak urine, and sometimes growl. The father couldn't walk the dog, although the animal loved walks, and couldn't even feed him unless he put down the bowl and walked away. The contrast between the dog's joyous affection for the mother and children and his fear of the father was troubling the whole family, making the father moody when the dog was about.

Since this family had always been close and truly wanted to remain so, the problem was solved simply by using the first motto of dog training: Food conquers all! Postman was given only water in the morning and spent the rest of the day trying to coax the mother or children to feed him, but with no results. When the father came home, he opened a can of dog food, laced it with some pieces of salami (a special treat), put the bowl down, and stepped back only a few feet. For a long time, Postman looked from the bowl to the father, then to the rest of the family. Finally hunger won out, and he approached the bowl, on his belly, leaking drops of urine in fear. He gulped his meal, eyes on the father, and immediately retreated.

The following day the routine was repeated, but Postman was less frightened and approached more rapidly. As time went on, the father moved closer, until Postman was at the dish before it left his hand. Then, before Postman was given his meal, Dad offered him pieces of salami from his hand. At first they had to be dropped on the floor, but after only a few trials, the dog caught them in midair and then accepted them from his hand. The next nights were spent training Postman to follow Dad for the salami bribes. It was not long before Postman was running down the garlic-paved road to the loving father.

For those who love their pets, cruelty to animals is incomprehensible. Recent research has found that animal abuse is closely linked to other forms of abuse. Thus senseless animal abuse can serve as a warning, indicating the need for therapy. James Hutton, a British social worker, examined families that had been reported for cruelty to animals to determine if they were known to other social agencies for problems like child or wife abuse. He found that most of the families that had been investigated for cruelty to animals were also known for other serious psychiatric and social problems. Thus if agencies were to share files, animal abuse could be a good early warning for abusive behavior toward people.

Dr. Randall Lockwood, when at the State University of New York at Stony Brook, designed a test in which patients in a child abuse treatment program ascribe meanings to drawings of scenes involving animals that may be at risk, such as when family members arrive home to find the dog standing by an overturned trash can. These modified thematic apperception tests and extensive interviews indicate that such patients often ascribe a variety of roles to the animals, including those of scapegoat and protector of a vulnerable family member—patterns that are similar for families with abused children. Lockwood, like Hutton, finds that animal abuse is very common in families with a history of child abuse. From this study valuable diagnostic measures may aid in identifying people with potentially distorted views of life before they commit acts that hurt themselves and others.

Animal cruelty is thus receiving some serious legal and scientific attention, both to protect animals and to better understand the people involved. There is far less commitment to understanding zoophilia, which is often addressed only when it occurs in conjunction with other psychiatric disorders. Few people appear willing to speculate, if only transiently, on its occurrence as part of a normal relationship.

One of the great taboos of our culture is using an animal as a collaborator in sexual activity. This prohibition is probably more effective than the prohibition against incest with children. Since the pet has the status of *favored* child in the family, sexual exploitation of pets is seen as a particularly loathsome kind of incest.

Boris Levinson, who was among the first people to use dogs in the therapy of disturbed people, hypothesized that one of the main reasons people resist sterilizing their dogs and cats is that they recognize the animal's sexuality and appreciate it, either vicariously or directly. For some, watching dogs mate is repulsive, but many enjoy watching and may even hold the animal. Others, especially youngsters, enjoy watching, even masturbating at the same time. Undoubtedly, for many people, animals provide the first real insight into how sexual intercourse is accomplished. Dr. Heini Hediger, a European zoologist who has spent most of his career working in zoos, reports that the sexual behavior of zoo animals is a major attraction.

People's treatment of animals often includes behaviors that at least mimic intimate human behavior: gentle touch, petting, soft and loving speech, scratching almost any part of the body, and kissing. Words of frank affection accompany these gestures and are openly used. But for the vast majority of owners and handlers of animals, the interaction stops short of actual or prolonged genital contact; for a few people, it does not.

In their research on people's sexual behavior, Dr. Alfred Kinsey and his associates asked questions about animal contact, but only after the person being interviewed had developed trust in the scientific purpose of the interview and believed that the researchers made no social judgments. They did not ask whether the person had sex with animals but how often, as if to imply that a positive answer would not be surprising or shocking. Between 40 and 50 percent of farm boys, especially city-bred boys now living on farms, indicated some actual sexual activity with animals, perhaps in response to the unavailability of females in the religious or moral setting of the time. Eight percent of urban men, mostly adolescents, also reported such activity. Only 3.6 percent of adolescent urban women reported similar activity— 74 percent of it with dogs—and in only 1.2 percent was there repeated genital contact to orgasm. The behaviors included genital contact and masturbation—dogs and cats were encouraged to lick the person's genitals, and actual coitus was performed with the animal.

Education was strongly associated with this behavior: the higher the education, the more likely sexual activity was. This may reflect some reporting bias, as it is generally assumed that better-educated people are more open with investigators, but the more educated people also reported increased involvement with other, less traditional forms of sexuality, such as a greater variety of sexual positions during intercourse with people. Generally, educated people are less tradition-bound and more experimental. It should be noted that Kinsey's findings on the incidence of zoophilia were that "no other type of sexual activity . . . accounts for a smaller proportion of the total outlet of the total population for both males and females."

While in graduate school, Beck attended a psychiatry class taught by Dr. John Money. A female patient agreed to be interviewed before the class. She complained that she always developed a psychosomatic case of stomach gas (belches) whenever she tried to have sexual intercourse with her husband. She also tended to gently feel the genitals of the young babies in her care. Almost in passing she mentioned that she did have intercourse with the family dog. She had been in therapy for many years but had never mentioned this aspect of her troubled life because she felt the doctors would not understand. She was more afraid of the judgment that might be passed on her activity with her dog than of being unable to have normal intercourse or being a pedophile. It was only after she heard Money lecture on zoophilia at her church that she realized she needed to discuss this problem, and she sought his help. (Incidentally, Money gave such lectures because he believed that this problem has been driven so far underground that people were not getting the help they needed. He was apparently correct.)

In another report a man and woman, their fourteen-year-old daughter, and the family's Doberman arrived at the emergency room of a veterinary hospital. They wanted the dog examined for any venereal diseases that could be transmitted to the daughter because they caught her having intercourse with it. The fascinating aspect was that their first response was not to go to a psychiatrist or a gynecologist but a veterinarian. The dog was examined and cultured for leptospirosis and found healthy. There was no follow-up.

In New York City the Department of Health received a

call from a woman who said that she was picked up by some men with a dog while she was hitchhiking. They drove to a secluded place and made her have intercourse with the dog while they watched. She was concerned about disease. She refused to give her name or come in for an examination, and there was no way to confirm the truthfulness of the story. In any event, it indicated that for some, voyeuristic and rape fantasies include roles for animals.

In fact, pornography using dogs, horses, and pigs is relatively common and available. Beck collected data by visiting a peep-show theater and observed patrons depositing quarters to view films of sexual action; nearly one-third of the choices involved animal subjects. Many of the paperback books and magazines being sold there combined human and animal partners. In large cities one can find newspaper advertisements for "party" dogs that are specially trained to service people.

Such cases are not common, but they and others like them provide additional evidence that animals, especially dogs, can be "people" or "family" in a most intimate way. Sexual interaction can be a chance or even accidental encounter, a fantasy, or a full-blown sexual act leading to orgasm for both partners. The feelings about sexual encounters with animals are more important than the actual acts themselves, and we will examine them later in the book.

In the context of this chapter, however, it must be recognized that zoophilia can be a kind of incest, and thus our reactions to men having intercourse with animals are different from our notions about the equivalent acts for women. Men having intercourse with farm animals is a subject of humor and mild contempt, like masturbation. This attitude is reflected in our response to jokes about farmhands and heifers. Women having intercourse with animals, however, is not regarded as humorous. The idea is frequently horrifying and is used in fantasy as a means of punishing or degrading women. Yet women's sexual engagement with animals is continually fascinating to men. It is perhaps no accident that in the three cases cited before—the only ones in our files—the human partners are women. This combination of horror, degradation, and fascination is identical to the feelings surrounding the idea of the male child committing incest with his mother.

Apparently, in our best and most innocent affectionate interchanges with our pets, and in some of the worst, the animal still acts as a kind of child. What value does the pet's childlike status have for us? In brief, defining a pet as a kind of child permits us to nurture the animal and to gain all of the benefits that such nurturing provides.

When Katcher was on a radio call-in show devoted to the health benefits of pets, a woman told him she had learned how much her pets meant to her when she had had open-heart surgery. Her heart stopped, and she felt herself floating over her body. At that moment she thought, "I can't die, my dog needs me." The surgery was five years ago, and since then the dog has been replaced. But she will never be without a dog, because her pet pulled her back to life.

Pets, houseplants, and gardens pull us into life by requiring care that must be performed day after day. They do not vary much from year to year, and they require simple skills and some patience. They are the kind of cyclical activities that once marked all human life and therefore pull us back into the security of cyclical time. The little acts of caring, feeding, watering, tending, and protecting all call forth a response, and the sum of the acts leaves the caregiver with the feeling that he or she is needed. The reciprocal feelings of caring for something and being needed are lines that can hold us to life. The solemn act of feeding an animal is often the first real connection that a child makes with the living world, establishing him as a caretaker. Some eighty years later, the same person, who may now seem to have little to offer any other human, can continue caring by setting out some crumbs for the winter birds. The pleasure in the act is the same, and the feeling of being needed is the same.

When people become depressed and cease caring, they

fall prey to illness and accident. This increased vulnerability is reflected in an increased death rate. Some illness may come from the failure to maintain normal patterns of eating and exercise. However, depression and the experience of giving up can produce subtle pathological changes that disorganize the body chemistry, reduce resistance to infectious disease, and accelerate the progress of chronic degenerative diseases, such as coronary-artery disease and cancer.

Psychiatrists have identified a syndrome they call helplessness/hopelessness, whose victims no longer believe that they can improve their lives and stop trying. The syndrome has been associated with greater rates of invasive cancer and even a vulnerability to sudden death. The kind of deaths reported by anthropologists that result when someone feels he has been the target of witchcraft may be an example of the lethal effect of this depressed emotional state. The frequent accounts of people dying suddenly after the death of a relative are also evidence of the deadly aspects of despair.

When people maintain patterns of caring, whether for a house, a garden, pets, or other people, they are protecting themselves against despair, against giving up. They are rewarded by feeling needed. The word "care" has many meanings, however, and one of them is "worry," as when someone is burdened with care. You do worry about the things you care for. Unfortunately, the association of care with effort and worry leads us to conceive of old age as a period in which one should live a "carefree existence." After retirement, people are urged to give up their cares. It can be a lethal trade-off. The person who stops caring for something may have taken the first steps to the hopelessness/helplessness syndrome. And those who cope best with old age are those who continue the daily acts of caring, especially the most satisfying ones—care rendered to living things, such as pets and gardens.

Nurturing engages mind and body, and the alterations in emotion and body chemistry created when we care for others influence our health. To understand why we feel better and why we are healthier when we care for others, it is necessary to reexamine human evolution.

It is a reasonable hypothesis that the prolonged care of infants in primate and early human groups was facilitated and maintained by deeply rooted physiological, psychological, and social rewards. If child-rearing makes parents healthier and more socially attractive, their infants would have a better chance of survival. Survival of parents and their young would also be increased if competing adults without children were less attractive and more vulnerable to disease and death. If you wish to ensure the passage of your genes into the next generations, then stay healthy as long as you can, aid your children in the competition for resources, and then pass out of the picture rapidly when you become only another competitor.

The history of human evolution is a history of increasing time spent in nurturing infants as the size of the human brain increased. The continuing enlargement of the brain demanded that infants be born in an increasingly helpless state because more and more of the growth of the brain had to be completed after birth—the human pelvis is not large enough to accommodate the fully grown brain. It is reasonable to assume that as the period of infantile dependency on adults began to grow, members of the kin network became engaged in part of this child care. This would be an evolutionary efficient strategy, since kin fostering would also result in the passage of some of one's genes into the next generation. The progressive infantile dependence in succeeding evolutionary stages would extend the period of time and the kinds of people engaged in affectionate nurturing and also decrease the distinction between adult and childlike characteristics, blurring the distinctive traits that release affectionate care. One could hypothesize that greater generalization of the nurturing response would also extend to disabled and sick members of the band, resulting in a higher survival rate from illness and accident. There is some evidence for this generalization of nurturing in the fossil record. Archaeologists discovered an eleven-thousand-year-old skeleton of a dwarf adult male with disabilities that would have made it difficult for him to hunt or even to keep up with his nomadic band. For him to reach adulthood, he must have been fed and protected by others in his tribe.

When human beings began to rear other animals, perhaps by bringing home the young of adults killed in the hunt, they extended their opportunities for involvement in nurturing activities. The care of animals became facilitated both by the practical value of the animals themselves and by the pleasure and the physiological rewards of caring for the animals. If nurturing plants and animals had some of the same rewards as caring for other human beings, then we would also expect that the health of those groups practicing domestication would be improved by better nutrition and by the direct beneficial effects of the increased opportunity to engage in nurturing activities. Domestication of plants and animals also extended the opportunities for rearing human children. The limited resources available to nomadic tribes required them to space out childbearing, whereas the increased food resources and opportunity for permanent settlement afforded by agriculture permitted a greater frequency of childbirth.

Agriculture was fully established some ten thousand years ago, providing for humankind a continual and almost universal contact with animals and engagement with the nurturing of plants and animals. This engagement persisted throughout the history of civilization until the last two hundred years. In those two centuries—only ten to fifteen generations, a trivial time in the genetic history of human beings —there has been an extraordinary disengagement of people from care of animals and plants. This process began well before the Industrial Revolution with the enclosure and expropriation of public lands and with a shift in agricultural practices to support trade in grain, wool, and cattle.

Changing patterns of agriculture, with the displacement of small or peasant farmers, continued into the beginning of this century in Europe and continues in South and Central

America to this day. Since the Industrial Revolution, there has been an enormous shift of people into cities, away from any contact with the rearing of animals or the care of gardens and orchards. In the space of two centuries, the United States and western Europe went from a population that was only 10 percent urban to one that was 90 percent urban. In the United States, by 1910 there were fewer farm workers than industrial laborers, and now farm labor makes up only a small fraction of the workforce. Many of those remaining laborers have tasks that are divorced from the care of animals, such as seasonal harvesting. In these relatively few years, there has been a radical transformation in the physical relationship between human beings and other living things, with a very large part of the population being excluded from contact and care of living things other than their own children.

This shift has made us particularly dependent upon our pets for the opportunity to nurture others. For instance, Gail Melson, at Purdue University, has noted that by preschool, children can appropriately appreciate the difference between dogs and puppies, cats and kittens; they know that adult animals are caregivers, not babies. Boys usually increase their knowledge about animals with age, but their interest in, and care for, human infants generally decreases; this not true of their interest in, and care of, animals, perhaps because pet care is not associated with gender, as with the care of human infants. Boys, in particular, may be introduced to the importance of nurturing with the aid of their pets.

The human family has contained domestic animals for thousands of years. It has been said that "to be a good human, one needs to be first a good animal." In *Pets and Human Development*, Levinson noted that the "values of pet ownership in promoting normal child development may be summarized as follows. A child who is exposed to the emotional experiences inherent in playing with a pet is given many learning opportunities that are essential to wholesome personality development. His play with the pet will express his view of the world, its animals, and its human beings, including his parents and peers." It appears to us that companion animals are our children's children, and the best thing we can do for our children is to help them be better parents.

It is this healthful, and sometimes life-saving opportunity that we build into our culture we refer to when we describe pets as members of the family. Yet pets can sometimes be even closer than a family member; they can be a part of the self.

Four

Pets Can Be Self

IT'S A TRUISM that people pick pets to suit their own personality. Aren't Afghan owners different from people with Dobermans? "Typical" images include the tall, long-haired, bouncy young woman with her Afghan; and the plump, middle-aged woman with too much jewelry, too much makeup, and a toy French poodle or a Persian cat. That some people look like their pets is a long-held conviction, evident in numerous cartoons. All these notions reflect an ancient belief that people and animals can share identity and change one into the other.

Perhaps the nightmares of early humans involved their kin turning into beasts with devouring teeth and tearing claws. Such fantasies have been recorded in early drawings, in clay and stone figures, and finally in words, all depicting half-human and half-animal beings that change from human to animal form. Egyptian gods wore the head of a dog or a hawk on a human body; Greek gods such as Poseidon and Zeus took on animal form to carry off women; Circe changed men into swine. Christianity may have erased the pagan gods, but St. Christopher still bore the head of a dog. And medieval artists relied heavily on animal symbolism to depict the stories and lessons of Christianity.

Today vampires and werewolves are still part of our mythology and are continually reanimated in film. People who can become cats, and alien creatures who can become human beings, are recent film myths. In Eugène Ionesco's satirical drama *Rhinoceros*, people became rhinoceroses, charging about in angry futility. A persistent belief is that of the wild child who is raised by wolves and takes on their habits, or even, in one television drama, their eyes. A "true" account of such a child appeared in *Weekly World News* of October 19, 1982, under the title "Howl of the Wolf Boy." The story described his flesh-eating habits and nocturnal howling. Discovered among a wolf pack in the Indian jungle, the boy, newly named Pascal, was adopted by Mother Theresa's nuns, who, over the skepticism of the doctors examining Pascal, believed they could educate him. This is but one in a long series of such stories.

Just as people are believed capable of taking on the form of beasts, they can also assume what we perceive as animal characteristics. Part of our vocabulary for describing human behavior and feelings is based on this perception: "greedy as a pig," "bitchy," "going ape," "after him like a pack of wolves," "chicken," "swinish," "bullheaded," "monkey see, monkey do," "catty," "birdbrained," "snake in the grass," "sheepish," "elephantine," "bullish," "bearish," and so on. The list seems endless. Animal metaphors are used because animals are assumed to be constant in appearance and behavior, so that their appearance can stand for their behavior, while human appearance can be deceptive. As Shakespeare said, we can "look like the innocent flower but be the serpent under't." But because we use animals to represent aspects of human behavior, our vocabulary makes us think of ourselves as a zoo of behaviors, each represented by an iconic animal.

At some level we believe that human beings are an uneasy conjoin of animal and angel. Behaviors that are not shaped by the rules of social convention are described as animalistic, and people who are excessive in their anger or desires are described as animals. Scientists speak of the organization of the human brain as a troika of reptilian, mammalian, and human elements. Clearly the Freudian id is an animal, continually escaping restraint and controlling some part of our actions. Even those who believe in neither the Freudian animal brain nor the evolutionary animal brain expect that children start life as animals, as natural beings, and then through learning and the acquisition of restraint become human, and hence cultural, beings. However, the natural child—the animal—still lives within the envelopes of learning and social restraint.

Yet there is a way of relating to animals that is different from the junctures implied in animal metaphors. A real animal—a pet—can be made part of the self and loved as one's self. Understanding how people love themselves in a pet animal begins with the fantasy life of the infant, played out with the stuffed animals of the nursery, and continues with such adult idols as God and country. Since all these ideas can be embodied in the form of animals, they are all related, and all help explain the overflowing love between ourselves and our pets.

INFANT FANTASIES AND IDEAL MOTHERS

The infant has no words and lives only with images in its consciousness, reconstructing the world with mental pictures. The mind of the infant is the silent world of dream images. The infant feels hunger as pain, which the mother removes by feeding. Later the pain of hunger stimulates a fantasy of a nurturing mother that has the force of a hallucination, since the infant can't distinguish between external and internal reality. This hallucination alone can calm the infant's hunger and replace the real mother for a while, becoming the image of an ideal mother that is only good. All the bad feelings attached to the real mother are split off into another being. The mother that restrains, washes, walks away, takes things away, and even hurts is separated from the complete mother, whom the infant perceives as both good and bad. By dividing the image of the complete mother, infants create two mothers—a good fairy godmother and a wicked witch.

The child will eventually learn that the two polar beings are aspects of the same real mother, but this tendency to split real beings into opposite images continues throughout life. Some adults still think, for example, that communists are all bad while born-again Christians are all good; women are either saints or whores; men are macho or wimps; people are either part of the problem or part of the solution. Learning about reality is learning to put such split images back into composite flesh-and-blood beings. Yet for infants and adults, the split images of good and evil can be simple and comforting tools for organizing the world.

Animal metaphors provide graphic images of good and bad feelings and behaviors assigned to good and bad feelings. For example, we equate lions with bravery, jackals with cowardice, elephants with good memory, squirrels with forgetfulness, ants with industry, and grasshoppers with indolence. By giving behavior or feeling a form, animals permit us to visualize actions as split or as ideal images and to store those images in the wordless, unconscious level of the mind that generates both dreams and poetry.

STUFFED ANIMALS AS IDEAL MOTHERS

Each child, then, may have two fantasy mothers, one all good and the other all bad. In his dreams and in his waking imagination, he is comforted by one and threatened by the other.

The child's imagination is augmented by children's literature, which is peopled by beings who are simple signs of either virtue or vice, and by the fantasies that parents themselves create centering on the world of stuffed animals and security blankets. The child's room can be turned into a soft menagerie, with stuffed animals of all kinds filling space on crib, bed, floor, and shelf. The child with thumb in mouth, blanket or stuffed animal in hand and against cheek, has become part of our stock representation of childhood. Like thumb-sucking itself, security blankets and special teddy bears have become over the years more tolerable to parents, less of an aberration, more like a developmental phase.

Whether it is tolerated or not, the stuffed animal or even the more amorphous blanket is usually given a name and an identity, and the child is encouraged to talk to it, sing to it, greet it, and say "night night" at bedtime. Parents may even elaborate on the child's attachment and fantasies by telling him that the object loves him or will be there at night to protect him. The stuffed animal may be used to reinforce parental wishes: "Teddy would want you to take your medicine." Sometimes parents fall into a technique like doll therapy with such suggestions as "Tell Teddy what you want for your birthday" or "Well, if you won't tell me what's wrong, tell Teddy!" All these social responses confirm the reality of the object for the child and aid the child in his attempts to make the teddy bear or soft panda or other animal into an ideal object capable of loving him, protecting him, and making him feel safe. The child's belief is partially confirmed by the object's behavior. It never scolds, hurts, confines, or restrains him, and it is there when he needs it—soft and constant.

The psychologist Dr. D. W. Winnicott perceptively called these cloth creatures transitional objects, meaning that they help the child move out into the world without the mother. The object becomes a kind of portable mother, ensuring the child's safety when the real mother is not there. Being safe, the child can then form new attachments and interests independent of his real mother.

Children use their stuffed animals during transitions, particularly from wakefulness to sleep and from sleep to a new day. At these moments the world is more threatening, more difficult to keep in order; the silent comfort of the animal provides security, just as it first did when the mother left the room for the night. In confronting new situations or in seeking some independence from the mother, the child feels safer with the trusted stuffed animal. It is, then, an ideal piece of the mother, the part that makes the child feel most secure. And unlike his real mother, it always comforts, never punishes with anger, never interferes with his explorations, and is always there when he wants it.

It is impossible to underestimate the power of stuffed animals. In Dr. Harry Harlow's famous experiments with "cloth mothers," a baby monkey isolated from its mother and raised only with a stuffed animal could learn to master strange environments, lose fear, and explore what was around it. The stuffed animal was the only mother the infant monkey knew, and without "her" it would spend its time crouching, rocking, and gnawing on its fingers, unable to move at all. Certainly the cloth mothers were not enough to enable the infant monkeys to become normal adults, but they were more powerful than anyone had anticipated.

PETS AS IDEAL MOTHERS AND LOVING CHILDREN

The stuffed animal is one of the models for a child's later relationship with a living pet. A pet begins to acquire, as the child gets older, some of the characteristics of the ideal mother. The enormous love between people and pets seems to resemble the perfect love of the ideal mother.

The anthropologist Dr. Constance Perin first suggested that the pet could be a symbolic equivalent of the mother. In a paper delivered in 1980 she wrote:

I began to look into the nature of the mother-child bond thinking that those feelings of idealization, of ambivalence, of complete devotion [that we have toward our pets] might take their strength, their force, from this source. . . . . Above all, it is the theme or structure around which dogs are shaped as the symbolic vehicle of that excess of human love, an idea about love apart from any real person, for the superabundance of love after infancy has no rightful human object in our society. Yet the original symbiosis is recollected. Dogs give "complete and total love," "utter devotion," "lifelong fidelity," the "one-person" dog. Speechless, yet communicating perfectly, the mute and ever-attentive dog is a symbol of our own memory of that magical once-in-a-lifetime bond.

The idea that the love and devotion that we feel flowing from a dog is an idealization of mother love is a brilliant insight but only provides us with half the picture. Systematic observations about what people do with their dogs and other pets are required to complete the picture.

There is no doubt that most people treat a pet as a child. They talk to the pet and touch and play with it as they would with a child. They feed and respond to its sexuality and its excretions as if it were a child. They place it in the family as a child. The unfortunately common practice of abandoning dogs and cats once they have matured reinforces the impression of the pet's position as a child, suggesting that these animals are most attractive when they are most childlike. In our myths, the more adultlike wolves, not dogs (see chapter 8), have nurtured children from Romulus and Remus to Kipling's Mowgli to Mother Theresa's wolf boy. Nana in *Peter Pan* is a singular exception of a nurturing dog.

Other aspects of our behavior toward dogs and even cats suggest that there are idealized ideas about mother love attached to them. Perin mentioned our inflated ideas about the dog's devotion and the superabundance of his love. We also train dogs to be continually attentive to us, even when we ignore them. This attentiveness mimics the mother's role, as does our feeling that the dog's attentiveness provides a feeling of safety and comfort. Last, and most obvious, the dog is a territorial predator that protects our home and turns his teeth against dangers from the outside.

The truth is that with our pets we are both mother and child, simultaneously or alternately, with the pet playing the opposite part. When we greet our pets in the morning or on returning home in the evening, they are transitional objects, permitting us to enter new territory or a new day or to safely return from foreign territory. It is no wonder that we want to see our pets first when we return home; what child doesn't first look for its mother when returning from school or play? When we walk with our dogs in strange or dangerous places, the dog is our loyal protector, as the teddy bear once was, dispelling our fears.

In play, we and the dog are both parent and child, alternating control and pursuit. Roughhouse that is mixed with petting and touching makes us mothers playing with a toddler. Sitting quietly with the dog, ruffling or playing with his fur, makes us infants touching mother as we drift off into fantasy or makes us a mother touching an infant to calm herself and her child. The pet in the bed is an animated version of the stuffed animal, which when hugged became part of mother —the most primitive of all kinds of transubstantiations.

Although, as we will discuss in chapter 11, Lassie can be a bitch, she does seem to play the part of the mother with consistency. Dogs, by virtue of their size, their real ability to protect and even rescue us, their constant attention and their pack-animal devotion, fit the role. What of cats? They are small, and in the wild they are solitary animals. They are not devoted, malleable servants; their most ardent lovers describe them as aloof, untrainable, and a bit self-centered. Can cats teach us to alternate between being a loving parent and a loved child? Certainly cats do greet their owners at the threshold; being highly territorial animals, they are closely associated with the home. We pet them, and they respond to our petting. We feed them, care for them, play with them, and laugh at their foolish antics. They share our beds. Certainly we can enjoy loving them and feeling their acceptance of our love as love reflected.

However, cats are probably not associated with the

mother in the same way that dogs are. We would like to suggest that cats can be parents too, but the cat is more likely to be equated with the father, an errant, selfish, demanding, and wayward one who monopolizes the mother's love and gives little in return, the selfish, narcissistic lover who doesn't work and can be faithless and rejecting. Cartoons continually make an equation between a tomcat out on a prowl under the moon and a drunken husband holding on to a lamppost for support. The suspicion and anger that many people feel toward the cat is a child's anger at an unworthy father who claims mother's love without earning it. That anger is often expressed when cats are cast in such threatening roles as familiar spirits or servants of the Devil. It is also expressed in the various hate-cat books, such as Simon Bond's *101 Uses for a Dead Cat.*

PETS AS SELF

Because we alternate the roles of child and parent with our pets, the feeling of mutual love and devotion is understandable, not only because the pet carries some of the idealized attributes of the mother but also because the pet is the self. In mothering the pet, we are mothering ourselves. In being mothered by our pets, we are recreating, as Perin suggested, the faith of the infant in superabundant love. However, most of the activity between person and pet casts the pet in the role of child—in essence, an infant loved by a human mother. However, the pet could also be seen as a *representation of oneself as an infant.* Therefore the pet is the self as a child, still suspended between nature and culture, no longer part of nature but not yet trained to live in adult society. In loving our pets, we love and keep alive our own childhood.

Every human being feels at some time an estrangement from nature and from free contact with his or her own inner nature. The price of learning a culture is imprisonment within that society, away from nature. Rarely do people formally mourn their lost childhood; they are too busy growing up. Yet the child mourning a dead pet at a mock funeral is in fact mourning both the loss of the animal and of her own childish nature. This feeling was expressed by Gerard Manley Hopkins in the poem "Spring and Fall: To a Young Child":

> Margaret, are you grieving
> Over Goldengrove unleaving?
> . . . .
> Now no matter, child, the name:
> Sorrow's springs are the same.
> Nor mouth had, no nor mind, expressed
> What heart heard of, ghost guessed:
> It is the blight man was born for,
> It is Margaret you mourn for.

As we grow older, we lose our animal nature. It is not merely the child's change in behavior with age that constitutes the loss. After all, any animal can be trained and still be an animal. Rather, it is a change in the operation of the unconscious mind that leads to our progressive estrangement from the world of natural creatures.

In a unique study of children's dreams, Dr. Robert Van de Castle noted the change in frequency of dreams containing animals as children grow older. When the child is younger than ten years of age, 30 to 50 percent of dreams contain animals. After that, there is a consistent decline in the frequency with which animals act in dreams. For children between the ages of fourteen and sixteen, animals appear in fewer than 14 percent of dreams; and after the age of eighteen, dreams of animals decrease to fewer than 7 percent. The perception of the animal as a child in conscious thought and the association of children with animals in literature mirror the operation of the unconscious mind. Maturity is a separation from the animal part of ourselves. The animal within dies so that the child can become an adult.

Later we can relive life as a child through a pet; however, we experience being loved as if we were children, loving as if the pet were a child, and being a child simultaneously. In some sense, then, the life with a pet recreates a childhood that never was. By the time the child can love as actively as we love, and are loved by, pets, the intense bond between mother and child is already being loosened. The child, able to run about actively, hug, tussle, and talk, is already conscious that mother's love must be shared. Precisely because pets have the ability to recreate a mythic love for the self, they can be used to requite love when human love has failed.

The identification of owner with her animal is not all fantasy. The owner can shape the animal's behavior, control its movements, feed it, clothe it, dress it, bejewel it, and doctor it, transforming the animal into a picture that suits the person's own vision. The animal can be trained to express aggression as well as loving submission. It can externalize a narcissistic concern about beauty, being clipped, shampooed, and clothed as frequently as the owner wishes. The owner can regulate the pet's presence, another important attribute of a vehicle for the self. Every time the owner returns home, the animal is there; at home the owner can spend as much or as little time with the pet as she wishes, and at night the pet can share the bedroom.

The belief that the pet is part of one's personal identity is reinforced by the social response to people with pets. As any politician knows, being pictured with a dog is just as good as being pictured with a baby, for people with pets are perceived as more approachable, more attractive, and more trustworthy than people alone.

In England, Dr. Peter Messent followed people on their walks through city parks and found that people with dogs were much more likely to be engaged in conversation than people who were walking alone. People with pets were even more approachable than mothers with small infants. The same kind of results were observed in another study, by Randall Lockwood. He showed subjects a series of relatively ambiguous pictures of people in a variety of common social settings. There were two similar sets of pictures: in one there were only people, and in the other there was a pet with one of the people in each scene. The subjects were asked to rate each of the people in the pictures according to several scales. The results were predictable. People with pets were perceived as being more socially attractive and as having more desirable personal characteristics. Pets changed the people's social identity for the better.

The conclusions of Messent and Lockwood were confirmed in a whole variety of studies that found that animals paired with people made the people more attractive. Lynette Hart and her colleagues found that handicapped children were noticed and talked to ten times more frequently when they were out with their service dogs than when they were walking alone. Katcher and Beck, working with Ruth Zasloff, found that pictures of prisoners or people with disabling neurological conditions were perceived as significantly more attractive by college students when the subjects in the pictures were paired with an animal.

PETS AND NARCISSISTIC LOVE

Psychiatrists use the term "narcissistic love" for the practice of using another being as a vehicle for expressing love of the self. The narcissistic lover is relatively insensitive to the identity of the being he loves and tends instead to recreate that being by projecting onto it whatever qualities he wishes. The narcissistic lover also wants complete possession of his love and constant attention. Loving oneself in another always leads to a desire for fusion. Narcissistic lovers are, of course, easily disappointed when the love object insists on having an independent identity. Don Juan is the classic narcissist. He demands to possess each woman he is attracted to, but once he does, he finds that they are not what he wanted, and he must go on to another conquest.

One solution to the narcissist's dilemma is a pet. Animals have so little identity of their own that the owner can project the attributes he chooses without contradiction. He can also control their behavior and movements so that their presence and attention never fail.

We do not mean to imply that the fifty million pet owners in this country are zoophilic Casanovas. Some people do use pets to express narcissistic love with little real perception of the animal's needs and are determined to turn the animal into a reflection of the self. But for most of us, the situation is more subtle. Most people who have pets become well aware of their animal's true nature simply by caring for it each day. However, virtually all of us use pets to reflect a love that we, not the pets, feel. All of us need to be loved unconditionally, and the ability of pets to reflect that love back at us satisfies a basic need. Pets can become a kind of psychotherapist, reaching even withdrawn people who do not sense love from any other human being.

Using pets to provide unconditional love is not a problem. It is part of the real attraction and utility of pets. Problems arise when people are unable to care for the real animal because they are blinded by their fantasy image of it. Many of the animals turned in to shelters or abandoned on the streets are victims of people who fell in love with the idea of having a cute puppy, kitten, exotic animal, or purebred dog. When their expectations were defeated by the animal's real behavior—soiling the carpets, chewing the furniture, demanding too much attention, barking or crying at night, shedding hair, and making it difficult to get away for weekends—the love was rapidly withdrawn and turned back toward the self, and the animal was discarded.

Christmas and Easter are especially bad times for animals. Animals given as gifts symbolize the loving feelings of the giver. The recipient of the gift may have little tolerance for the animal once the holiday is past. Whether the animal is a gift for the self or for others, experience and growth of the animal can defeat and contradict idealized dreams, and the animal that once mirrored love is frequently abandoned.

The sad defeat of narcissistic love is illustrated in the case of a young woman who brought her medium-sized female dog in to our behavior clinic, complaining that the animal was attacking her, and she had deep scratches on her abdomen and thighs. Investigation revealed that the woman was taking the dog to bed and clutching it to her like a teddy bear or lover. The dog was simply trying to escape her tight embrace and in the process had inflicted the scratches. The woman had never been bitten, and behavioral testing at the clinic revealed the dog to be a passive and compliant animal. When the dog's behavior was explained as a normal response to excessive constraint, the owner wept, saying that she could not fall asleep without hugging her dog. She had been depressed for years and was absolutely alone, with no friends. She wanted to give the dog tranquilizers so that it would not struggle in her embrace. When this suggestion was rejected, she started crying again and asked to leave. Her animal had failed her. It was not a teddy bear or a perfect lover.

Narcissistic love can also interfere with the proper care of animals. One of the ways in which a pet's life may be better than ours is in the manner of the pet's death. Veterinarians are permitted to practice euthanasia and can give the pet a comfortable death when illness becomes too painful or debilitating. When Katcher was first learning about how people responded to the death of their pets, Dr. Marc Rosenberg, a wise veterinarian, described how to prepare pet owners for euthanasia when they are closely bonded to their animals: "Some owners are so closely bonded that the pet is a part of themselves. Any threat to the pet is a threat to their own life. I have to get them to separate from their pet; to see it as an animal with its own life. Frequently I will ask them what they liked best about their pet. Then I will ask if the pet can do those things any more. Sometimes they then will be able to see that the animal can no longer be their pet and they will permit euthanasia." Owners have to give up the narcissistic quality of their love to permit their pet to die a decent death.

Exotic animals, which may not be loved as dogs and cats

are loved, can also be a narcissistic adornment that is used expressively by their owners. People might own snakes for the pleasure of a challenging hobby and not necessarily because they are in love with evil. Yet someone who chooses to keep poisonous snakes in an apartment—like the man who vanished from his New York City rooming house and left his cobras behind (see chapter 12)—is to some degree enamored of the lethal potential of the snake. The same fascination seems to attract some people to spiders and others to carnivorous fish, such as piranhas, Oscars, and Dempseys. A popular way to use piranhas for amusement is to starve them for a week, buy a number of goldfish, and put them in the tank and watch the killing frenzy.

People who keep wild cats—lynx, cheetahs, and even lions —are decorating themselves with killing power. Sometimes the infatuation with the meaning of the animal can lead to its complete neglect. One New Yorker kept a coyote in a dark cellar surrounded by its own feces. When the animal was confiscated, the man could only talk of its beauty and what that had meant to him.

We do not mean to imply that the exotic pet is always an immediate statement about the owner's personality or emotional balance. Truly benign people may own snakes, and truly malevolent ones may own doves. We do mean to suggest, however, that animals act as a kind of living heraldry to help people proclaim the distinctness of their own identity. And this is as true of dogs, cats, and parakeets as of monkeys, lions, and snakes. As pets, they help us define ourselves, for better or worse.

Five

Talking, Touching, and Intimacy

TALK

WHEN WE BEGAN our study of touch, we did not plan to study intimacy. We were only interested in the way people stroked their pets, and we were planning to contrast our subjects' physiological states during verbal (talk) and this kind of nonverbal (touch) communication. Fortunately for us, our subjects defeated our intentions, and we learned something new about intimate dialogue with pets.

For several years Aaron Katcher and James Lynch had been studying the effects of touch on seriously ill patients at the coronary care unit of the University of Maryland Medical School. Without disturbing either the patient or the nurse, they could observe the nurse touching the patient. The patient was continuously wired to a cardiac alarm that recorded the heartbeat. They observed that when the nurse touched the patient to take his pulse, the frequency of arrhythmia was reduced.

They saw similar phenomena in the shock trauma unit, where patients who were badly damaged in automobile accidents were brought for emergency treatment. They, too, had to be monitored continuously to prevent them from falling into shock or respiratory failure. Some were artificially paralyzed with the drug curare to prevent them from resisting the action of the respirator, which they depended on, as the pain of their broken ribs would have prevented them from breathing enough oxygen. Even these patients, who could not move a single muscle, would respond with changes in heart rate and blood pressure when a nurse touched their wrist or arm.

At the same time, they were also looking at the physiological costs of talking. They had studied hundreds of normal subjects: children, adults, students, patients, fellow doctors and nurses, patients with hypertension, and unsuspecting volunteers who were attending their lectures. The results of that long series of experiments were consistent and troubling: every time people talked, their blood pressure rose, and it remained elevated as long as they continued talking. The rise occurred whether they were talking about the little pleasures of the day or its petty angers. Something about the act of talking itself, independent of the emotion carried by the talk, caused the rise in blood pressure.

Katcher and Lynch intended to contrast the excitation produced by talking with the calming influence of touch and to continue the study with healthy people, not hospitalized patients. Unfortunately, the very nature of a study of touching makes both the observer and the subject self-conscious. Touch is a part of our communication used to qualify the emotional meaning of what we are saying or intending. People are hardly aware of how they include touch in a conversation. When they become directly aware of it, the interaction becomes awkward or strained. It is actually easier to perform sexually before an audience, as William Masters and Virginia Johnson found out to their surprise, than to use gentle natural touch to express affection. The motions of sexual stimulation are in the foreground, and the quality of our performance is improved when we concentrate on what we are doing. By contrast, the unconscious act of affectionate touch is disrupted by such concentration. Fortunately, people are relatively unself-conscious about petting dogs, much as women are not self-conscious about petting babies. The researchers designed a simple experiment. A client from the veterinary school clinic would be taken into a quiet room without his dog. He would talk to the experimenter, and then his dog would be brought in and he would pet it. Continuous measurement of blood pressure would answer questions about touch and talk. Once designed, the experiment was turned over to Erika Friedmann, who had conducted the heart disease study described in chapter 1, and two undergraduates, Melissa Goodman and Laura Goodman.

The students ran several pilot tests on subjects to shake down the experimental design and reported that blood pressure was lower when people were petting their dogs than when they were talking. However, no subject just petted the animal; they all talked to the dog at the same time. The plan to contrast talking and touching performed separately had to be scrapped. Later Katcher and Lynch realized that asking someone to stroke a pet without talking is like asking someone to caress a child or spouse without talking—impossible in most situations. The experiment was then redesigned to contrast pet owners talking to people and talking and touching their pets. The results can be presented in a simple graph.

All the readings in this experiment are elevated because, to keep the subject's arm free to touch the animal, researchers recorded blood pressure from the calf, which produces a higher reading. Blood pressure was highest when the subjects were talking or reading to them and lowest when they were greeting—that is, talking to—and petting their dogs. When they were resting quietly, doing nothing, blood

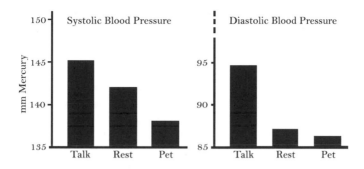

pressure was between the two other readings. Statistical analysis showed that the changes in systolic blood pressure were significant, meaning that it was unlikely that chance variations in blood pressure could have produced these results. The changes in diastolic blood pressure were similar to the changes in systolic blood pressure, but their significance was less certain.

Since that first conclusion that, unlike talking to people, talking to animals reduces stress and blood pressure, the validity of the observation has been confirmed by many other investigators. Gentle touch-talk dialogue with animals is always less stressful than talking to adults or strangers. If you ask people to describe the times when contact with their pets is most important, they usually tell you that they enjoy greeting their pet as they come home from work. That greeting and the accompanying dialogue of words and touch decreases or eliminates the stresses of the day.

In the experiment in which Katcher and Friedmann observed the stress-reducing dialogue between people and pets, they also were struck by the way in which people talked to pets. They recorded the dialogue and filmed the subjects' faces to make a permanent record of facial expression. We have already described the way in which pet owners talk to their animals—with softer, higher-pitched voices than normal, their conversation punctuated with simple questions, such as "Whatcha doing?" and with their attention fully on the animal to the exclusion of all else. They also observed that when the subjects shifted attention from pet to experimenter, they invariably reverted to a normal, louder voice. When they were talking to their animals, it was as if they were trying to shut out the rest of the world and, by whispering, make sure that the talk was for the animal only. One woman was quite conscious that she was shutting out the other people in the room, and after she talked a while to her cat, she would raise her voice and tell what she had been saying to her animal. Katcher and Friedmann saw another striking change later, on the television tapes. When the subjects talked to a researcher, their facial expressions were unremarkable except for a look of slight apprehension, perhaps because of the television camera or the novelty of the experimental situation. They tended to smile with the kind of tight, forced smiles that people normally use in anxious situations, and their faces sometimes seemed lined from the strain of the situation. When a subject turned his face down to talk to his pet, or even at the moment when he saw his pet being brought to him, there was an immediate change in facial expression. The smile became gentle, unforced, more relaxed. The facial features seemed to smooth out, and lines of tension were erased from the brow and around the eyes and mouth. Subjects looked younger and less forbidding, and the women seemed prettier. The changes were obvious to anyone who looked at the films. Soon after the experiment, an Adelphi University documentary film unit started making a film about this research called *Intimate Companions*, and they duplicated the study and photographed people talking to people and talking to their pets. As part of the film, Katcher and Friedmann analyzed the results. The people whom the Adelphi group photographed had the same response. One of their subjects was an elderly New England lawyer with a seamy face and a severe expression. Yet when he was given his dog to hold, there was the same softening of both voice and facial features. Talking to his dog, he looked younger, friendlier, and much more approachable.

The voice tones and style of speech used when communicating with pets resemble the baby talk used with infants. The facial expressions are, however, different. Those used with infants tend to be exaggerated, as if the parent or other adult were training the baby to express feeling with the face. Facial expressions used with animals are much more relaxed, more comfortable, and are clearly marks of intimate dialogue. That intimacy makes petting and talking to a dog feel good: it relieves tension and makes you feel more comfortable and appear more comfortable, more relaxed, and more attractive to others.

In working with both dog and cat owners, cats on occasion posed some problems. The cats needed more time to accept their new surroundings. On one visit the cat was reluctant to emerge from the carrying box, so the owner put the carrier open on the floor while the background interview was conducted. The owner and the interviewer went to another room, and after a wonderful, and long, discussion about cats, returned to the room—the cat was still quietly resting in the carrier. Most cats, however, eventually explored the room and began routine interactions with their owners.

In order to test whether the talk-touch interaction that occurs with dogs and cats is a general response that people have to companion animals, people who have pet birds were also examined. Volunteers were once again solicited from the university community, and subjects were interviewed by appointment. They were asked to bring their birds to the laboratory at the veterinary hospital, where they were interviewed without their birds in the room for about fifteen minutes, and then their birds' cages were placed beside them. The subject removed the bird from its cage and continued to answer questions. The subjects were asked to interact with their animals as they usually do, and again all not only had no difficulty demonstrating the interaction but also conducted themselves as if no other people were present. The topics covered by the interview were general and nonthreatening, designed to elicit general interactional behavior with both interviewers and the birds.

Again, the interviews were videotaped, with the equipment in full view of the subjects. The tape showed that more than 90 percent of the owners treated their birds like members of the family. Bird owners, like cat owners, spend more time talking to their pets than do dog owners. All three types of pet owners are just as likely to talk to their animals as they would talk to another person. And like other pet owners, people talk to birds with the same facial expression and voice inflection. They also believe that birds, like other animals, express some sort of jealousy when attention is diverted away from them and that birds, like dogs and cats, show a definite loyalty to one or two specific people—usually those who spend the most time with them. With all of our pets—whether dog, cat, or bird—talk is an essential component of the person-pet relationship. The dialogue we engage in with our pets creates companionship, and companionship is one mechanism through which the pet exerts a positive influence on health.

TOUCH

No matter what kind of emotional bond people have with their pets, touch is an essential part of that relationship. Touching reduces stress and, combined with gentle talk, creates a feeling of intimacy, closeness, completion. The word "pet" is derived from an agricultural term for an animal reared or mothered by hand, implying that a pet is a child within the family. The use of the word as a verb meaning "to stroke, touch gently, or fondle" reflects the belief that touch necessarily accompanies any mothering. Without touch, animal and human children will die or grow up stunted and emotionally deformed. We know how important touch is for the infant, but we know much less about the importance of it for the person who cares for the infant or the pet. Petting animals is one of life's most common joys; it is also an image that is closely associated with childhood in our culture: a toddler, with both fear and delicious anticipation, reaching out to pet a dog; a dog licking a child's giggling face; a child clutching a wriggling puppy. Because petting animals is such a happy cliché for simple pleasure, we take it for granted and are no longer even aware of it. Because pets are often defined as children, we touch them as if they were children. We touch animals with freedom and indulgence because animals have the capacity to call forth an immediate, childlike response that is usually not constrained by the rules of our culture. The ability of puppies to elicit instant affection and intimacy is another expression of the very primitive and immediate nature of our relationship with animals. Since starting this research, we have watched hundreds of people touching and holding adult dogs and puppies and have examined an even larger group of photographs of people petting dogs or clutching puppies. What impresses the informed eye is the similarity of gesture and facial expression regardless of the subject's age. The picture of a four-year-old girl holding a pup or of an eighty-five-year-old man stroking a cat in his lap bear striking similarities to each other. When they hold animals, mental patients and disturbed children lose the stigmatizing facial expressions that make them look "crazy." Animals have the capacity to call forth an essential kind of affection that is not changed by age or warped by the experiences that destroy or gravely injure one's ability to love other human beings.

When we started our examination of how people touched animals, we had to begin as if we had never seen anyone touch a dog or fondle a cat. We began by asking Laura to sit with a placid golden retriever named Emily in the waiting room of our veterinary clinic. Emily's real owner, Missey, who was also a student, had trained the dog to attend class and politely sleep through endless boring lectures and laboratories, making Emily an ideal "cover dog." Her capacity for sedate inertia allowed Laura to observe clients without being conspicuous. Laura sat with a notebook, coding the behavior of the clients and their dogs. In this situation, they were ideal subjects, as both were anxious and in need of comfort, and it was quite natural that their mutual needs should be expressed by touch. First we compiled a "dictionary," or list of the basic gestures of petting, which were used to evaluate the sequence of gestures made by the clients and pets in the clinic. The dictionary contained such items as "hand resting on dog," "arm around dog," "scratching," "massaging," "stroking," "grooming," "squeezing," "sounding pat," "grasping," "hugging," "kissing," "leaning against," "dog in lap," and many more. Each item was then qualified regarding the part of the pet's body being touched. We also had to specify the owner's response to the animal's own touching behavior— subtle responses such as eye contact and obvious ones such as talking. The dictionary alone helped uncover new information about the meaning of touching animals. Most entries were familiar to all of us, but two special kinds of touching caught our attention.

One day, as Katcher examined Laura's growing list of entries, he found a category called "idle play." "Well," Laura explained, "when someone is touching his dog—for example, playing with its fur, picking at it, or just stroking with his mind somewhere else, just doing it and not thinking about it—that's 'idle play.'" Not satisfied, Katcher asked to be shown, and they returned to the clinic waiting room and watched. He recognized it at once. He had been watching it all his life but now really saw it for the first time. A woman was sitting with her border collie, which rested against her thigh. The woman was staring off across the room, but her eyes were not focused on anything particular. A book was on her lap, closed over her thumb, and her free hand was on the base of the dog's neck, slowly gathering up hair between the thumb and forefinger, letting the hair roll between her fingers, dropping it, and picking up another strand. The dog seemed to pay no attention to her touch: he was looking at the other animals in the waiting room with no great interest and no noticeable muscle tension. The owner was obviously in reverie.

This sight immediately triggered in Katcher a strong memory of his three-year-old son Jonathan sitting on the front steps of his house, a leg and his trunk gently pressed against those of his friend Oliver. Both children were sucking their thumbs, but Oliver also rested an arm on Jonathan's shoulder and was gently twisting a spiral of Jonathan's hair around his index finger. Both children were staring at the cars in the street without really seeing them. They were content in their mutual and separate worlds, and while they sat with each other, they were free to let their thoughts roam in a private internal world. That image in turn called forth a montage of memories: Jonathan rubbing his nose with the ear of his stuffed toy, sucking his thumb and looking out at nowhere before falling asleep; Paul, Jonathan's older brother, sitting in his father's lap watching *Sesame Street* and slowly moving his index finger in a circle over the hairs on the back of his father's hand; a student, eyes off in space, chewing on the eraser of her pencil and rolling a strand of her hair about her index finger; Greek men in Thessalonica with their worry beads.

The presence of dreamy, inattentive, reverie-inducing touch is so much a part of life that once it is recognized, it is seen everywhere. Just before leaving the clinic that day, we spent a few moments delighting in the sight of a mother with a six-year-old child in her lap and a small schnauzer on the chair next to her. The daughter was playing with her mother's hair with one hand. The palm of the child's other hand was beneath the palm of the mother's hand that circled her waist, and her thumb was moving over the back of her mother's hand in a slow, gentle, back-and-forth motion. Her mother's other hand was on the back of the dog, gently scratching his fur. All three were staring out across the room with a kind of contented blankness.

In the next chapter we will describe how such sights as tropical fish swimming in a tank, ducks on a pond, cats playing in a room, dogs running in front of you on a walk, and leaves moving in the wind can induce a state of reverie or even suspend thought altogether as the mind concentrates only on the world around it. This kind of absorbing gaze, which can also be elicited by events such as open fires or surf or shadows moving as you walk, has the same physiological effects as meditation and can relax people enough to produce a significant reduction in blood pressure. Touching and the combination of idle touching and gazing can also produce the same relaxing reverie. Unfortunately, we have largely forgotten how to use either sight or touch to produce this kind of relaxation. When it occurs, it is almost by accident, and most people do not know how to use either touch or gaze to reduce the stresses of life.

Having identified the elements of our "petting dictionary," we became interested in differences, including gender differences, among people in the way they pet animals. American men have always been stigmatized as being more touch-inhibited than women, giving less touch and wanting less touch. One of the outcomes we were eager to determine was whether there was a difference between the way men and women touch dogs. Do men touch more or less frequently than women? Do they use the same touching gestures? We used Laura's dictionary to make a checklist for rapid observations and then asked her to observe five minutes of interaction between 110 randomly chosen owners and their dogs. When the data were analyzed, we obtained the following straightforward table.

Kind of touch	Men (47)	Women (63)	Total (110)
Hand resting	26%	27%	26%
Arm around	21%	11%	15%
Idle fingering	47%	46%	46%
Scratching	23%	17%	20%
Massaging	19%	28%	25%
Stroking	23%	37%	31%
Pat	28%	19%	23%
Sound pat	11%	5%	7%
Kissing	0%	5%	3%
Restraint	9%	6%	7%

Men used some forms of touch more frequently than women and vice versa, but the differences were small and insignificant, according to our statistical tests. Men and women touched their dogs as frequently and for just as long during the five-minute observation period. There were no significant differences between the sexes.

This result says something about the role of pets in our society. Among Americans, boys and men are trained to look upon public displays of affection as effeminate, unmanly. Boys rapidly reject their mothers' kisses and are embarrassed when they are fondled or touched publicly by their relatives. It may be acceptable for women to affectionately touch a male friend in public, but men tend to touch to indicate possession rather than affection. The adolescent male gesture of throwing an arm tightly and awkwardly around a girlfriend's neck as they walk is an example of a possessive gesture. Men are less likely to fondle, hold, and kiss children in public, and certainly they find it difficult to touch each other affectionately—kissing and hand holding between men raises the suspicion of homosexuality. More than women, men simply tend to confuse affectionate touching with sexual overtures. While one of the beneficial effects of women's liberation has been the liberation of men to be more affectionate with their children, they are still relatively out of touch with the need to be affectionate with touch. Therefore, the ability of men to touch dogs with the same gestures used by women and as frequently as women suggests a special role for pets in modern male life. A pet may be the only being that a man, trained in the macho code, can touch with affection. This suggests that a pet may have a special role as a man's child, a view that is supported by our observations of pets and health.

Using the data that Laura recorded in the clinic waiting room, we determined that age made little difference in the way owners touched their animals. After that analysis we concluded that the petting gestures people use with animals are learned early in life and are not shaped by the same inhibiting conventions that shape the behavior we learn as adults.

FEELINGS OF INTIMACY

Our study of people touching their pets in the clinic and elsewhere led us by a slightly circuitous route to an examination of human intimacy. Intimacy is the feeling of closeness, absorption, affection and mutual sensitivity that must be reflected from one person to another. Intimacy is almost the essence of companionship. Without it, no matter how many people are around us, we can feel alone. Worse, we can feel we are not ourselves or have no self because there is no intimate who can reflect our own feelings. When we are intimate, we feel that we are in some ways complete and that we complete another. The word "communion" describes the effortless, blended intermeshing of expression that we think of as intimacy.

The strength of our belief in the wordless understanding of animals is evident in the accounts of animals with psychic powers: horses that can locate lost children or dogs that know of their masters' deaths thousands of miles away. If the animal does not require words for understanding, it is easy to believe that it has psychic powers. Even scientists, such as veterinarian Michael Fox, have seriously entertained belief in the psychic ability of animals to track people, a phenomenon labeled *psi* tracking. Serious attempts have been made to document these powers of animals by studying the physiological and brain-wave response of animals to "thoughts" sent by their owners from distant rooms. As we discussed in chapter 2, many people, especially adolescents and the isolated elderly, use their pets as confidants, attesting to the belief that the animal is a sensitive listener. When you ask how people confide in their animals, the replies are quite similar. When teenagers are troubled, for example, they go out to the barn, start to comb their horses and, in the silence, experiencing close physical contact with the animal, they begin a monologue, punctuated with such questions as "What do you think, Ranger?" As described earlier, a child who is too upset may not speak but will let the horse lean or nuzzle against her, frequently with no eye contact between person and animal; both just look off into nowhere but feel the presence of another. With adults the intimate discourse begins at the front door. The furious greeting of a dog or the gentler rubbing of a cat's arched back against a leg is such a contrast to the meanness of the day that the animal is picked up and held and hugged like a talisman of safety and sanity. With big dogs the hugging tumbles into play, usually brief, and then the talk begins. It is like an interior monologue, sometimes punctuated with mock inquiries of the animal, sometimes with eye-to-eye contact right after a question, sometimes with the dog's head held by the jaw, prolonging eye contact, and then the answers are supplied for the pet. At other times the person sits down and the animal sits alongside, keeping some part of his body in contact with the owner. Small animals come to the lap then. As long as the animal maintains static contact, the owner continues talking or reverts to ruminating about the day, touching the fur of the pet in that idle, unconscious way we have described earlier.

This intimate dialogue is in many ways similar to the touch-talk intimacy we have with each other and with children. When you comfort a sobbing child, you just cuddle and stroke and say very little, perhaps repeating a word or two, such as "there" or "all right" or "okay." When the pain is deep or the child is little, you ask no questions; you just comfort. With a very little child who is sick and restless, you may sing or hum, rocking his body against yours. Words are unnecessary; each is content with what the other is doing. Between people in love, there are times when comfort means simply holding each other and saying nothing. If one person talks, it is often without looking at the other, and the stroking goes on beyond the awareness of either.

Some of the same characteristics are found in other intimate relationships. Carl Rogers observed that patients were most satisfied with psychotherapy when they felt that their therapist had two critical attributes: empathy and a nondirective stance. Rogers perfected a very simple technique for keeping the patient talking without imposing the therapist's sense of direction onto his talk. The therapist simply repeated the last phrase or sentence of the client as if it were a question. "I am feeling terrible!" "You are feeling terrible?" "Yes, I just don't know if I can make it through the day." "You don't think you can make it through the day?" The procedure sounds patently stupid when it is laid out in this simple fashion, but it always works. The patient's monologue continues almost uninterrupted. The strength of the technique is such that it works even on the most highly trained professional, as Katcher discovered when it was used on him. The Rogerian technique has the form of conversation, but the analyst uses almost no words at all.

Sound familiar? A Rogerian analyst is not unlike a Labrador retriever. The Labrador retriever is certainly not directive. He gives no advice and never interjects his opinions about your life, your successes and mistakes. He never criticizes your judgment about men or women or money. He is perceived as empathetic, and he keeps your conversation going by nuzzling, by looking with the kind of wide-eyed inquiry that dogs sometimes have, by resting next to you as you play with his fur. The retriever, of course, has a great advantage over the analyst. He can touch you, lick your face, let you kiss and hug him whenever it feels good. Most therapists are constrained by their training not to touch patients except in the gravest emergencies, and then touch is likely to be brief and rarely repeated. The difficult art in therapy is achieving a mutual feeling of intimacy without touching.

By looking at therapy in this way, we can recognize that we have one-way conversations with intimate companions in which very little of substance is said. In the light of this general statement, the ability of a dog or a cat to provoke a feeling of intimacy is completely understandable—it is natural and inevitable. Recognizing the ability of animals to be our intimates brings us face-to-face with an important revelation. We immediately recognize how unimportant words are for loving dialogue and how we have learned to overvalue the exchange of information. In chapter 7 we will describe how animals can be used as therapists, and in chapter 13 we will suggest that we must learn to say less, not more, in order to be better confidants and intimates for the people we love.

Recognition that the dog, cat, or horse can be an intimate is as old as the first tale in which a human being had an animal companion. In such narratives the intimacy is usually suggested by having the animal talk, which also permits the storyteller to further the action by having the animal offer information. However, the rhetorical device of the talking animal obscures the real basis of our intimacy with animals. They are intimates *because* they cannot talk. If they were capable of the tiresome moral instruction that they produce in children's stories, they would be no different from people. Instead they keep their silence. They ask no questions; they say no words that hurt; they offer no advice. There is no way they can fail a test of intimacy and disallow the past.

Every psychiatrist, no matter how analytical, how Rogerian, must speak at some time or other, and that speech can reveal an ignorance that destroys months of imagined sensitivity and close understanding. We feel ambivalent about people because they both hurt us and please us with words. Parents, the people we love most intensely when we are most vulnerable, must continually hurt us with words because they are continually educating us to new tasks. Children who have emotional problems are exquisitely sensitive to parental disapproval, and they anticipate similar correction from therapists, who generally try to correct this fear by playing with the child. Boris Levinson used his dog as a wordless therapist whom the child could approach in safety. When the dog and child were established in play, Levinson would join the game, directing his attention to the dog, not the child. Thus a triangle was formed in which the two significant people, doctor and patient, could feel good in each other's presence through their involvement with a third being. Later the therapist and child could establish a direct relationship.

Levinson describes the importance of the dog's capacity to establish a loving dialogue without words as follows:

> The child's need for cuddling should be met by selecting a pet which is cuddly, is not threatening, does not scold and does not expect the child to be on his best behavior. A greater understanding of the child's need for cuddling, love and affection by animals and human beings would lead, quite frequently, to more rapid recovery in many children. It also appears that all children have an intense need to master someone or something that does not talk back, that accepts one regardless of what one is. This is overwhelmingly prevalent among disturbed children who especially do not want to be judged. They want to be accepted, admired and permitted to regress as far as possible without being berated by someone or something loved and without feeling the consequent guilt. Disturbed children have a strong need for physical contact but are afraid of human contacts because they have been hurt so much and so often by people. Since the hurt is not associated with the dog, this conflict resolves itself. They will permit a dog to approach them and they will pet the animal while telling him all about their difficulties. A dog apparently poses less of a threat because he can satisfy the child's need for physical contact without the painfully embroiling emotional entanglements that the child already knows accompany emotional involvement with humans.

Samuel Corson, writing about the use of animals as therapeutic aides with adult patients in a mental hospital, sees the primary virtue of the animal as having the "ability to offer love and tactile reassurance without criticism." He documents in adults the same therapeutic triangulation described by Levinson. Patients who are unwilling to approach or talk to a therapist are able to reach out to an animal. After playing with, touching, and talking to the animal, they begin to talk to humans again. The presence of the animal makes talk safe, whether that talk is directed toward the animal or toward another person. In very diverse circumstances— with patients in an old-age home, with autistic children who have never spoken, and with disturbed children who do not talk at school—the presence of an animal has drawn speech from the mute. Not only is it safe to talk to animals, but for some it is exceedingly important because only through feeling intimate with an animal can they feel safe enough to reach out to another human being.

Knowing that dogs, cats, horses, and other animals can give us the feeling of intimacy and permit us to use the language of intimacy says a great deal about this essential feeling. Like parents with infant children, who do not understand the meaning of a single word, pet owners do not feel alone in the presence of their pets, who also do not understand words. They enjoy a state of relaxation that is fulfilling and restorative, without the assault of words. Despite all of the animals who talk in myth, fable, and children's stories, we prefer them without words.

The pet often has the status of the youngest child in the family.
Photo courtesy of Pet Food Institute.

Sharing social occasions and celebrations with our pets indicates their membership in the family.
Photos courtesy of Pet Food Institute.

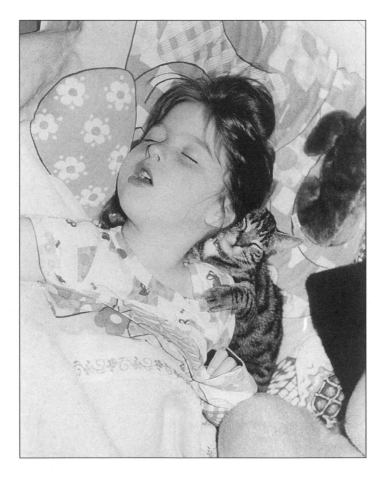

Stuffed animals, and later pets, have characteristics of the ideal mother. *Photo courtesy of Pet Food Institute.*

A child's healthy emotional development can be encouraged
by caring for a pet. *Photo by Mary Bloom.*

Pets allow you to be alone without being lonely.
Photo courtesy of Pet Food Institute.

Six

Looking at Life

SOME YEARS AGO Aaron Katcher was hiking alone in the Austrian mountains when he encountered a wild animal, a breathtaking experience that he remembers well: "I had bent down to examine a dew-covered, low-growing mountain flower when, suddenly, being aware of some presence, I slowly raised my head. Not fifteen feet away was a mountain chamois. This delicate fawn and I looked eye-to-eye for a time that was both endless and shorter than the time between breaths. Even as I let out my stopped breath, it spun away up the slope." The clarity of the moment has remained with him, and like other brief contacts with secretive wildlife, it left the impression of time standing still—a cliché, perhaps, but an accurate description of the feeling. There is an even more intense feeling: the awareness of the animal's presence before it was seen and the impact of its returned gaze leave a tingling sensitivity in your own body that marks the presence of the uncanny, a prescience that is older than words or perhaps even consciousness.

In a more mundane way, pets share this ability to draw our vision and fill our visual memories. Cats delight the eye by delicately walking among vases and sculpture or stalking a piece of string or exploring an empty paper bag. They are almost never self-conscious, and they do not use your direct gaze as an invitation. While walking in a park or wood, the wandering trail of the dog as it explores its environment gives our gaze a path to follow and a place to rest. The dog's form and motion provide a foreground for the confusion of natural scenes and make visual choices for us. Alternatively, the sight of a sleeping dog can induce a sense of relaxation and well-being.

We did not originally relate our thinking about stress and relaxation to the leisure pastimes of looking at living things and at the inanimate objects that imitate life, such as clouds, flame, and surf. It was a film documenting the treatment of Bethsabee, an autistic child, that inspired us to examine the calming influence of our living environment. Bethsabee's treatment began when the mute six-year-old girl saw a dove fly through her classroom. Fortuitously, the record of that dramatic awakening was caught on film by Dr. Ange Condoret, a French veterinarian practicing in Bordeaux, who pioneered the therapeutic use of animals in nursery schools. He had placed a variety of animals in a nursery school that had both normal children and youngsters with emotional problems and learning disabilities. In the course of photographing the children's play with the animals, he caught the critical event that started Bethsabee's therapeutic progress. Bethsabee had been in a foster home since birth, kept confined to a room, usually in a bed, and continually drugged. When Condoret first saw her, she could not abide being left in a room with a closed door. She avoided all human contact, kept her eyes averted at all times and refused any touch from the teacher and the other children. When touch was forced upon her, she remained still and rigid. When she was left alone, as she preferred, she played only with objects, usually blocks, and accompanied her play with wordless noises. Her face was expressionless save when she cried.

One day, after she was well acclimated to the class, Condoret and his colleagues attempted to introduce her to a dog. She stiffened as usual and touched the animal only with the block she held in her hand, but for one instant the film recorded a flicker of eyes, the briefest attempt at some kind of direct glance. Other contacts with the animal elicited no response; her attention was fixed on her blocks. Another time, a dove was brought into the classroom, and again there was no response. Then, quite by chance, she was seated in front of the dove when it took flight. The record of that event on film is one of the most striking human transformations imaginable. Her eyes followed the dove, and her face was illuminated by a smile, the first one anyone had seen from her. Looking at the film and running through the scene again and again, one is struck with wonder each time the sequence appears. Her face loses the withdrawn, inward, immobile expression of a severely disturbed child, and she becomes an apparently normal girl radiating joy. The dove was encouraged to repeat its flight, and Bethsabee's gaze again was drawn to it, and again she smiled. From that moment Bethsabee began to change. She became able to examine and touch the bird when it was still. She gradually accepted touch from her teachers and classmates and began to explore her own body. At times she would alternate between touching herself, touching her teacher's hand, and bringing her teacher's hand to touch her. Over the next months she began to join games and speak her first words.

There is no way of knowing what conclusions to draw from Bethsabee's story. Her attention to the dove's flight might have been a chance event that signaled some internal change, one that would have occurred with or without the dove's movement. To know for certain would require many more trials with withdrawn children. Yet in some sense the film that documents Bethsabee's encounter with the dove is so compelling that one is not sure how much more conviction would come from other experiments.

The rest of the chapter will explore the influence that looking at animals has on essentially normal human beings. As we performed these rather cool scientific experiments, we were thinking of the power of animals to draw our gaze, the power in Katcher's encounter with the mountain chamois and the power that drew Bethsabee's attention to the world of the living.

EXPERIMENTS IN OBSERVATION

From our work with the touch-talk dialogue between people and pets, we knew that pets make us feel safe and calmed us. Yet sometimes the sight of an animal alone is enough to lower our anxiety and tension. A graduate assistant working with Peter Messent in England reported that if students were waiting to take an examination and were given a questionnaire to measure anxiety, the students' anxiety was lower when they took the test in the presence of the experimenter's dog. To follow up this observation with a physiological measure of tension, Katcher and Erika Friedmann worked with a dog and a group of children. The children were recruited by James Lynch's sons, and one at a time they entered Lynch's comfortable family room to find either Friedmann alone or Friedmann accompanied by a friendly dog. Once the child was in the room, his blood pressure was measured both while resting quietly and when reading aloud from a book of stories. The children's resting blood pressure was significantly lower when the dog was present. Friedmann with a dog was safer than when she was alone. The children's blood pressure was elevated when they read aloud; however, blood pressure while reading was lower when a dog was present, suggesting that the children felt that their reading performance was going to be evaluated more benignly when an animal was present. Some children saw the dog when they first came into the room, and for others the dog entered later. The children who saw the dog when they first entered had the lowest blood pressure, suggesting that the initial sighting of the dog labeled the whole situation as safe.

This experiment stimulated many other investigators to try to duplicate or augment this original work. Over the years, as we have listened to or read these reports, we have been pleased to find our conclusions that the sight of pets could lower stress confirmed over and over again. New findings were also reported. As expected, the subject's own dog reduced stress more effectively than a strange dog. Other activities that directed attention outward toward the environment were just as effective in producing relaxation as the presence of the dog. When the subject could simply watch the dog, relaxation was more complete than when he or she was distracted by some task, such as mental arithmetic.

Dogs and cats are more than an intriguing object to watch. To study how the sight of animals to which we are not so closely bonded can influence us, we chose an aquarium as the focal point. The aquarium was landscaped with rocks and living plants and stocked with tropical fish: four gracefully swimming angel fish, ten bright-neon tetras, two pairs of red swordtails, a number of tiger barbs for a little active chasing, two shy catfish to enliven the bottom of the tank, and an algae eater to keep the walls of the colony transparent. The first subjects for our relaxation experiment were a group of students and university employees, all of whom were relatively young and had blood pressures at the low end of the normal range. Subjects in the second group were older and all had clinical hypertension. The experiment itself was simple. We brought each volunteer into a somewhat cluttered laboratory and seated him or her in a comfortable lounge chair with support for the head and arms. We explained the nature of the experiment and wrapped the upper arm with the cuff of a device that automatically measured blood pressure at sixty-second intervals. The first blood pressure readings were always higher than the subject's normal resting reading and reflected the subject's uncertainty about the experimental situation. The participants were then asked to read aloud for two minutes to obtain a stressed blood-pressure level. (As we described earlier, reading aloud or talking to people always raises blood pressure.) Subjects then watched a blank wall for twenty minutes to permit the blood pressure to fall to a normal resting level. Finally they watched the fish tank for twenty minutes. We asked them to fill their minds with the sight of the fish. No other suggestions were made. The results of the experiments are given in the graphs below.

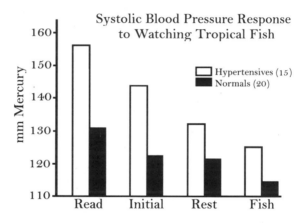

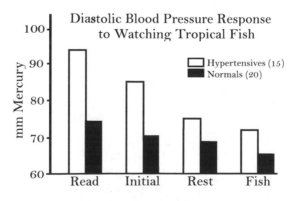

Watching the fish lowered blood pressure and produced a state of relaxation. The subjects' blood pressure began to fall when they looked at the blank wall, but it fell even more when they watched the fish. Of course, the highest blood pressures were recorded when the subjects talked to the experimenters. The changes in blood pressure for the hypertensive subjects were large: more than a twenty-five-millimeter decrease in systolic blood pressure and a sixteen-millimeter decrease in diastolic blood pressure. This magnitude of change is clinically significant; more important, the average blood-pressure level of the hypertensive subjects fell to levels within the normal range while they were watching the fish.

In other experiments we observed that blood pressure would fall even if subjects watched a tank with only plants and no fish. The moving plants and the bubbling of the filter seemed to have the same effect as the fish, although subjects watching an empty tank could not sustain their calm for very long. Before the twenty-minute observation period was over, they became bored and restless, and blood pressure levels began to rise. The calm induced by watching fish also reduced the subjects' response to stress. When we asked them to read aloud at the end of the study, blood pressure rose less than half as much as it had at the start of the experiment.

One of Katcher's patients, Erik F., discovered this "fish tank therapy" on his own and unwittingly confirmed the experiments. Erik was a general manager for a group of women's discount clothing stores operated by a parent manufacturing company. The company, only six years old, depended on fast growth. At times cash flow was precarious, and the management relied on its chain of retail stores to generate a relatively reliable fund of money. The stores multiplied faster than management could train competent sales personnel. Continually pressured to meet sales quotas, Erik had to pass that pressure on to the stores and compensate for ineffective managers. The managers, knowing their failings, apply a counterpressure of complaints and demands on Erik for larger stocks of the more salesworthy goods. After a day such stressful situations, Erik found himself unable to face the stored-up needs of his wife and children without a drink or two at a downtown bar with like-minded colleagues. After several months of mobile drinking, he found a quiet bar that he liked. It had an aquarium that was brightly lit against the dim amber tones of the bar and booths. After a few visits he went without company, glad to be without conversation. He sat, drank, and watched the display of moving color in the fish tank. He also tended to nurse one drink rather than to down several. His fixed attention on the fish and the slowness of his drinking led the bartender to ask ironically if he was there for the booze or the fish. The irony was effective, and Erik realized that he was there for the fish. The drink was simply the price of admission.

That weekend, with a hunger for action built up by months of pushing against unyielding people, he converted his study into an aquarium. He took his two older children and ranged through a pet shop, buying tanks, filters, water treatments, heaters, pumps, plants, and fish, all at once, purchasing by pointing without bothering to learn names. Later, after one shelf collapsed and fractured a forty-gallon tank beyond repair, and after many of the fish died over the following weeks, he bought some books and talked about replacements with the salespeople. He and his sons soon became adept at keeping fish and plants alive, then breeding live-bearers, and most recently setting up and maintaining a saltwater tank. He shares caring for the fish with the older children, the youngest being permitted sometimes to look but not touch.

Now Erik comes home directly after work, enters the house through the study door without greeting anyone, and watches his fish. He will sit like a stone, only his eyes moving, for twenty to thirty minutes. First he will just watch the fish, making his mind empty of everything except for their color and motion and the bubbling sounds of the aerator. After a few minutes of filling his mind with the fish, he will begin to review the day, but always keeping part of his mind on the motion of the aquarium, so that the events of the day are reviewed at a distance, muted by being projected on so rich a screen. When the residue of the day has been purged in this fashion, he arises and joins the family. Only later, after dinner, will he undertake the care of the fish with his children. His wife still resents not being greeted immediately when he returns from work. She says it makes her feel as if she and the home are a trial for which her husband must prepare himself. Yet she treasures the time he now enjoys with his children and, trial or not, prefers fish to alcohol.

We have demonstrated the calming influence of fish tanks even under the most difficult of circumstances. After the 1981 International Conference on the Human-Companion Animal Bond, at which the physiological effects of watching fish were first reported, we conducted a demonstration for a national television news program. Two hypertensive subjects, Barbara and Larry, were asked to come in for a "photo-demonstration" without telling them they were to be part of a network program. Each arrived and was faced by the television crew, cameraman, sound man, announcer, and producer. With the lights, camera, and microphone, each subject in turn sat before the tank and watched the fish. Barbara's diastolic blood pressure was 118 when she began and fell to 85 as she sat and watched, a drop of 33 millimeters that reduced her blood pressure from the hypertensive to the normal range. Larry, who was taking medication for hypertension, was able to reduce his systolic blood pressure from 170 to 128, a fall of 42 millimeters. This relaxation was accomplished under the gaze of a camera and crew and with the knowledge that they were performing for millions.

Katcher himself has been changed by the fish tanks in his office. Like Erik, he uses them to obtain a "shot" of calm before returning home on those days when he cannot take his usual medicine—a brisk twenty-block walk from the office to home. More frequently he uses the tanks to stay calm during irritating telephone calls that break his concentration. He tolerates these calls with much more equanimity when he floods his visual cortex with the sight of the fish while his abused auditory centers have to deal with the demands of the caller.

Like the other blood pressure experiments, these studies

were replicated in both the United States and Europe. In addition to the scientific attention, the experiments were widely reported in the media, and this publicity had its effects. Dentists began to place fish tanks in their waiting rooms, and a new industry grew up: maintaining fish tanks, fresh and saltwater, in the offices of doctors and dentists who were too busy to do their own maintenance. Hospitals followed, placing large aquariums in their waiting rooms, especially waiting rooms for families with children. The response was so great that an October 23, 1986, article in the *Wall Street Journal* noted, "Aquarium sales are up sharply from the early 1980s, thanks partly to a 1983 University of Pennsylvania study indicating that aquarium viewing reduces blood pressure."

We now knew that the sight of animals was an effective calming agent, but why? The relaxing influence of attention to exterior sights or sounds was demonstrated by John and Beatrice Lacey, psychophysiologists renowned for their early studies of blood-pressure and heart-rate responses to psychological stimuli. More than thirty years ago, they studied the physiological responses of subjects to different kinds of laboratory tasks. They measured heart rate, blood pressure, and the activity of the palm's sweat glands, a good index of anxiety. They found that when a subject was required to think, the signs of nervous activation increased. Blood pressure and heart rate increased, and the palms secreted more sweat. Subjects became stressed and anxious. The more troublesome the mental work, the more physiological activation occurred. However, when the subjects were asked to attend to the external environment—wait for a light to flash, listen to music, or listen to instructions—the heart rate and blood pressure fell and the palms became drier. Essentially our experiments with the fish tanks uncovered the same thing: we relax whenever any neutral visual event draws our attention outward and interrupts our ongoing train of thought.

These results have been confirmed over and over again. Of course, not all external events reduce stress and anxiety.

Watching a bloody, violent movie will cause blood pressure and heart rate to go up. Television is an example of a non-relaxing pastime. Americans spend an average of four to seven hours a day watching it, and it is recognized as addictive, chosen over play, talk, games, and a whole variety of social events. Yet no one has advocated watching it as an alternative to meditation, biofeedback, or yoga. Why? It is certainly hypnotic enough.

The answer partly lies in the fact that television must continually excite and arouse viewers to keep their attention on the content of the program. The viewers are expected to set aside their own thoughts but pay attention to the commercial messages and the program content. In order to capture the viewers' attention for the content, they must not be permitted to lapse into peaceful reverie, as one does in front of a fish tank. They must be continually stimulated. The camera moves, sound changes constantly in volume, scenes shift every few seconds, and programs include violence or sexual arousal. The technique of television presentation prevents its images from being too relaxing. Yet if you turn off the sound, a football, basketball, or hockey game can approximate the experience of watching tropical fish. You are no longer concerned with the progress of the game but only with the way the images move, reforming and repeating the action. It becomes a neutral event, repetitive and calming in the way that the motion of fish is calming.

After hearing of our research, a California firm began aggressively advertising a television tape of fish swimming in a tank. The image was designed to be projected onto the wall of an office to calm the staff. Unfortunately, television tapes tend to become monotonous after the first few viewings because the fish always move in the same way. Since that time there has been a progressively larger number of relaxation tapes on the market that feature the sights and sounds of nature. The ones we have watched have been effective the first few times they are viewed. However, there is a difference between watching life and watching the imitation of life, as we will discuss later in this chapter.

Like television, driving a car focuses our attention on visual events. However, the driver must also remain constantly alert to his own car and the other vehicles around it, ready to react to any change in position or acceleration. The visual background rushes by so fast that we can only see large objects that persist in frontal vision during a long approach or smaller objects that can be instantly recognized. Looking through the window of a moving car is much like watching television. The images are in constant motion and succession. Only the boldest features can be seen because the task of driving demands too much attentiveness. The beauty of distant mountains, sunsets, huge vistas of shore and sea can be appreciated from a car, but not the quiet detail of a tree or pond. Both television and driving suppress ongoing thoughts, replacing them with arousing sensations that are only marginally more pleasant. Television arouses us to keep us watching; driving does so to keep us alive. Neither one reduces stress or induces relaxation.

CONTEMPLATION AND HYPNOSIS

To continue our experiments on the beneficial effects of looking at animals, we decided to see whether we could increase the effectiveness of contemplating a fish tank by combining it with the hypnotic state. What better place to test our theories than in the stressful environment of a dentist's office? Most people fear dental visits and the built-in discomforts: insertion of the needle and the pressure of the anesthetic injection, the unpleasant wooden feeling of a numb face, the drilling, the pounding necessary to extract a recalcitrant wisdom tooth, the pain that surfaces once the anesthetic wears off. Both the imagined dangers and the reality are unpleasant enough.

Hypnosis has the unique ability to focus the minds of even severely apprehensive patients. Like our use of the fish tank, one method of hypnosis depends on fixation of attention on some point, light, or object. The subject remains quiet and listens to the hypnotist's voice. Everyone remembers at least a few films with "Svengalis" who reduced their victims to sleepwalkers by forcing them to stare at a pendulum or a crystal or directly at the hypnotist's eyes. Lionel Barrymore as Rasputin, charming the czarevitch out of his hemophilia by swinging a pocket watch in front of his eyes, is one famous instance. Katcher witnessed such a scene in reality when, to his utter delight, a visiting lecturer put a subject into deep hypnotic trance within ninety seconds by swinging two crystal chandelier ornaments in front of his eyes.

To describe the similarity between hypnotic induction and quietly gazing at a tank of fish, we can quote from Ainslie Meares's *A System of Medical Hypnosis*, a respected text on hypnotic technique.

The Induction of Hypnosis by the Direct Stare

Braid's Method. The use of a bright object to fix the patient's gaze . . . is still probably the most widely used method of induction in medical practice. All manner of things can be used as the bright object: a bead, a crystal pendant, a ring suspended by a cotton thread, a watch held by its chain. An ophthalmoscope light is effective and has the advantage of suggesting a medical rather than a magical procedure. In each case, the bright object is held in front of the patient at a level which is slightly higher than is comfortable for him. The result is that the upper eyelids are under some strain, they tend to tire, and the suggestions of heaviness of the eyelids become more effective. . . . The Metronome . . . has long been used in the induction of hypnosis as a means of tiring the senses by monotonous auditory stimulation. The type of metronome which is commonly used by piano teachers is quite satisfactory. Some therapists use specially designed metronomes in which the pendulum carries a small reflecting mirror. A strong spotlight is directed so that the mirror comes into its beam at the end of each swing of the pendulum. The patient is placed in such a position that the light is intermittently reflected into his eyes. This mechanical aid provides a monotonous sensory stimulation of both eyes and ears, as well as fixing the patient's gaze. . . .

The Hypnodisc . . . produces patterns of color and form

when it is rapidly revolved in front of the patient, and so produces monotonous visual stimulation.

Obviously, our fish tank would act as such a hypnotic
stimulus, but we wanted to determine precisely how effective
it could be. Under other circumstances people might be able
to relax by watching the fish in a tank, but in a dentist's office
many of them become so frightened as they wait that they
are unable to concentrate. They pace or fidget, chew gum
nervously, flip the pages of a magazine without reading it,
and so on. In the grip of such anxiety, it is impossible to focus
on any object in the real world. Hypnosis overcomes this
fragmentation of attention because the hypnotist is able to
focus the subject's attention narrowly. Hypnosis has few essential characteristics, but the two closest to its core are sug-
gestibility and the focusing of attention by the means we
have described, among others.

We used forty adult subjects who were having an elective
extraction of a third molar (wisdom tooth). They were
brought into a laboratory for an hour, forty minutes of which
were spent in relaxation in front of a fish tank or a poster of
a mountain stream in the French Alps. Half the subjects
were hypnotized and half were not. Another group of ten
subjects served as controls and were asked to sit and relax
for forty minutes without any specific instructions. All subjects were told that they could sustain their relaxed state
during the surgery that was to follow. Surgery was performed in the clinic, with subjects receiving local anesthesia
but no other drugs. The dentist doing the extraction did not
know the type of relaxation used. Blood pressure and heart
rate were measured during surgery, and both the dentist and
an independent observer rated the patient's outward emotional state. At the end of the procedure, the patient rated his
own level of relaxation during surgery.

Predictably, the subjects who were the least anxious to
begin with could pay attention to the fish tank and relax by
turning their attention away from the threat of the extraction. The most anxious subjects could not focus on the fish

tank at all. Their blood pressure might fall for a few minutes as they watched, but then it would rise again. Sometimes it would cycle, falling when they were paying attention and rising when they could no longer concentrate. Toward the end of the forty-minute experiment, they would become visibly restless, and their blood pressure would return to the elevated starting level.

As a whole, the results again demonstrated the ability of simple contemplation to induce calm. Patients who contemplated the fish tank and/or were hypnotized were significantly more relaxed during surgery than those who contemplated the poster or the control subjects. The dentist and the observer also noted that the patients contemplating the aquarium behaved in a more relaxed fashion than the other patients.

The effects of hypnosis did surprise us. We had thought that hypnosis would improve the effect of contemplation by focusing the subject's attention; however, hypnosis did not improve the results of aquarium contemplation. The patients who watched the aquarium in a normal state of mind were as relaxed as those who watched the aquarium under hypnosis. The results were quite different with contemplation of the static poster. There the hypnotized subjects were much more relaxed than the subjects who watched the poster in their normal state.

These results suggest that contemplation of an aquarium can be a simple and effective procedure for helping anxious patients relax before surgery. For some patients, at least, it may be as relaxing as the more cumbersome and difficult procedure of hypnosis. In the application of these results, however, it should be remembered that the patients were not just placed in a waiting room with an aquarium. They were told to expect relaxation and increased comfort and instructed how to use the fish tank for contemplation. To obtain similar results in the application of this experiment, other patients should be given similar instructions.

Although aquarium contemplation may be as effective as

hypnosis overall, the results suggested that there may be some patients who would benefit more from hypnosis. We measured how anxious the patients were at the start of the study, and looked at the relationship between their fear of dental procedures and their level of relaxation during surgery. In both groups that used contemplation in their normal state of mind, the most anxious subjects relaxed the least during surgery. The differences in relaxation between the most and the least anxious were greater in the poster contemplation group, but they were still present in the patients who contemplated the aquarium. In the subjects who were hypnotized, there was no relationship between dental anxiety and outcome. The hypnotic relaxation could help the very anxious subject as much as the calm subject. Thus hypnotic relaxation may be useful for the very anxious patient, while contemplation of a fish tank can be used as a simple, general procedure for the broad range of surgical patients. Perhaps natural objects of contemplation should be routinely incorporated into the medical environment as a simple and effective means of inducing relaxation.

Animals are not the only natural phenomenon that can induce relaxation. As we were pursuing our work with fish tanks, another investigator from the field of landscape architecture was carrying out another series of quite different investigations with similar results. Roger Ulrich and his colleagues had been investigating the effect of watching pictures of natural scenery on subjects' level of arousal. They found that pictures of moving water, large trees, mountain vistas, and open grasslands bordered by forest were all perceived as more attractive than pictures of buildings or pictures with people in them. These natural scenes were more effective in relaxing subjects who were recovering from the stress of examinations or from donating blood than pictures of buildings and people. These results seemed to mirror our work with the fish tank.

In a more realistic clinical experiment, Ulrich randomly assigned patients who had experienced a surgical operation to one of two types of rooms. One kind of room had a view of a park with trees, and the other had a view only of another building. The patients assigned to the rooms with a view of a park used less narcotic medication for the relief of pain and were discharged from the hospital a day earlier. Having a view of trees decreased the pain experienced by these surgical patients and speeded their recovery. This was a finding almost as powerful as our observation that pets could affect the progress of heart disease.

THE POWERS OF OBSERVATION

Green leaves, trees, and birds are almost everywhere, even in cities. Yet many people ignore the world around them and turn instead to some form of packaged relaxation, such as transcendental meditation (TM), preferring to learn the difficult task of focusing attention on nothing or on a single word or symbol.

TM is one of the enduring types of meditation. For twenty minutes twice a day, the practitioner silently repeats his own personal, secret mantra, which is revealed to him only after completion of a "training session," for which he must pay tuition. TM was chosen by Herbert Benson, a professor of medicine at Harvard, as the focal point for a study of the claims that meditation reduced stress and protected the practitioner against the adverse health consequences of anxiety and stress of modern living. Benson ran a series of experiments in which he studied the physiological effects of the technique alone, without any of the religious indoctrination or symbolic associations. After years of experimentation, Benson convinced himself that the effect of meditation was nonspecific and common to a wide variety of meditative or relaxation techniques. He defined four basic elements of what he called the relaxation response, the subjective state produced by meditation:

> The first element is a quiet environment. One must "turn off" not only internal stimuli but also external distractions. A quiet room or place of worship may be suitable. The nature

mystics meditated outdoors. The second element is an object to dwell upon. This object may be a word or sound repetition; gazing at a symbol; concentration on a particular feeling. For example, directing one's attention to the repetition of a syllable will help clear the mind. When distracting thoughts do occur, one can return to this repetition of the syllable to help eliminate other thoughts. The third element is a passive attitude. It is an emptying of all thoughts and distractions from one's mind. A passive attitude appears to be the most essential factor in eliciting the Relaxation Response. Thoughts, imagery, and feelings may drift into one's awareness. One should not concentrate on these perceptions but allow them to pass on. A person should not be concerned with how well he or she is doing. The fourth element is a comfortable position. One should be in a comfortable posture that will allow an individual to remain in the same position for at least twenty minutes.

It is perhaps a little difficult for us to equate something as informal as watching a fish tank with meditation, but we can certainly feel the similarity between the relaxing effects of sitting quietly before a fish tank and reverie, the dreamy state that you fall into in front of a fire or while watching the surf pound on the beach or clouds pass in the sky. Reverie is a passive state of mind. While the eye is fixed on the external world—the fire or clouds—thoughts pass in and out of the mind of their own accord. They are distant and dream-like—no attempt is made to think particular thoughts or ignore others. Gaston Bachelard, in a book with the imposing title *Psychoanalysis of Fire*, talks of reverie before open flames:

> The dream proceeds on its way in linear fashion, forgetting its original path as it hastens along. The reverie works in a star pattern. It returns to its center to shoot out new streams. And, as it happens, the reverie in front of the fire, the gentle reverie that is conscious of its well being, is the most naturally centered reverie. It may be counted among those which best hold fast to their object or, if one prefers, to their pretext. Hence this solidity and this homogeneity which give it such a charm that no one can free himself from it. It is so well defined that it has become banal to say, "We love to see a log

fire burning in the fireplace." In this case it is a question of the quiet regular controlled fire that is seen when the great log emits tiny flames as it burns. It is a phenomenon both monotonous and brilliant, a really total phenomenon: it speaks and soars, and it sings.

The fire confined to the fireplace was no doubt for man the first object of reverie, the symbol of repose, the invitation to repose. One can hardly conceive of a philosophy of repose that would not include a reverie before a flaming log fire.

Dr. Konrad Lorenz, winner of the Nobel Prize in 1973 and one of the founders of modern animal behavior studies, was wise enough to see the similarities between fires and aquariums:

> A man can sit for hours before an aquarium and stare into it as into the flames of an open fire or the rushing waters of a torrent. All conscious thought is happily lost in this state of apparent vacancy, and yet, in these hours of idleness, one learns essential truths about the macrocosm and the microcosm. If I cast into one side of the balance all that I have learned from the books of the library and into the other everything that I have gleaned from the "books in the running brooks," how surely would the latter turn the scales.

The fire offers constant novelty yet is always the same. Natural objects of contemplation, the sights that induce reverie, have these properties in common: the combination of beauty and monotony, novelty and constancy, sudden beauty that passes and is indistinguishable from the next flash. The movement of brightly colored fish in a tank or unconfined above a tropical reef, the passing of birds through a forest, the pattern of clouds—all have this dual property of having points of instantaneous beauty that attract our gaze but lapse without notice into an essential constancy. In this sense the sea, the fire, and the moving patterns of birds or clouds in the sky are all similar.

If the living part of nature has such an ability to calm, why is relaxation such a problem for so many? Perhaps because we are no longer trained to find relaxation by focusing our gaze on the world around us. The inability to look is a product of the anxious arousal of urban life. In cities there is little nature to observe, and people are usually too distracted to see what is there. Life is represented by people or pests that we do not wish to see. Living in cities, then, is a continuing exercise in not seeing. We avoid looking at the dirt, the litter, the garbage, the dog excrement, the graffiti, the worn crumbling buildings, the angry faces of the crowd, the sad, dirty people who live and beg on the streets, the garish displays of goods we do not want. We not only ignore the sights of the city, we try to ignore the smells, the sounds of traffic and people, all that movement.

Some people do come to cities to gape and look and feel, but once the novelty wears off, it can be replaced by a sense of being overwhelmed by chaos. What is an exciting novelty for tourists is noise for residents, who must filter out all the background in order to maintain some kind of relative calm. The need to filter and control the sensations of the city has generated a market for boom boxes and Walkmen, which create a cocoon for their users, making them insensitive to the sights, sounds, and smells of the world around them. That insulation is necessary because the wearers of electronic cocoons cannot turn their attention outward to their environment without being painfully overwhelmed. All too frequently there is nothing pleasant to look at in their urban world.

The ability to see the world around us is not actually lost in cities, because it was never really learned. Modern schooling, designed for urban children, does not teach them to see the world. Success in school is based upon the ability to recognize words and use numbers. Only those two skills bring the rewards of success to the child. There are no rewards for insightful seeing into the real world. Science does not encourage children to look at the life around them because it is taught as the study of the hidden or invisible. The important events in science are those that the unaided eye cannot see— the hidden processes of physics, chemistry, and biological metabolism. Vision is used for the classification of dead specimens, to put plants and animals in conceptual boxes, the way dead beetles and butterflies are put in physical boxes. Many university students know the details of atomic structure and the twists of the DNA helix, yet almost none of them can recognize the trees that shade the campus or describe their leaves or tell how a bud unfolds or how a cat moves when it runs or how a dog places its feet when it walks. Even students who have had pets of their own cannot describe their animals' behavior—how they play or fight, how their bodies change to signal their intentions. They have never been rewarded for looking critically at the world around them.

Perhaps the joyous scene from Steven Spielberg's movie *E.T.*, in which the children rebel against turning a living frog into dead parts, indicates a change in the way children are taught in school. They can be taught to look at living things, to follow ants and beetles and trace their trails, to learn to recognize the trees about them so that they are more than background, to watch animals move and signal to each other, and to learn to pick out the individual from the confusion of nature. We need to instruct our children in a visual, living biology that enables them to see the world about them, and through that kind of seeing to help them understand the kind of peace and deep, relaxed comfort that the informed sight of the living can bring. In our work with hyperactive children at the Devereux Foundation, which is described in chapter 7, the sight of animals and nature was highly effective in reducing symptoms of hyperactivity and in helping the children to concentrate and learn.

Knowing all of this, we still did not have a general enough explanation of why looking at so many different forms of life or lifelike events had the same relaxing, hypnotic effects. There are two interrelated ideas that could have a broad enough scope. The first could be said to come from the independent thought of two remarkable men. The earlier is Henry David Thoreau, and his insight is found in that great work about nature, *Walden*. After looking at the forms in the sand formed by the melting ice, he wrote:

When the frost comes out in the spring, and even in a thaw-ing day in the winter, the sand begins to flow down the slopes like lava, sometimes bursting out through the snow and overflowing it where no sand was to be seen before. Innumerable little streams overlap and interlace one with another, exhibiting a sort of hybrid product, which obeys half way the law of currents, and half way that of vegetation. As it flows it takes the forms of sappy leaves or vines, mak-ing heaps of pulpy sprays a foot or more in depth, and re-sembling, as you look down on them, the laciniated, lobed, and imbricated thalluses of some lichens; or you are re-minded of coral, of leopards' paws or birds' feet, of brains or lungs or bowels, and excrements of all kinds. It is a truly *grotesque* vegetation, whose forms and color we see imitated in bronze, a sort of architectural foliage more ancient and typical than acanthus, chicory, ivy, vine, or any vegetable leaves; destined perhaps, under some circumstances, to be-come a puzzle to future geologists. . . .

When I see on the one side the inert bank,—for the sun acts on one side first,—and on the other this luxuriant fo-liage, the creation of an hour, I am affected as if in a peculiar sense I stood in the laboratory of the Artist who made the world and me,—had come to where he was still at work sporting on this bank, and with excess of energy, strewing his fresh designs about. I feel as if I were nearer to the vitals of the globe, for this sandy overflow is something such a fo-liaceous mass as the vitals of the animal body. You find thus in the very sands an anticipation of the vegetable leaf. No wonder that the earth expresses itself outwardly in leaves, it so labors with the idea inwardly. The atoms have already learned this law, and are pregnant by it. . . .

The feathers and wings of birds are still drier and thinner leaves. Thus, also, you pass from the lumpish grub in the earth to the airy and fluttering butterfly. The very globe continually transcends and translates itself, and becomes winged in its orbit. Even ice begins with delicate crystal leaves, as if it had flowed into moulds which the fronds of water-plants have impressed on the watery mirror. The whole tree itself is but one leaf, and rivers are still vaster leaves whose pulp is intervening earth, and towns and cities are the ova of insects in their axils. . . .

Thus it seemed that this one hillside illustrated the principle of all the operations of Nature. The Maker of this earth but patented a leaf.

Thoreau saw a common pattern in nature, and many years later, Benoit Mandelbrot described the mathematics behind those patterns, the irregular regularities that make up the structures of living things and are now described as fractals. Snowflakes are all roughly the same, but no two are exactly the same. The trunks and limbs of a tree, the branching of arteries, the arterial tree, and the joining of streams to form the trunk of a great river all have the same approximate structure, and they can all be described by the mathematics of chaos, fractal geometry. Perhaps it is the general fractal structure behind the patterns in surf, running water, fire, and the repetitive motions of schooling fish that makes them relaxing and gives them their hypnotic quality. This explanation is, however, too general. To seriously entertain this hypothesis, we would have to know whether all patterns generated by fractal mathematics are relaxing, or whether only certain ones have this property. We would also like to know if there are fractal patterns that are relaxing in themselves, although they do not look like any of the events that we know to be relaxing. These questions still await investigation.

The second possible explanation comes from E. O. Wilson, the Harvard biologist who founded the field of sociobiology—the investigation of the genetic roots of culture and social structure. Wilson has suggested that the human mind evolved in the company of animals and amid the natural world. The realities of hunting and gathering would reward those with the ability to pay close attention to animals and vegetation and discriminate most carefully between different species. If the human mind was shaped by the demands of scouring nature for food over millions of years, then it is highly plausible that we have an inborn tendency to pay attention to natural forms and motion. If our minds are programmed in this fashion, then natural events and animals in motion would have an innate capacity to draw our attention outward, and in so doing would produce a state of relaxation.

Whatever the reason, life is meant to look at life. Samuel Coleridge gave an unparalleled description of the restorative value of love springing from the sight of life. The ancient mariner, cursed with the dead albatross, is redeemed when he is overcome with love at the sight of living color in the water about his ship, love for the beauty of animals he would never touch or tend in any way.

> Beyond the shadow of the ship,
> I watched the water-snakes:
> They moved in tracks of shining white,
> And when they reared, the elfish light
> Fell off in hoary flakes.

> Within the shadow of the ship
> I watched their rich attire:
> Blue, glossy green, and velvet black,
> They coiled and swam; and every track
> Was a flash of golden fire.

> O happy living things! no tongue
> Their beauty might declare:
> A spring of love gushed from my heart,
> And I blessed them unaware.

Seven

Pets as Therapists

IF SIMPLY LOOKING at life—at the world around us and the animals in it—can benefit normal people, then direct contact with pets can be even more rewarding and restorative for those beset with troubles, as the following case histories from the work of Samuel and Elizabeth Corson and Leo Bustad illustrate.

> Patient Sonny was a nineteen-year-old psychotic who spent most of his time lying in his bed. The staff tried unsuccessfully to get him to move about and interact. Nothing seemed to interest him; he would not participate in occupational therapy, recreational therapy or group therapy. In individual therapy he remained withdrawn and uncommunicative. His drug regimen (haloperidol and other drugs) did not improve him. A work-up for electroshock therapy was begun. A token (reward) system was introduced, but again Sonny showed little response.

Before starting the electroshock therapy, it was decided to attempt to use a dog as a component of the token reward system. . . .

When the psychiatrist brought the dog Arwyn, a Wire Haired Fox Terrier, to Sonny's bed, Sonny raised himself up on one elbow and gave a big smile to the dog's wildly friendly greeting. The dog jumped on Sonny, licking his face and ears. Sonny tumbled the dog about joyously. He volunteered his first question: "Where can I keep him?" Then to everyone's amazement, he got out of bed and followed the dog when she jumped to the floor.

The health care team at the home meets to decide which resident can derive the greatest benefit from living in the private therapy room. The current resident, Marie, was chosen because she had no family or friends, would not communicate, and remained curled in the fetal position with no interest in living. She also had sores on her legs from continual scratching. When other measures failed, she was moved in with Handsome (the resident cat). Whenever she began to scratch her legs, the cat played with her hands and distracted her. Within a month the sores were healed. She began to watch the cat and to talk with the staff about him. Gradually she invited other residents in to visit with him. Now she converses with strangers, as well as the nursing home staff, about the cat and other subjects.

A frail elderly man was brought to the nursing home from the local hospital. He had been discovered in a severely malnourished and confused state in a rural farmhouse, living alone in filth. Once his condition stabilized, he was brought in restraints to the nursing home since he refused to eat. Each day he worked to free himself from restraints and remove the feeding tube. It then was reinserted since he refused to eat. The staff was unable to break this cycle until an aide found the Center's three kittens in bed with him. When the cats were removed, he became agitated. A reward system was devised whereby the cats would be returned to him if he ate. He gained forty pounds and interacted with other residents. The cats were the bridge that brought him back to reality. The director of nursing stated that otherwise she believes he would have died.

These case histories give us some idea of the force behind the idea of animal-assisted therapy (AAT). Yet when we think about it, the fact that pet therapy is successful is not remarkable at all. Much of what we have been saying throughout this book indicates that pets should have therapeutic value. If the loving devotion, the soft touch, the constant companionship, and the attentive eye and the uncritical ear of the pet are so attractive to so many of us, they should be even more important to those who have been wounded by other people or deprived of the comforts that friends, family, and children bring.

We believe that animals can make a unique contribution to therapy because of their capacity to make people feel safe, loved, and worthwhile. Thus they have a role in the treatment of those who can no longer be helped by other people. Most patients who are depressed and withdrawn, helpless and hopeless, have been hurt by words. Animals do not use words, and patients can safely approach them when they cannot approach people.

As noted in chapter 4, animals can assume the role of that perfect mother we imagined in infancy, the mother who is embodied in the teddy bear or the security blanket. Later this same feeling of overflowing love and uncritical acceptance is attached to pets, and they retain the ability to evoke this love from people who have been hurt by other human beings. Perhaps the most remarkable ability of animal therapists is their capacity to call forth speech from those who have given up speaking. Pets can do this because the love they stimulate in people is unambivalent, unalloyed with the distrust and fear that frequently color even loving relationships with other people. Freud recognized this remarkable aspect of our love for animals, and he wrote in a letter to a friend:

> It really explains why one can love an animal like Topsy (or Jo-fi) with such an extraordinary intensity: affection without ambivalence, the simplicity of a life free from the almost unbearable conflicts of civilization, the beauty of an existence, complete in itself. And yet, despite all divergence in

the organic development, that feeling of an intimate affinity, of an undisputed solidarity. Often, when stroking Jo-fi, I have caught myself humming a melody which, unmusical as I am, I can't help recognizing as the aria from *Don Giovanni:* "A bond of friendship unites us both."

Freud was unwilling to describe a therapeutic role for pets. Yet as we have noted in chapter 5, there is a resemblance between the intimate dialogue between a patient and a silent, empathic therapist and the dialogue between people and their pets. Dr. Jan Loney made the same association with regard to pet therapy:

> Not only is the pet safe and attractive, it has the capacity to modify the identity of the environment and other people in the environment. The therapist who comes with the pet becomes less dangerous, and the patient can reveal more of himself. Just as the therapist becomes less forbidding and more human, the patient with the pet is perceived by others as more human, and hence less "sick" and more treatable. This in turn becomes a self-fulfilling prophecy.

In chapters 5 and 6 we demonstrated that children and adults felt much safer in stressful circumstances when a dog was present. Animals make good therapists because they make people feel secure. In Loney's experience,

> The staff that includes a canine therapist has at least one colleague who is without vanity and ambition, who has no "pet" theories, who is utterly unconcerned with role or status, who is free of intellectual pretensions, who does not fear emotion, and who does not feel that he is being underpaid. In truth, an inspiration and a model for us all.

Loney later observed that a child therapist is "optimistic, empathetic, sincere, alert, sensitive, straightforward, relaxed, spontaneous," like a Boy Scout, who is "trustworthy, loyal, helpful, friendly, courteous, kind, obedient, cheerful, thrifty, brave, clean, and reverent." This description may better fit the family dog; in fact, Loney further notes that the American Kennel Club standard for the Samoyed is "intelligent, gentle, loyal, adaptable, alert, full of action, eager to serve, friendly but conservative." By now the similarities among therapist, Boy Scout, and dog should not be surprising.

Professional therapists have come to value animals as therapeutic aids in treating simple problems, such as loneliness in the elderly, and more complex disorders, such as severe autism in children. In what has come to be known as AAT, animals have found a place in the home and in settings such as prisons, nursing homes, and other institutions. One of the pet's primary functions in therapy has been to act as a bridge by which therapists can reach patients who are withdrawn, uncooperative, and uncommunicative. When such patients are brought in contact with pets, they often have an immediate emotional reaction, exhibiting the same kind of joy that would be expected from anyone. After a few sessions with an animal, many of these patients will respond to the human therapist and then to other people, when previously such social contact had been impossible. For example, older patients who have not talked in years and children who have had difficulty talking at all have been stimulated to begin speaking in the presence of animals.

It is well known that after admission to a nursing home, the elderly person often exhibits depression, helplessness, disorganization, or rapid deterioration of health and psychological well-being. At the very least, animals in nursing homes provide a valuable distraction and a source of amusement. But to be more than a diversion, they must alleviate some problem and usually facilitate some therapeutic goal. Animals can promote activity by requiring feeding and walking; animals can foster a sense of security by their bonding behaviors. They can even stimulate the patient to think by encouraging interest in learning more about the animal and by fostering an awareness of a part of nature or the immediate environment. Gerontologists Judith Gammonley and Judy Yates note that "It is this bonding relationship, used therapeutically, that differentiates AAT from animal entertainment."

The presence of animals in nursing homes poses special problems because these facilities are not like the home environment. Their residents are relative newcomers to their surroundings, which often include living and eating quarters smaller than the ones they were used to in their own homes. And while there are some risks associated with any active intervention and animal contact in general—including animal bite, allergy, diseases transmitted by animals, and falls caused by the animals or by their excreta—to date there is no indication that AAT programs are particularly dangerous, and there are few reports of adverse effects. Dr. Robert Anderson and his associates at the University of Minnesota surveyed 284 Minnesota nursing homes with visiting and residential animals and found no cases of pet-related infections over a twelve-month period. Dr. David Walthner-Toews conducted a survey of 150 U.S. and 74 Canadian humane societies for prevalence of AAT programs and experience with animal-transmitted diseases and found that 46 percent of U.S. and 66.2 percent of Canadian societies had AAT programs. Dogs and/or cats were employed in most—94 percent—but rabbits (28 percent), pocket pets, such as hamsters, mice, and guinea pigs (15 percent), and birds (10 percent) were also used. Most workers were concerned about rabies, ringworm, and external parasites, but few actual problems were found. AAT programs appear to cause few health problems for people, and most therapists feel that the programs are an acceptable risk if it lessens the despair that often comes with loneliness.

In nursing homes and psychiatric institutions, where custodial care is about all that can be provided for the patients, pets benefit both patients and staff. Working in such institutions, where no one is really expected to improve, can be depressing and demoralizing. But the introduction of AAT tends to make staff members more optimistic, and in turn they treat the patients with more recognition of the patients' essential humanity. For elderly patients, animals may substitute for the grandchildren who do not visit. The presence of animals may even encourage the grandchildren to become closer to their grandparents. For older patients the pet is also a means of regaining contact with their childhood. It is a tool for reminiscence and reverie. The animal's lack of sensitivity to the older patients' age, wrinkles, smells, and debilitated condition provides a kind of social validation, a sustaining belief that their essential identity is unchanged and that in some real respect they are still what they once were.

AAT is relatively easy to provide and can involve nonprofessionals. Many humane societies and zoos have programs that bring animals to nursing homes at no cost to the institutions. They have no difficulty finding young volunteers to bring the animals to the institutions. Knowing the value of recreation and visitors—any visitors—the institutions welcome the free programs. Often staff personnel have well-trained dogs or cats that they gladly bring to work rather than leave at home.

From *Family Circle* and *Vogue* to *Science* and other specialist journals, the use of animals in therapy is viewed as the newest addition to holistic medicine. And while skilled and careful therapists have observed the benefits of AAT, they have not yet been confirmed by the kind of controlled experiments that test the value of more conventional therapeutic agents. Critics rightly note that AAT has not yet undergone rigorous evaluation. As we have seen in preceding chapters, pets are not always the answer; in fact, they can sometimes cause problems of their own. But these problems and the failures are often not even reported. If they are, it is certainly not with the same intensive focus as the successes of AAT programs. Most reports about AAT also pay little attention to long-range effectiveness. Even so, there is certainly enough evidence to continue the existing programs and to devise new ones. We hope that AAT will be given the scientific testing it so rightly deserves.

A BRIEF HISTORY

The intensity of recent interest in animals as therapists has made it seem that AAT is a new phenomenon. It is not. Animals have always made people feel better in a general way, but therapy requires healing an illness. It is not clear when this role for animals officially began. In Greek mythology, Chiron—a centaur, or half-man half-horse—was the first physician and the teacher of Aesculapius and could be considered the first pet therapist. In the 1700s horses were used in the therapy of a variety of diseases, but the first clear reports of AAT came from the York Retreat in England, founded in 1792 by the Society of Friends. From the beginning, William Tuke, a Quaker merchant, felt that animals would enhance the humanity of the emotionally ill. Patients could "learn self control by having dependent upon them creatures weaker than themselves." The retreat provided rabbits, chickens, and other farm animals from which, in modern parlance, the patients could learn self-control by positive reinforcement. At the time, this was a vast improvement over conventional treatment, and even now it would be beneficial in most institutions.

In 1867 pets were part of the treatment for epileptics at Bethel, in Bielefeld, Germany. Bethel is now a five-thousand-patient facility for the treatment of physical and mental disorders, and animals—dogs, cats, horses, birds, farm animals, and even wild animals—are still part of the treatment. Caring for them is a major part of the program. Unfortunately, there has been no systematic record by which the effects of the animals can be evaluated.

The first well-documented use of animals in the United States was in the rehabilitation of airmen at the Army Air Force Convalescent Center in Pawling, New York, from 1944 to 1945. The program, sponsored by the American Red Cross, used dogs, horses, and farm animals as a diversion from the intense therapeutic programs the airmen underwent. After the war there was no longer a need for the program, and again no records exist.

In 1966 Erling Stordahl, himself blind, established Beitostolen in Norway for the rehabilitation of the blind and those with disabilities. Dogs and horses were used to encourage patients to exercise. Many patients learned to ski, ride horses, and live more normal lives that could include some sports activities.

PRESENT RESEARCH: AN OVERVIEW

The current interest in the value of companion animals to human health was generated in large part by the work of Boris Levinson and Samuel and Elizabeth Corson. Their courage in using animals as therapists before there was a "bandwagon," as well as their own gentle warmth and wisdom, have been as inspirational as their scientific work.

Levinson was the first child psychologist to build the use of companion animals into a self-conscious diagnostic and therapeutic technique. When he presented the results of using a dog as a cotherapist, there was a good deal of snide resistance to the concept. His reports were not given serious attention and were even ridiculed with such comments as "Do you share your fee with the dog?"

Oddly enough, Levinson was able to demonstrate that his colleagues were more willing to *use* animals in therapy than to talk about it in scientific meetings. He sent a questionnaire to a random sample of more than four hundred psychotherapist members of the clinical division of the New York State Psychological Association. The vast majority answered; more than one-third had used animals at one time or another, and more than 58 percent had recommended pets for their outpatients. More than half felt that animals could best be used to treat the adjustment problems of children and adolescents—anxiety states, behavioral disorders, depression, obsessions, phobias, physical disabilities, schizophrenia, severe deprivation, and uncommunicativeness. Levinson's books and subsequent papers give numerous case studies of the roles that pets, mostly dogs (including his own dog, Jingles), play in the treatment of young patients. He published his findings in two books: *Pet-Oriented Child Psychotherapy* in 1969 and *Pets and Human Development* in 1972.

Samuel and Elizabeth Corson conducted one of the earliest scientific studies to evaluate the effects of animals in an institutional setting. Recognizing the difficulties of finding an appropriate control, the group they chose to work with was patients who had failed to respond to any traditional form of therapy—individual and group psychotherapy, drug and electroshock therapy, occupational and recreational therapy. In effect, the patients served as their own controls; because nothing worked before, any change must be due to the Corsons' experimental treatment. Ethics demanded that patients continued to receive other forms of therapy during the study, which is a common problem facing all researchers in the field.

The experiment design was simple; patients were introduced to dogs (and some cats) in the kennels, on the wards, or at their bedsides, whichever was convenient. They could choose the animal to be considered theirs during the course of the study. Patient and pet enjoyed many sessions together, and many sessions were videotaped to permit analysis of the patients' interactions with the animals and with the human therapists and to document any changes. The analyses showed that most of the patients became less withdrawn, answering a therapist's questions sooner and more fully. Subjectively, the patients appeared happier—the immediate response that makes so many converts to AAT. Only three of the fifty patients absolutely failed to respond.

The Corsons emphasize the importance of the personality of the dog in the therapeutic match between patient and pet. They used dogs that could be described as "aggressively friendly," "shy-type friendly," and even "withdrawn, extremely shy." This last, relatively unattractive animal was chosen by one patient who said, "I felt that this dog needed me."

One patient of the Corsons was described at the start of this chapter. Another is of particular interest because she needed to change from one dog therapist to another as she improved. After her recovery she appears on tape as an attractive, vivacious young woman. She was admitted to the hospital in a manic state and chose a dog that she described as being manic. The patient and the dog would run actively about the grounds of the hospital, each enjoying the other's pace. At one point, when the patient was starting to lose her manic drive, she realized that she could no longer keep up with the dog and collapsed on the grass. The dog, perhaps in disappointment, perhaps to encourage her to move, urinated on her twice. The shock of this rejection crystallized her awareness of how much she had changed. The "manic" dog made her realize how her own manic behavior made life difficult for her family and friends. She then chose a more disciplined border collie as her pet-companion for the rest of her hospital stay.

The Corsons' introduction of quantitative analysis and their genuine respect for their subjects encouraged many researchers to introduce animals into hospital settings. A totally different experimental design was undertaken by Clark Brickel in a hospital-based nursing-care facility in California. Instead of using individual animals on a one-to-one basis with each patient, Brickel introduced a single mascot (a cat) into each ward. He based his findings on observations made by the staff. While some negative aspects were reported, such as concern about fleas and allergies, the overall impression was that the cats improved the patients' responsiveness, offering them pleasure and enhancing the general milieu of the treatment setting. Ward mascots may be easier to integrate into institutions and have as many positive effects as individual pairings of patient and pet.

We also compared the impact of animals on group therapy in matched therapy groups who met either in a room that contained some finches or the same room without birds present. The thirty-minute group-therapy sessions were held five days a week for ten weeks. The psychiatric inpatients were more comfortable talking and participating in group-therapy sessions in the presence of birds than they were in the same room without animals present. Pre- and post-evaluations demonstrated that the group that met with the birds present had significantly fewer feelings of hostility and were released earlier than the group that met without the birds sharing the therapeutic environment. The observation that people feel safer and can share more openly in the presence of animals appears to be especially important in trying times.

In another study pets were used as socializing agents with chronic psychiatric patients. Drs. Mary Thompson, Robert Kennedy, and Sue Igou, working in a Maryland hospital, used a variety of patient evaluation questionnaires completed by the staff to determine the effects of spending three hours a week for six weeks feeding, grooming, petting, and handling animals. Different animals were used each week, including dogs, kittens, a cat, guinea pigs, and a parakeet. In general, the patients who had animal contact showed more improvement than those who participated in other activities. However, the more severely troubled did not significantly improve; in fact, their scores were worse. The number of subjects was too small to explain this negative finding.

When the person who is institutionalized happens to be a child, contact with an animal is almost universally beneficial. In chapter 6 we discussed the dramatic awakening of Bethsabee, an autistic girl, whose recovery could be dated from the moment she watched a dove take flight. The dove was the first living thing that claimed that child's attention.

Many sensitive teachers and parents have observed the fascination that animals have for autistic children, and how they display affection and a kind of sociability with these animals, which are rarely directed toward people. Recently, Oliver Sacks offered a sensitive description of the autistic condition in a collection of essays called *An Anthropologist on Mars*. In that work he tells the story of Temple Grandin, who was autistic but became world-renowned for the design of facilities for animals. She said she always had a feeling for the psychology of animals, but she had difficulty in understanding the minds of people. Sacks notes, "I was struck by the enormous difference, the gulf, between Temple's immediate, intuitive recognition of animal moods and signs and her extraordinary difficulties understanding human beings."

If individual autistic children and adults respond to animals, sometimes when they do not respond to people, can contact with animals be used therapeutically for autistic children? Laurel Redefer, a doctoral candidate in the educational psychology graduate department at the University of Pennsylvania, determined to find out. She worked under the supervision of Dr. Joan Goodman, and they designed a carefully controlled study in which observers coded the behavior of the autistic child with the therapist, and later with the animal and the therapist. The observers were trained by observing test videotapes until they could code behavior in the same way. The child was studied with his or her therapist for a prolonged period so that the investigators knew the behaviors were stable, and then the dog was introduced. Later, after a series of sessions with the animal present, the therapy sessions were continued without the dog. The results were unequivocal. In the presence of the animal, there was more social behavior, and less typical autistic behavior, such as flapping motions of the hands. The social responses were first directed at the dog and later at both the therapist and the dog. The children learned to play games with the animal, and over time the games with both the animal and the therapist became more intricate. Importantly, the increased social behavior was accompanied by increased verbal behavior —the children talked more.

Some years later, Aaron Katcher and Carol Campbell tested the reliability of Redefer's observations by working with more severely disturbed autistic children in residential treatment. Again working with videotaped therapy sessions, they observed the same findings: more social interaction, less typical autistic behavior, closer proximity, and more touch between patient and animal and patient and therapist. One child, who used speech only in an echolalic manner—that is, repeated words in meaningless sequences in inappropriate situations—paid no attention to a rather boisterous, untrained, and highly playful dog for the first three sessions. On the fourth session, he came into the room with a broad smile and called the dog's name. Later, in a perfectly appropriate manner he ordered the dog to sit, saying "Sit, Buster! Sit!" In the next session he again ran into the room but dived under a table, remembering there was a ball under there, and fetched it to throw to Buster, who promptly brought it back, to continue the game of fetch. Similar bursts of social competence were seen with other patients. No one made a significant "breakthrough," but most children made small gains, demonstrating to the staff that they had the competence for a social and emotional life under the right conditions.

Just several months ago, at a meeting devoted to the impact of companion animals on health, we had the pleasure of seeing four young Spanish investigators win a research award for a case study of AAT with an autistic child. Their study was carefully constructed, and they presented some scenes from their videotapes. It was startling to see the same behavior with dogs that we had observed in our work. The children began their social dance with the animal by petting it on the tail, apparently unsure, at first, whether they could read its face. Later, when more confident, they began to pet the animal face-to-face, as normal children do.

Before leaving the story of AAT with autistic children—certainly a promising avenue for the stimulation of social responses, including language—it is necessary to discuss the publicity that has been given to the reports of interactions between autistic children and dolphins. That work illustrates the inherent problems with the mass-media credulity about AAT, especially when combined with the cultlike feelings centered around contact with dolphins and whales. In 1978, Dr. Betsy Smith in Miami, Florida, began using dolphins to capture the attention of autistic children. Some of those unresponsive children did engage eagerly in water play with the dolphins. She cites one instructive case history.

Michael Williams is an eighteen-year-old who has been labelled nonverbal autistic since the age of six—a child who does not normally reproduce human sounds. At the second encounter session with the dolphins, Michael began to make a dolphin clicking sound to get the dolphin Sharkey's attention to participate in the ball tossing play. Before this day, he had never approximated this signal before. This was verified by his parents and his teacher. Michael continued to "click" with the dolphins at all sessions. Listening to the tape, it requires close attention to distinguish Michael's "click" from Sharkey's click, although his "click" is easier to separate from Dawn's and Holly's clicks. To date, when Michael sees an advertisement billboard or a TV commercial with dolphins, he responds by "clicking" at the dolphin image. Six months after the project came to a halt, Michael began furious dolphin clicking in a local drugstore. Mrs. Williams found him clicking at a rubber flotation device shaped like and painted like a dolphin.

One year after the project was halted, Michael's class went to the Seaquarium on a field trip. Michael broke away from the group, went to the project area and stood outside the locked gate clicking to the dolphins inside. During the fall of 1981, NBC's *Amazing World of Animals* sent a film crew to record Michael's first encounter with the dolphin Sharkey in over a year and a half.

Michael began to click as soon as he heard Sharkey's signals in the filming area. He sat on a platform, engaged in water play with Sharkey, and "clicked" with Sharkey for over three hours of a TV crew's demands for retakes.

Similar, well-publicized clinical encounters were continued by David Nathanson. Unfortunately, none of the dolphin research used any other animal as a control to determine whether contact with dolphins was any more attractive to autistic children than, for example, a Labrador retriever swimming in the same pool. Clinical observations and the experiments just cited suggest that animals as diverse as doves, turtles, dogs, and hedgehogs may be highly effective in engaging the attention of autistic children. It is a pity that many anxious parents have gone to great trouble and expense to seek out contact with dolphins when a trip to a local pet store might have accomplished the same effect. At present we have no evidence that contact with dolphins has any advantage over contact with any other kind of animal for any purpose. Having said that, it must be recognized that the cult of the dolphin is so firmly established in our culture that no evidence will dissuade people from believing that swimming with these engaging animals is not the best means of coming into direct contact with the healing powers of Mother Nature. Nonetheless, people who are concerned about protecting dolphins question the wisdom of exploiting these animals for an imagined benefit. There is a legitimate question about the ethics of keeping dolphins in captivity for a therapy that may better be provided by domestic animals. Even the so-called swim with the dolphins programs, which keep the animals relatively "free," may be stressful for the dolphins and unsafe for people.

Just as animals have been used to help hospitalized patients, they can also be used with adult outpatients seen in the psychiatrist's office. In the late 1970s, Michael McCulloch assessed the role that animals played in thirty-one of his cases in which animal-owning patients had depression resulting from medical illness. Fifteen of them had a close attachment to the animal, and sixteen considered the pet to belong to another member of the family. The responses of the two groups were surprisingly similar. Most patients reported that their animals made them feel secure and needed, distracted them from their worries, and made them laugh. Those with a primary bond were also more physically active. In general, pets helped these people cope with feelings of depression, loneliness, and isolation and promoted a sense of play and humor. McCulloch concluded that the use of animals should be considered for outpatients with symptoms of chronic illness or disability, depression, role reversal, negative dependency, loneliness and isolation, a sense of helplessness and hopelessness, low self-esteem, and absence of humor.

The type of patient who can best be helped by a pet is illustrated in one of McCulloch's case histories of a former pet owner who was helped by a therapeutic pet after a prolonged battle with severe medical illness:

Mr. E. B. is a fifty-six-year-old married father of six who was referred for psychiatric evaluation because of depression. He was essentially in good health until he developed severe nephritis in 1972 at which time his renal function rapidly deteriorated. By 1976, he required renal dialysis. He received a kidney transplant from his son in 1976, but this was rejected and he was returned to dialysis. In May of 1977, a second transplant was attempted from a cadaver; but this was also rejected, and once again he returned to dialysis. . . .

He was noted by his internist to be increasingly despondent and was placed on a low dose of antidepressant, which he tolerated fairly well in spite of his dialysis. However, his mood continued to deteriorate: he was noted to be very irritable with his family and very belligerent and argumentative. He was also observed to withdraw from other family members and friends. He did not enjoy his usual interests. His wife had gone to work which left him at home alone during the day.

Although he was collecting a disability income, he and his wife had completely reversed roles. She went off to work and obtained the paycheck and he stayed home. He reported feeling increasingly useless, very angry at his physical restrictions, and imprisoned by his dialysis machine. He began to view himself as a burden to the rest of his family, and at times he wished that he would die while on the machine. His life was devoid of humor and everything seemed morbid and gray. . . .

After discussing it with his family, they agreed that it would be worthwhile to obtain another dog.

Considerable time was spent in finding the right animal as he wished to get another basset pup (their last dog had died in 1970). He became very much interested in contacting various dog breeders and finally going to pick out the dog. Within two weeks, his spirits were improved, his activity level was increased and with the arrival of the seven-week-old pup the tension in the household markedly decreased.

The dog became a natural focus for family members. The antics of the animal caused laughter that had been conspicuously absent in the household for many months.

The patient's spirits continued to improve. He was noticeably less angry and seemed very involved and interested in the training of the animal. The patient's communication with other family members took on a much more positive note, and he reported feeling much less preoccupied with his illness and was more willing to be physically active in walking and training the dog. He also stated that it was nice to be needed again. . . .

He has continued his low dose of antidepressants, and he has remained absorbed in his pet dog which he has named "Hope."

McCulloch also gave criteria for cases in which using animals is inappropriate, such as when a patient is too ill to care for the pet or when worrying about the animal would make the patient worse. There are times when an animal is a nuisance or too great a responsibility for a person, or a patient's previous experiences with animals may have been such that the patient will not derive any comfort from further animal contact.

Michael McCulloch was shot to death in his office by a deranged former patient on June 26, 1985, and his unique contributions and insights are very much missed.

The way in which AAT programs can be studied with the careful use of a control group and objective measurement of results can be illustrated by the study of the therapeutic effects of AAT with at-risk children in residential treatment for severe attention-deficit hyperactive disorder (ADHD). For years Katcher had searched for a way of validating his clinical intuition that the AAT program run by Dr. Sam Ross at Green Chimneys was a highly effective way of treating children at risk. At Green Chimneys children from the worst neighborhoods of New York go to school at a working farm that is also devoted to the conservation of wildlife and rare breeds of domestic animals. There they learn how to care for animals and grow vegetables, help in the rehabilitation of wildlife, and explore the natural settings contained within Green Chimney's acreage. They also participate in therapeutic horseback riding programs and learn about ropes and climbing in Outward Bound courses. It was always a pleasure to visit Green Chimneys and talk with Ross about his visionary ideas about the therapeutic value of farming and nature, but research was almost impossible. Every child at Green Chimneys went through their animal program, and no one in his right mind would deprive one of those children of that experience to form a control group. Katcher had to wait till he had the opportunity to begin an AAT program at another treatment center where it would be possible to use some sort of controls.

The opportunity came when Leonard Green, the director of the division of the Devereux Foundation that was charged with developing new kinds of therapy for children in residential treatment, gave his support for a trial of AAT at Devereux. Katcher and Gregory Wilkins worked with boys between the ages of nine and fifteen who were in residential treatment at the Brandywine Center of the Devereux Foundation in Pennsylvania. Most of the students were diagnosed with ADHD. This implies that they were impulsive, had difficulty learning situational rules governing behavior, were highly distractible, had limited social skills, and as a result of all of these problems experienced consistent failure in school. In addition, more than half of these students were aggressive, noncompliant, socially disruptive, resistant to control, and frequently violated age-appropriate social norms and the rights of others. Accordingly, they were diagnosed as also having conduct- or oppositional defiant disorders.

As a result of their inability to inhibit impulsive behavior and to direct attention consistently in sustained and flexible ways, children with ADHD are, from early life on, subjected to conflictual and unrewarding social interactions with parents, siblings, peers, and teachers. Moreover, both conduct disorder and attention-deficit disorder are serious risk factors for criminal behavior later in life.

A controlled crossover experimental study was designed with the random assignment of fifty children to one of two voluntary experiences complementing their regular education. The control procedure was a course similar to Outward Bound, where the children learned such activities as rock climbing, canoeing, and water safety. We chose an experience like Outward Bound as a control, knowing that skill-based programs of that kind are thought to have therapeutic value on their own. To make the test stringent and fair, we needed a control experience that would be helpful and attractive to the children. The experimental treatment was a nature education program for five hours during the school week: the Companionable Zoo program. After six months the Outward Bound group was taken into the nature education program, and the students in the original experimental group were returned to their regular school program. They were, however, permitted to visit their animals in their free time. The reason for the partial crossover was the strong belief that it was unethical to separate the children from their pets.

The focus of the nature education program was a four-teen-foot-by-thirty-two-foot building that housed a collection of small animals: rabbits, gerbils, hamsters, mice, chinchillas, iguanas and other lizards, turtles, doves, and chicks. One of the two nature educators had a dog, which was present most of the time. The students in the nature education program were given only two general rules: they had to be gentle with the animals, which included talking softly while in the zoo, and they had to respect the animals and each other and avoid speech that devalued each other or the animals. These rules were designed to facilitate behaviors that demanded motor inhibition and impulse control. Through speaking softly and being gentle, the student was better able to focus his attention on the animal. The use of the term "respect" was a deliberate attempt to define the animals anthropomorphically as a means of helping the children to think reflexively with the animal as an intermediate object (that is, to think about their own feelings by reasoning about the animals' feelings and relationships).

The first task given the students was learning the general requirements for care of animals and the proper means of holding them. The second task was learning the biology and care requirements for the animal that the child chose to adopt as his pet. After adoption, there were some twenty-one other knowledge and skill areas that a child could learn, such weighing and measuring their pets and charting their growth, computing food and bedding requirements, breeding their pets and caring for the mother and young, and demonstrating a pet to children in other special-education classes at the Devereux Foundation or adults in rehabilitation hospitals. The educational and learning tasks of the zoo program were designed to be comparable in scope to the very school tasks that these students experience with antipathy, avoidance, and failure.

The program also included hikes through the Devereux campus, fishing and camping trips, and visits to local state parks, to pet stores, to farms, and to a veterinarian's office. On these trips the children learned about the water cycle, the basic aspects of wetlands, pasture, and woodland, and the identification of indigenous birds, trees, reptiles, and small mammals. The zoo had spaces for "guest" wildlife, such as insects, amphibians, and reptiles that the children found. These animals were housed in the zoo a few days for identification and then returned to the wild. In addition to their regularly scheduled times, the children in the program could visit the zoo to care for, or play with, the animals on their free time after breakfast, at lunch, and after school.

The evidence unequivocally demonstrated the effectiveness of the companionable zoo program. The animals caught and held the children's attention, and attendance was significantly greater in the zoo than in Outward Bound. Not only did children want to come to the zoo; they also learned actively. In one term the average student progressed through eight skill areas completely and partially completed three or four more, even though there were no other direct rewards for learning once a child adopted a pet. Some students who had made no progress in the regular school program for as long as four years rapidly accomplished learning tasks in the zoo. More than 80 percent of the children made a good clinical response to the zoo education program. Impulse control was consistently better in the zoo, and aggression and violence were almost absent. Children frequently had to be restrained and medicated because of explosive outbursts in both the residences and the classroom, but no child ever had to be restrained in the companionable zoo, although from the frequency of restraints during the school day, we would have anticipated thirty-five incidents or restraints during the first six months of the clinical trial. Teachers were able to use a visit to the zoo as a therapeutic intervention to calm children who otherwise might have been restrained or medicated.

To measure changes in behavior in the children's regular school program—the best test of the efficacy of the AAT—we used the Achenbach teacher report form, the best-developed, empirically derived scales to rate behavior. Completed by the teachers, these scales demonstrated a significant reduction of symptoms in the classroom. We concluded that animal-assisted therapy and education can have a large, persistent, and broadly distributed therapeutic effect on highly aggressive emotionally disturbed children and adolescents with severe learning difficulties. These effects include a decrease in agitated and aggressive behavior, better cooperation with instructors, enthusiastic engagement with learning, and improved behavioral control in their regular school classes.

As dramatic as these effects were, they were also strongly influenced by context. Immediate changes were seen in the zoo programs, and these carried over to the school within six months. However, we never observed improvement in the less-structured milieu of the residences, and the positive effects on behavior were always greatest within the zoo program. The results we observed in measuring self-esteem with the well-respected Piers Harris children's self-concept scale illustrated the power of context. When we tried to document improvement in self-esteem after entrance into the zoo program by having the children fill out the Piers Harris in their regular classrooms, we observed no significant changes. We found significantly higher self-esteem in the zoo context when we contrasted children who filled out the form in the zoo with children who filled out the form in the classrooms.

We have described this experiment at length to indicate that it is possible to conduct controlled clinical research with AAT and that such research, at least in this instance, has demonstrated that clinical intuitions derived from careful observation of individual cases can be validated by carefully designed experiments.

ASSISTANCE DOGS

Animals, especially dogs, that help the blind navigate through a normal environment are widely known and accepted. Alysia Zee, a social worker and guide-dog user, queried other users about the roles their animals played in their lives. They often reported that the dogs gave them confidence to deal with other people and a sense of independence. Obviously guide dogs are much more than simple prosthetic devices, such as crutches or canes. Whatever benefits sighted people derive from pet ownership are added benefits for blind pet owners.

Over and over again, guide-dog users told Zee that the "dogness" of their guide dogs infused them with confidence and vitality. The dogs also returned them to the world of the sighted by restoring their self-esteem and linking them to all those who love dogs. As we noted earlier, the presence of a dog makes it easier for others to make contact. If this is true for the sighted, how important it must be for the blind! What follows are a series of direct quotes from guide dog users.

I feel so lonely sometimes, so left out and kind of overburdened. Tali is the only one I can turn to for comfort. She can't get too much love; just stroking her soft fur and thinking how grateful I am to her for all her dedication cheers me up.

I have read about and experienced blindness as a social stigma, a negative difference. My dog seems to serve as a link between me and regular people. Some barriers are broken down; they approach me less fearfully, and our mutual love of animals and, sometimes, dependence on them as companions bring us together. Somehow they think I'll have the insight to understand their attachment to their pets, and I do.

My dog has the basic values I believe in—health, activity, positive outlook and trust. I feel so proud when I'm with him, in control and able to conquer my environment. I sense that people around me are admiring and awesome, and I like that respect. Sometimes people can be so curious, so invasive with a blind person, and the dog reminds them that I have power too. I am not helpless and deficient; I can manage.

When I applied for my first job as a medical typist, some people complained about Duffy, her shedding, etc., but I stood up for her, explaining about the training she had had and her good behavior. I didn't realize before that I could be so outspoken and convincing. The secret of success is belief in yourself and an ability to win others. Duffy and I are a winning duo.

When I lost my sight, I became quite idle and despondent. My dog gave me a reason to live again. My family had been so upset and overprotective, but they respected my need to take care of and have control over my dog. It was my first real independence in months. I had felt so uncomfortable outside with people noticing I couldn't see, but they genuinely admired Angel, and I don't feel ashamed any more.

On hearing Zee deliver her talk at the 1981 Conference on the Human-Companion Animal Bond, we realized how differently a person feels toward blind people who are using canes and blind people with dogs. As she pointed out, blind people with canes seem a little bit dangerous in their vulnerability. People worry about them but do not quite know how to approach them to offer help. Blind people with dogs seem so much more in control; we feel neither apprehensive nor protective, and we admire how the person and the dog work together. More recently dogs have also been trained to accompany the deaf. What a relief it must be not to have to worry about someone coming up behind you, about missing a telephone call, or sleeping through a smoke alarm. Dogs make most people feel less alone, a special blessing for the deaf, who often suffer from a magnified sense of loneliness. Presently there are five major centers that train dogs for the blind and two that train dogs for the deaf. This latter function requires somewhat less intensive training, and more centers for such dogs will probably be developed. These animals permit their masters to navigate public thoroughfares with greater safety and agility. There are even a few monkeys trained to fetch objects for para- and quadriplegic people. This is a new idea and very expensive, but it may someday prove to be another contribution that animals make to our lives.

If one holds that therapy must be curative, dogs that guide the blind and deaf are not in themselves therapeutic—the dog does not improve vision or hearing. Ostensibly the dog is serving as a prosthesis, a device that is an extension of the body to serve a particular function. It should be remembered, however, that the loss of a sense often leads to other psychological impairments that may prove to be as much, if not more, of a handicap. Besides serving as guides, dogs and other animals may be very important to the person.

RIDING PROGRAMS FOR THE DISABLED

Probably the best-established use of animals in school and institutional settings is in riding programs for youngsters with disabilities. In the United States and Great Britain, children with a wide variety of physical disabilities, including cerebral palsy and spastic muscle disorders, are encouraged to exercise, learn balance, and share a normal sense of competition by learning to ride. Natalie Bieber, who supervises a therapeutic equestrian program for physically disadvantaged students at a school in Connecticut, defines her goals as giving students self-confidence and self-esteem by their ability to control a horse, providing recreation as well as exercise, stimulating the students' curiosity and awareness of the environment, and enhancing social and emotional adjustment and growth. The program includes riding and classroom activities. The students' interest in horses can be used to motivate learning in general.

The North American Riding for the Handicapped Association, in Ashburn, Virginia, maintains information about cooperating programs, certifies instructors, and assists in developing new programs. The association has a network of regional programs.

ANIMALS AND THE OLDER ADULT

No single aspect of pet-facilitated therapy has been given more attention recently than the introduction of pets into facilities for the aged. One reason, as we mentioned, is the immediate visual and emotional impression made by the loving responses of the deprived older people to the animals. Although animal enthusiasts have been bringing animals into homes for the aged for years, it was the work of the Corsons that drew serious attention to the phenomenon. The hero of their investigations is a patient called Jed, and his story deserves retelling.

> Jed was in his late seventies and had been a nursing home resident for twenty-six years. He was admitted to Castle Nursing Homes, Millersburg, Ohio, in 1949, after suffering brain damage in a fall from a tower. At the time of his admission he was believed to be deaf and mute as a result of his accident.
>
> Through the ensuing years Jed was antisocial and often appeared to be unaware of those who cared for him. . . . Jed's only form of verbal communication was gruntings and mumblings which were incoherent and not necessarily used

to make his needs known. He spent most of his time sitting in silence, apparently deaf, with intermittent outbursts of mumbling to himself.

In 1975, shortly after the arrival of the Corson "feeling heart" dogs at the Castle Nursing Homes, the administrator, Donald DeHass, brought the dog Whiskey (a German shepherd, Husky cross) to visit Jed. Jed's reaction was immediate—he spoke his first words in twenty-six years: "You brought that dog." Jed was delighted and chuckled as he petted the dog.

With the introduction of the dog, the communication barrier was broken. Jed started talking to the staff about "his" dog. The nurses noted an improvement in Jed's disposition and in his interactions with the staff and other residents. Jed started drawing pictures of dogs and now has a large collection of his canine drawings.

One of the most extensive programs involving pets and the aged is the People Pet Partnership Program, operated out of the Veterinary College at Washington State University in Pullman, Washington, and directed by Dean Leo Bustad. Two case histories from the People Pet Partnership Program were cited at the start of this chapter; others can be found in Bustad's book *Animals, Aging, and the Aged.*

Bustad notes that one must be careful in matching the pet to the person. In one old-age home in rural Washington, someone thought that a cage of playful gerbils would amuse the residents. When the animals were placed in the day room, the retired farmers were not amused. They tried to destroy the cage so that they could "stomp" the animals. After all, that is what they did to rats on the farm.

Just a few years ago, Judith Siegel at UCLA studied nearly one thousand non-institutionalized older adult Medicare patients. Those subjects who owned pets appeared to experience less distress and required fewer visits to their physicians than nonowners. While animal ownership generally had value, the most remarkable benefits to health were for those who owned dogs. Most of the owners noted that the pets provided them with companionship, a sense of security, and the opportunity for fun/play and relaxation. Animals allowed people to experience bonding. Siegel suggested that pets have a stress-reducing effect. As a result, support has grown for protecting the pet-ownership rights of senior citizens who live in the community and for encouraging animal contact for those in long-term nursing home settings.

For older people, who may be less mobile and who may have few or limited companions, animals provide family and friendship, something to care for and to be recognized by. Talking to animals when alone is normal and rewarding, companionship on demand is available when needed, and appreciation for the relationship is shown.

PRISONS

Prison is a metaphor for isolation and loneliness. Putting vengeance aside, most people agree that prisons at best should rehabilitate and at worst should confine people humanely. There are many stories of animals in prisons—unfortunately not well-documented—indicating that they make life within more human, if not humane. The so-called Bird Man of Alcatraz attracted national attention by converting his incarceration into a productive life by learning about, and caring for, the birds that visited the prison. In 1975 David Lee, a social worker at Lima State Hospital for the Criminally Insane (now the Oakwood Forensic Center) in Lima, Ohio, introduced fish and parakeets as mascots in the hospital. The inmates included murderers, rapists, and other violent criminals. The ward mascots proved so popular that Lee initiated a reward system whereby the inmates could work toward owning their own pets. Initially only small animals, such as gerbils, rabbits, fish, and caged birds, were permitted. There was no evidence that the incarcerated animal owners were ready to reenter society; however, permitting the prisoners to care for small animals resulted in significant reductions in the frequency of fights and almost completely stopped suicide attempts. The relationship between the prisoners and the animals in Lima has been documented in a film, *HiYa Beautiful*, distributed by the Latham Foundation. The film shows that the animals give the prisoners a focus for living. Caring for them, building their cages, raising some of their food, and learning about their needs directed the inmates' attention. The exchange of tenderness and caring between human prisoners and the small animals permitted the men to express the need for affection and gentle touch, which were absent from prison life. The animals did for these violent, angry men what other human beings could not do. The prisoners were too angry at people—their reflexive rage was too ingrained, too automatic, to be overcome by other people. The animals were able to stimulate a kind of love and caring that was not poisoned or inhibited by the prisoners' experiences with people. The renewed gentleness transformed them, not by making them open toward other human beings but by giving them an area of concern that they wished to protect. In addition, as is often the case where AAT programs exist, there were improved relationships with the staff. Animals facilitate a positive communication between the caregivers and those receiving the care, whether in prisons, schools, nursing homes, or hospitals, just as animals facilitate communication in the more normal settings of everyday life. This is an important aspect of all AAT programs.

One of the most recognized prison pet placement programs is at the District of Columbia Department of Correction, where selected prisoners in the Central Facility, Lorton, Virginia, were given pets—mostly birds, fish, and small mammals—by the volunteer program People, Animals, Love. The program was developed and organized by Dr. Earl Strimple, a veterinarian in Washington, D.C. We conducted a study at this facility to determine whether, in addition to the apparent improved spirits of prisoners in the program, there were behavioral, psychological, and physiological consequences of contact with pet animals in a prison setting.

The presence of an animal did not influence resting blood pressure. When subjects talked to the experimenter, blood pressure rose significantly, both when the pets were present in the room and when there was no pet present. However, when the subject was talking to the pet, blood pressure was significantly lower than when the subject was talking to the experimenters. There was only a small decrease in the number of offenses in the pet group during the first year after pet acquisition, although there was no significant change in the severity of offense. While the full spectrum of advantages of animal contact seen in nonprison populations may not be seen among prisoners, there is nonetheless widespread belief that AAT programs make incarceration more humane and help develop behaviors and interests that will benefit the prisoner when he returns back into society. At the very least, prisoners are exposed to interests and skills that may improve employment opportunities after release.

Animal programs can offer prisoners the opportunity to actually serve the general community. More than a decade ago, Bustad and colleagues at Washington State University developed a program at Purdy Correction Center whereby woman inmates could learn the care and training of dogs that would then be used to help people with disabilities. Versions of this program have been developed in other facilities around the country. Psychologists Paul Walsh and Peter Mertin found that a program that trained dogs for older adults and people with disabilities at the women's section of the Northfield Prison Complex in Australia did more than produce useful animals. The training experience improved the self-esteem and lowered the depression of the prisoners.

THE FUTURE OF AAT

In general, the use of animals in therapy is becoming more common. The use of animals with people in care settings is not rare or new. Unfortunately, most programs are undertaken with no attempt to assess their impact or general effectiveness. There is often no distinction made between just having animals around and real therapy. Nutritious food, friendly care, or even a pet may not be therapy in the strictest sense, but clearly the effects go beyond the obvious goals. In many situations animals may simply provide a sense of normalcy, a contact with better times, when pets were part of a normal life.

One of the benefits of public attention is that more researchers are attracted to AAT. One major goal is to distinguish the true therapeutic roles of animals and to determine how to maximize their positive impact in a cost-effective manner. However, AAT both benefits and suffers from the vast amount of attention it receives from the general public and the media. This spotlight has raised expectations beyond what any therapeutic method can accomplish. High expectations and the constant focus on apparent successes may blind us to the weaknesses of AAT and slow down research on how to improve it. Only in the past decade have there been rigorous attempts to document the salutary effect of animals on health, and we hope that rigorous clinical research will uncover the true value of AAT in the next decade.

GUIDELINES FOR ANIMAL THERAPY PROGRAMS

In the last few years there has been much popular and scientific discussion of AAT, which is limited to therapeutic goals; and animal-assisted activities, which include any recreational use of animals. Making this distinction has sharpened the goals of practitioners and set a more favorable climate for research. In hospitals and residential treatment centers where AAT is being practiced, the volunteers and professionals are writing precise objectives specifying what the therapy is meant to accomplish and noting how successful it was in meeting those expectations. In the better programs there are also rigid protocols for animal care and for monitoring the health and stress level of the therapy animals. Led by the Delta Society, a number of organizations are offering certification of animals for temperament to avoid the hazard of bite and injury. Despite these growing controls, there is continued need for vigilance. For example, a friendly dog that was captured by animal control in London, Ontario, was brought to a nursing home as part of a visitation program but soon developed signs of rabies. A total of forty-two people had to receive rabies prophylaxis at great trauma and expense.

Those involved in AAT must continue to develop better guidelines for the use of animals. The presence of animals in nursing homes poses special problems because these facilities are not like the home. At the very least, the number and kinds of animals permitted must be carefully considered. Only animals with which people are familiar and comfortable should be included. In addition to dogs and cats, many of the smaller mammals, such as birds and fish, can serve the same purpose while fitting into the living situation more easily. The involvement of humane societies in AAT programs has meant an emphasis on dogs, which may not always be appropriate.

Because disease-susceptible people tend to be concentrated in nursing homes, special attention must be paid to the health of the animals. Dogs should be well trained, housebroken, and free of internal and external parasites. Cats should be litter trained and probably declawed. Both species should arrive already neutered and with current vaccinations for all the common diseases. They should be kept away from food-preparation and linen- and utensil-storage areas. Special care should be taken that dogs and cats do not get underfoot and cause falls. Larger, older dogs that are trained not to enter a resident's room unless invited would be a valuable safety feature.

It is absolutely essential to have specific staff members responsible for the care of any animals on the premises. A veterinarian should examine all the animals with regularity and be on call. A sick or dying animal will not only pose health problems but will be a source of grief for residents. All personnel should be alert to any situation that may be inhumane or compromise an animal's well-being. It is of great importance that the rights of residents who prefer not to have contact with animals must be protected.

Humane societies that provide animals for the elderly who live alone should develop guidelines to assist the new owners in solving some of the common problems associated with animals, especially in crowded cities. Making the owner the target of anger because of dog waste, noise, or bites only serves to aggravate the feeling of isolation that often accompanies old age. There is yet another problem associated with placing animals with the elderly: who is to care for the animal if the person has to be hospitalized? We have found that many people are very concerned about the fate of their animals while they are incapacitated. It would be a tragedy if a senior citizen refused to accept needed medical attention because no one was available to care for his or her pet. Many humane societies will board animals in such situations, and a few hospitals are beginning to acknowledge the problem in their admission procedures.

Just as there are guidelines to protect human research subjects, there are regulations that protect animal research subjects. Most animals used in AAT are owned by the researcher or institution where the animal resides, but we should remember that any vertebrate that is owned or maintained by a university can only be used in ways consistent with *Institutional Animal Use and Care Committees.* Fortunately, most of the welfare concerns for animals used in therapy have been specifically articulated, and to the credit of most involved in the field, guidelines have been developed and continue to be improved.

The Cooperative Extension Service at Purdue University has developed *A Guide for 4-II Animal Care* for management practices, especially for farm animals, and Green Chimneys has produced *People and Animals: A Therapeutic Animal-Assisted*

Activities Manual for residential programs, with attention to space, maintenance, animal health, and even funding. The College of Veterinary Medicine at Washington State University has prepared guidelines for those interested in developing people-pet partnership programs based on their many years of experience, and they are available from the university. Mary Burch, one of the country's most experienced practitioners of AAT, has written *Volunteering with Your Pet*, an excellent handbook for volunteers interested in therapeutic visitations.

Most AAT programs involve animals in institutionalized settings, especially for elderly people, and the Delta Society has developed *Guidelines: Animals in Nursing Homes* to address everything from selection of the animals to evaluation of the program. The most complete guide is Delta's *Handbook for Animal-Assisted Activities and Animal-Assisted Therapy*, which includes guidelines for all kinds of programs. The chief recommendations are that the programs should consider the planned use of the animal, predictability of behavior and health, controllability in the special setting, and suitability for situation and client population; there should be standards for the treatment plan and the evaluation of the animal's role; and there should be an assessment of the facility that addresses the appropriate management of the animal, both while it is in service and while it is not. The handbook also includes the following code of ethics:

> Code of Ethics for Personnel in Animal-Assisted Activities and Animal-Assisted Therapy. These personnel must: (1) treat people, animals, and nature with respect, dignity, and sensitivity; (2) promote quality of life in their work; (3) abide by the professional ethics of their respective professions and/or organizations; (4) perform duties commensurate with their training and position; and (5) comply with all applicable Delta Society policies, and local, state, and federal laws relating to their work.

This code is an excellent start.

If AAT is ever to gain the acceptance of the medical community, we must conduct the research that distinguishes therapy from recreation. Without such research, government support and financial reimbursement through Medicare and Medicaid will not be possible. We need to balance our enthusiasm about the value of AAT with guidelines for its judicial use and to continue research to fine-tune its application and develop its potential diagnostic value. Most of all, we must conduct proper studies to validate its effectiveness and justify its implementation along with other forms of appropriate therapy.

Dorothy Iannuzzi and Andrew Rowan of Tufts University best stated the goals of AAT: "Reconciling the risks to the animals with their rehabilitation value is neither simple nor easy unless one follows the dictum that animals absolutely should not be used as means to an end." In other words, after a therapeutic session has ended, all involved—the recipient of the service, the therapist, and the animal—must have benefited from the experience. In this way, all society will benefit.

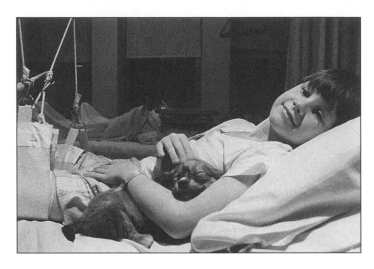

Animal-assisted therapy is effective for young and old alike, even for the most alienated. *Photos by Mary Bloom.*

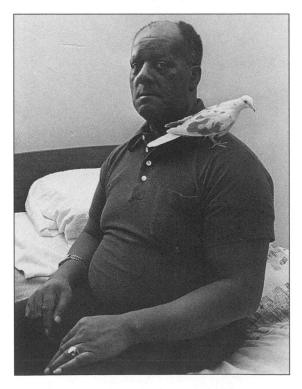

Guide dogs provide the sightless with self-confidence and a way to bond with other people. *Photos by Mary Bloom.*

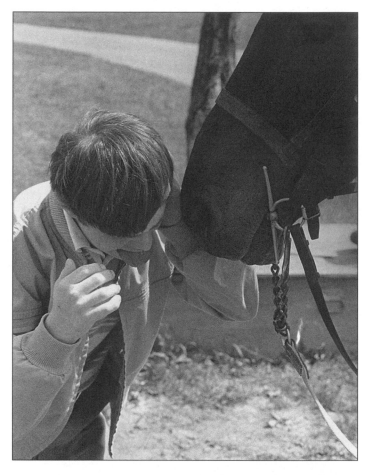

Many autistic children display affection and a kind of sociability with animals. *Photo by Mary Bloom.*

Pets provide the elderly with companionship and the opportunity for fun/play and relaxation. *Photo by Mary Bloom.*

For elderly patients, animals may substitute for the grand-
children who do not visit. *Photo by Mary Bloom.*

Eight

In the Image of Man

EARLIER WE DESCRIBED how people look for themselves in their pets. In chapters 9, 11, and 12, we will explore people's long-standing relationship with one of those pets—the dog. The dog deserves this close-up look for several reasons. For one, more than 48 million dogs enjoy blissful cohabitation with Americans. Then, too, through selective breeding the dog can almost be considered humanity's creation, making this animal, more than any other, the mirror of humankind's needs.

DOMESTICATION

Domestication is the process by which we encourage the breeding of animals with characteristics we desire and discourage or prohibit the propagation of those animals without the desired characteristics. This selective breeding alters the frequency of genes that control many traits in the breeding population. The genes themselves are not altered.

The long history of the dog's domestication has been described and discussed in other books, so here we will give just the highlights. The relationship between humans and dogs began some twelve thousand years ago, about the time people started living in villages. We know that domesticated dogs were around in the United States eight thousand years ago, because they have been found in Indian burial grounds of that era in the Midwest.

It is now generally accepted that dogs were first tamed, then domesticated, from the wolf—probably one of the smaller subspecies of *Canis lupus pallipes* or the now extinct *C. lupus variabilis*. These wolves undoubtedly trailed along behind prehistoric hunters, scavenging food and waste. At this stage the wolf was not so much loved as tolerated. An uneasy symbiosis must have developed in which the wolves warned the humans of approaching danger and may have even led early hunters to animals that both could eat. The humans, in turn, permitted the wolves to rest just outside the circle of light and heat, tossing them scraps. At this point the wolves were being tamed, not domesticated. Taming involves shaping the behavior of individual animals to be less fearful of humans by rewarding them with food when they approach and behave gently; it is a learning, not a breeding, process. Each new generation of animals must be tamed.

Eventually, especially as people began to settle in villages, they realized the value of these creatures as guardians, or at least as sentinels; as enticement, luring other animals to approach that could be caught and eaten; as a source of emergency food themselves; and as aids in the hunt, chasing and perhaps treeing prey. Early man began to capture and hand-raise the young wolf puppies. Many authorities believe that the keeping of young animals as pets is the root of the domestication process. Boris M. Levinson, in his *Pet-Oriented Child Psychotherapy*, noted that "Just as credible a reason as any for the domestication of animals is their use as pets. In other words, there is as much reason to believe that man's psychological needs were the primary cause for domestication of animals as that man needed to use animals for such material purposes as the saving of human labor and the satisfaction of a hunger for food." For safety's sake people preferred the smaller, tamer wolves, which had more manageable behavioral characteristics, and the process of selective breeding had begun. Perhaps, too, people selected for traits that helped them distinguish their new pets from their wild relatives. By doing so humans actually altered the evolutionary development of these wolves, creating, in time, an entirely new species. In a sense, man created the dog in his own image.

There are differences between wolves and dogs, to be sure; for example, wolves have more massive cheekbones if the muscle mass is included. The bone structure is not that different from some of the larger breeds of dog, like Saint Bernards. The wolf's teeth are larger, and this was probably a characteristic that people selected against when they started breeding from their early wolf stock. The differences between dogs and wolves today are *not* the kind of differences that separate species but are more like those that differentiate breeds of the same species. The floppy ears, curly tail, short legs and snout common in many dogs were developed by selective breeding; none of these characteristics exist in any of the wild species. There are fewer DNA differences among canids than among ethnic groups of humans, which are recognized as all of one species. All breeds of dogs and wolves have identical karyotypes (arrangement of chromosomes); wolves, coyotes, jackals, and all breeds of dogs are all interfertile, and cross-breeding occurs, even in the wild.

The traits that people preferred—and still do—are the juvenile traits, which would encourage playfulness, lessen aggressiveness in the adult, and make the animal a better companion, one that is easier to handle. Such a breeding program would also promote juvenile physical characteristics, which are usually considered more attractive—the wide eyes and short snouts of the puppy.

Though there is a hundred-fold range in size in dog breeds, their basic shape is similar. As Raymond Coppinger, from Hampshire College, noted in his studies, some of the very different-shaped dogs, such as the puglike (brachyce-phalic) and the borzoilike (dolichocephalic) long-shaped dogs, are victims of more recent intense human selection, which indicates that the genetic differences are allelomorphic—that is, changes in the rates and times of various developmental events occur (heterochronic shifting). Dogs and wolves start out the same, but there are differences in behavior and growth of body parts or expression of melanin (pigment) that account for the differences we see in the adult animals' behavior, shape, size, or color. This state, which is known as neoteny, can mean either early sexual maturation or retarded development of adult features, although the organism becomes sexually mature.

The idea that humans respond affectionately to the young of a species will probably not surprise anyone. We all know people who love kittens but hate cats, and unfortunately many thousands of pets, both cats and dogs, are abandoned or turned in to shelters once they mature. However, even when they are mature, dogs—and to some extent cats—are more infantile than their wild predecessors or cousins.

Exploring our preference for youthful traits, Dr. Stephen Jay Gould, in an oft quoted, insightful article in *Natural History*, traced the head proportions of Mickey Mouse throughout Mickey's more than fifty-year career. Over the years Mickey became more affable and vulnerable and less cunning. His appearance changed accordingly; his ears and eyes grew in proportion to the rest of his face, while his nose, originally long and pointed, became smaller and blunted. He was juvenilized to aid young and old fans in identifying him as worthy of our affection. The artists "domesticated" Mickey to make him a national pet. Gould summarizes the total impact of dog neoteny in his *Ontogeny and Phylogeny*, noting that "Selection for juvenile behavioral characteristics would not only make for a more tractable animal, with juvenile care-soliciting behavior and lack of species recognition, but serendipitously would also retard the onset of dispersing motivations and adult inflexible motor patterns, resulting in a tamable and trainable companion."

Similarly, the nonaggressive extraterrestrial creatures of *Close Encounters of the Third Kind* and *E.T.* are very different from the evil visitors depicted in other science-fiction movies. The formers' lack of aggression toward earthlings is clearly indicated by their large heads, wide, conspicuous eyes, and generally infantlike appearance. This is in sharp contrast to the creatures in such movies as *Alien* and *The Thing*, which have no redeeming juvenile characteristics or personalities.

Many of the animals that remain in the good graces of our culture are those that retain some of the physical attributes of the young, such as seals, dolphins, and squirrels. The killing of fur seals and dolphins is rigorously protested by groups who capitalize on the endearing juvenile qualities of these animals in their appeals for money to support their programs. Photographs of a baby seal looking pitifully into the camera, wide eyes and short snout clearly visible, or of a dolphin's "angelic" smile melt the heart of almost everyone.

Interestingly, it has been noted that human beings, *Homo sapiens*, have more in common with juvenile great apes, such as gorillas and chimpanzees, than with full-grown ones. The ability to stand erect, relative hairlessness, lack of a heavy brow, and relatively short arms are characteristics of very young apes and of people. As the ape matures, the pelvis rotates and forces the animal to stand and walk using its arms as well as its legs; the animal becomes hairier; a heavy brow ridge develops; and the face, arms, and body grow to the proportions recognized as the adult form. Human beings, however, never outgrow those particular infantile characteristics.

In addition to these infantile physical characteristics, humans possess many juvenile behavioral characteristics, including staying with their parents longer than the total life span of most animals and a need for touch and bonding, which most animals exhibit only during their immature stage of development. Man, not the dog, is man's first domesticated animal.

Animals were domesticated because we liked or needed them for one reason or another and wanted to continue liking them. As with Mickey Mouse, many of these animals—cattle, pigs, cats, and of course dogs—all retain many body characteristics and behaviors of the juvenile, even when they become sexually mature adults.

If the dog is basically just a "puppy" wolf, can some of the differences among breeds be varying degrees of neoteny? At Hampshire College, Lorna and Raymond Coppinger, who have reinstituted the idea of using dogs to guard sheep against predators (mostly feral dogs and coyotes), have made the intriguing observation that the dogs most suited for this guard work—the komondor, Saint Bernard, and Maremma —exhibit more arrested development than most other breeds; they all have short snouts and broad heads, and they even behave more like juveniles than other adult dogs, despite their great size. They are less likely to be predators themselves and are even more neotenic than most dogs. The Coppingers' article in *Smithsonian* documents many observations of caretaking behavior in these dogs and diagrams the body proportions to make a convincing argument that these dogs look and behave less predatory. In contrast, the most successful rural feral dogs are almost always breeds that have strong predator traits—German shepherds, collies, and their crosses are all more similar to wolves than to other breeds.

Although intense breeding has almost all but hidden the common ancestry of all dogs—the Saint Bernard is about 150 times heavier than the Chihuahua, and neither looks like a wolf—all dogs can theoretically interbreed and breed with wolves. While there are many reasons why you would not want to breed a Chihuahua with a Saint Bernard or wolf, it can be done through artificial insemination or breeding first to dogs of more compatible size. Eskimos today still breed their huskies with wolves on occasion, and dog-wolf hybrids are kept as pets by some people; however, they rarely make acceptable family pets.

There are many possible reasons for domestication. As we have already mentioned, dogs made good sentinels and hunting companions. Other animals were domesticated as food or to be helpful in other ways—transportation, for example. There may also be strong social reasons why people tame or domesticate animals. Historically, certain pets have been associated with status, class, and power—the exotic animal for the exotic person. Private European menageries once included cougars and greyhounds, while in Hollywood, movie stars may still use these animals as pets. The keeping of tamed, not domesticated, wild animals is often viewed as an exotic hobby for the wealthy. Even rare breeds of domestic dogs and other animals are in this category.

Our affection for dogs may simply be a way of expressing the love that a creator has for his or her creation. Dogs have become dependent on their creator for their existence; today they do not survive well on their own. And humans seem to have a special love for the things they create and nurture, be it a work of art, a garden, a child, or a dog.

There are more than two hundred pedigrees of dogs worldwide; many reflect our continuing need to create or to replace the status of pedigree now absent in most societies; we may no longer know our own heritage, but we can choose a well-bred dog of known lineage. In the United States each year, at more than 2,500 dog shows, people come from all over to view each other's (but preferably their own) dog crowned champion. It is the last vestige of our feudal heritage.

BEHAVIOR OF THE DOG

In spite of intense breeding, the dog does retain some of the traits of its wild ancestors. Many people, however, practically refuse to accept this, preferring instead to cling to what we call the Lassie myth.

In an average day's television viewing, dogs appear on a seemingly endless parade of dog-food commercials and sales pitches for everything from aspirin to automobiles. They are portrayed as an integral part of the American family. They gambol with the kids, roughhouse with Dad, and climb into the station wagon with everyone else for summer vacation.

In the movies they are rarely portrayed in any way but favorable, from the silly Pluto to the incredible Lassie. Vicious Dobermans or German shepherds might pursue James Bond or cause problems for American prisoners of war trying to escape, but they are seldom killed, at least on camera, although their evil human trainers are dispatched without mercy. In the long-running comedy television series *Hogan's Heroes,* the canine corps of German shepherds in the Nazi prison camp have gone over to the enemy (the Americans) and can be counted on not to interfere with any of the goings-on in the camp.

As for Lassie, this quintessential dog heroine still romps through reruns all over the country. She is relentlessly anthropomorphized. Not just a super dog, she would make a super person, always able to cope with the challenges of nature, from forest fires to wild animals, or with the emotional swings of her owners. She is gentle, noble, courageous, and tactful. Uncomplaining, she never sulks without good reason, and her human companions must regularly apologize for not understanding her better. She seems to tutor them in the nobler aspects of life. Incidentally, Lassie never urinates or defecates, never has to be taken for a walk (unless the family goes to the big city, which Lassie clearly hates), and never appears to require training for any of the extraordinary things she does.

The tremendous popularity of the motion picture *E.T.* can be understood in the context of the Lassie myth. Today's children are too sophisticated, cynical, and machine-oriented to accept the notion of an all-knowing dog. In some ways a space visitor with all the same attributes is more acceptable. Being an alien, he has the same problems, naïveté, and need of loyalty as a dog.

Given the model of Lassie, it is not hard to understand why children clamor for a Lassie all their own. What child— or adult, for that matter—would not want to have a friend like Lassie? How supportive it would be to have someone who would listen attentively and respond in all the right places, someone who would love, honor, cherish, comfort, and keep you "until death do you part"—in short, someone who would make certain that you or your loved ones never got trapped in an abandoned mine.

Needless to say, no dog is like Lassie; even Lassie is not like Lassie. If she is the American image of the ultimate dog and what is expected of our dogs, then it is not surprising that some real dogs do not remain in homes as cherished pets but are routinely abandoned or surrendered to animal shelters.

If there is no Lassie, what, then, is the true nature of the dog? The two major behavioral characteristics that have persisted from the dog's wolf ancestry and have accounted for the dog's success as a companion of man are the wolf's intelligence and its well-ingrained sense of social order. Stanley Young, one of the earliest chroniclers of wolf behavior in the wild, noted that wolves quickly learned to head toward the sound of gunfire during the heyday of buffalo hunting, distinguishing between themselves and the buffalo as targets and getting some good meat to eat. In the early sixties Dr. David Mech observed during his extensive study of wolves in Minnesota that wolves learned to avoid aerial hunters but tolerate biologists that used planes. Drs. Jerome Woolpy and Benson Ginsberg at the University of Chicago raised and trained wolves to accept human handlers and found that they remembered individual humans for at least eighteen months without further handling.

The social order of the wolf has been the subject of intense study and is based on the activities of the pack. In general, wolf packs include sexually mature adults, the young of the previous year, and the pups of the current year. Members of the group recognize their own and each other's place in the society. There is one linear hierarchy among the males and another among the females, with a dominant, or alpha, animal of each sex. Members of the pack have a complex means of communicating with each other, using sound, scent, and body postures. The wolf is very friendly toward members of its own pack. The great naturalist Adolf Murie, who studied wolves in Alaska in the early 1940s, reported observing few fights and bites among the animals and noted that adults would often share the care of the young.

Modern dogs have lost some of the precision of this society. For example, the males of only a few breeds will assist in the care of the young as wolves do. However, dogs do exhibit many of the same behaviors as wolves when they communicate with each other and with their human masters. Most people intuitively respond to some of the dog's signals—a wagging tail or a growl—in much the same way another dog would. The dog's preference for a pack dominated by a leader forms the basis for many successful human-dog relationships. When there is no clear hierarchy or when the animal, not the human, is the leader, we see problems in the family, including animal bites and inappropriate behaviors.

It is interesting to note that the closed wolf society requires the ability to identify territory clearly and to keep communications open among members of the group. Wolves often use scent to communicate and have evolved excellent control over their excretory processes. This bladder and anal sphincter control also made them more tolerable in early man's home, as they were not likely to soil the human's "den."

They also communicate with a string of postural and vocal signals, which may blend into each other and must be put in context. This is similar to what humans call body language—facial expressions and body gestures—which definitely communicates ideas and feelings.

Almost all the communication of wolves involves the relative position of body parts, such as subtle variations in how the ears and tail are held or variations in their vocalizations, from high-pitched whimper to deep bark. And much of this communication among wolves and dogs involves establishing and maintaining dominance through ritualized aggression.

In 1947 Rudolph Schenkel documented the subtle postures that wolves use to establish their relationships with each other. A series of challenges between animals of the same sex occurs, accompanied by apparently unimportant gestures: a stare, curled lip, growl, or stance over the other animal. In this way each animal finds its place in relation to the other, and a linear hierarchy develops. The alpha is dominant to all others; the beta is next in line, dominant to all but the alpha; and so on, with the juveniles all about equal to each other as they play out these behaviors until maturity.

Submissive behaviors are often the opposite of aggressive displays; the dominant wolf stands over its adversary with teeth showing, ears erect, and growling, and the subordinate wolf rolls over on its back, ears down, mouth closed, and whimpers. Rolling over or at least turning away to avoid direct eye contact is the opposite of approaching or biting.

The family dog, too, communicates by subtle shifts in position of the ears, mouth, and tail, accompanied by changes in body stance. When it is asserting itself or being aggressive, the dog's ears become erect, as does its tail and body hair, and it opens its mouth, exposing teeth—all behaviors associated with an intention to bite. Showing submission, as with wolves, involves the antithesis of these postures; ears and tail are pulled down, and the dog may even crouch with mouth closed. The dog signals total submission by carrying these behaviors to their extreme, rolling over on its side and perhaps even urinating. Dr. Peter Messent has diagrammed the common behavioral postures:

Schema of body language of the dog.

The diagram shows the various body postures and facial expressions by which the dog communicates, giving the consecutive changes from the normal stance to submission. From Peter Messent, *Understanding Your Dog* (London: Quarto, 1979).

As with wolves, the relative stances taken by two dogs are also important. The dominant dog will look directly at the submissive one; the subordinate will stand perpendicular to the other, avoiding eye contact.

At one time some behaviorists interpreted rolling over and exposing the underbelly, jugular vein, or other vulnerable portion of the body as an appeasement, giving wolves and dogs more credit for their knowledge of anatomy than is probably appropriate. These behaviors can be explained as simple modifications of the attack posture that are designed to inhibit an attack. Similarly, humans offer an open hand to indicate friendship—the opposite of making a fist or holding a weapon.

In dogs these signals are less well developed and finely tuned than in wolves. Perhaps our selection for the more juvenile traits and other alterations of body form, such as the curly tail and dropped ears of some breeds, has also lessened the effectiveness of the communication, and dogs often appear to be more aggressive both to other dogs and to people. Even so, dogs do use their ancestral postures to display dominance or to greet each other and their human companions. It only takes a little study and observation for us to recognize and appreciate these signals.

As a general rule, dogs appear more willing to accept people in their sphere than are wolves. Wolves born in captivity and hand-raised by humans are never as relaxed with humans as even wild stray dogs, which can quickly learn to accept human domination. Domestication is not simply a learning of the taming process but a true alteration of gene frequency that changes an animal's behavior.

THE DOG'S NEW PACK:
THE HUMAN FAMILY

All this brings us to a fascinating hypothesis: The relationship between dogs and people is rooted in the evolution of both. Dogs retain much of the behaviors of the young pack-oriented animal and thus accept people as members of their pack.

The first extension of such a hypothesis would be that a

dog and its owner are a true social group. Most loose dogs on the streets are alone, but if not, two is the most common number. About one-quarter of all free-roaming dogs travel in pairs, either male-male or male-female but almost never female-female. We suspect the sex of the human-dog pair is not significant; after all, this group is not going to mate or compete for a mate.

Within the family, the dog is a member of the pack. From the human's point of view, the dog is a member of the family, and from the dog's perspective, the family is his or her pack. Being somewhat of an alien in human culture, the dog is unlikely to be—and should not be—the alpha animal in the human pack or even to dominate any family member. When the hierarchy is confused, trouble arises, as we shall see.

What are the benefits or detriments for the animal and for the human in their social grouping? If survival and population increase are indicators of a favorable situation, then the dog is benefiting. Humans created dogs, and the population surely has thrived with human domination. Strays do not live as long or as well as dogs with human homes. The genetic diversity in dogs is greater than it has ever been—some say too great.

If the dog is thriving, is it the human who is in the dominant position? Dominance is not often considered to be a good trait; think of the dominating parent or authoritarian political leader who subjugates his people—conditions that certainly do not lead to well-being. But hierarchy is part of all social systems. Anyone who witnesses the greeting rituals of the well-socialized and subordinate dog that knows its place in the family cannot argue with the value of maintaining a clear hierarchy. That dog is a joy to have around, is healthy, and thrives.

The dog was domesticated to be a companion of man, not the leader of the human social pack. It was never intended to be an independent animal living on the social fringe or in competition with man. Unless we assume the full responsibility as the dog's leader, its alpha, we compromise the dog's existence and desired place in the human social fabric.

Our ambivalence about dominance in general explains some of our culture's ambivalence about dogs; one hears expressions of love and revulsion about the same canine traits. On the one hand, we want unquestioning loyalty and submission to our every whim, but the very traits that make the dog a reliable companion for the whole family are also referred to as fawning, cringing, and even bootlicking, which are not particularly endearing. People want and need submissiveness but may not respect it. Many dog-training books stress gentleness and reward-and-praise systems, yet England's Barbara Woodhouse, whose dominating approach makes even people obey when she says *"Sit!"* on television, is still the most popular dog trainer. Her methods stress total dominance over the dog. A dog that knows its place is a good dog.

Is being the leader good for people? Some of the human's benefits should be obvious by now. In addition to all the health benefits, consider the scene mentioned earlier, in which the well-socialized dog is greeting the family. Their faces reflect joy; they give and receive affection.

There may also be some subtler benefits that are never really appreciated. In almost every bookstore, there are books on how to be more assertive, how to not feel guilty while getting what you want and deserve, how to ask for a raise or just get your car repaired. Apparently we are in an age when there is some confusion about appropriate hierarchical relationships. Most of these books give you tricks that let you mimic the assertive personality—another example of acting as being. It is interesting to note that behaviorists often report that some of the most uncontrolled dogs live with families where there is no family dominance. The New York dog trainer Pat Widmer notes that she will not even try to train a misbehaving dog if the children in the family call their parents by their first names. This may be a generalization, but it can also be an indicator of a confused family hierarchy, which confuses the dog as well.

Perhaps all of us develop self-confidence from our relationships with our dogs. We learn appropriate assertiveness, dominance, and the responsibility of leadership. The dog, as an extension of the family, benefits from membership and contributes to the family in many ways, not the least of which is helping us with our mental well-being.

RULES OF THE GAME

Humans benefit from the games they play with dogs, as do the animals. For humans, games offer an escape from the complexities of life and a deepening of the bond with their companion animals. The dog enjoys the game in itself and is stimulated and exercised. Contentment is the same for both players. And the rules, once they are learned, never change. Here are some of the typical game interactions that have developed between people and dogs.

Perform means just that. The dog is asked to perform the tricks it knows and is rewarded for doing so.

Fetch is an obvious game, but the human must choose a place to throw the object that will extend the animal, making it search about or try to decide when the object will actually be thrown. If the dog has too much difficulty in finding the object, it will tire and begin exploring scents along the ground instead or just lie down. If the game becomes too routine, the human will become bored. The game of fetch may branch into either tug or keep away.

In *tug* the goal is to keep the object in the possession of both players. The dog must inhibit its natural tendency to inch up on the object, to get its teeth close to or around the human hand (an effective way of winning), and the human must not pull too hard to wrench the object away from the dog. If one party wins at tug, it can branch into keep away, or it may branch into tussle.

In *keep away* one player tries to get the object, while the other tries to prevent this by bringing the object close, but not quite close enough, for it to be seized. If it is seized, the game changes to tug, which can turn into keep away again.

Fetch branches into keep away when the dog does not return the object fetched but runs away with it, or when the human does not throw the object but keeps the animal leaping for it. Obviously, keep away can branch into tug or tussle.

Tussle is the game in which inhibition of possible competitive potential is most obvious. One common maneuver is for the human to grasp the animal with his hand around the lower jaw and fingers in the mouth and shake the animal's head. Alternatively, the animal's mouth may be held closed with the hand while it struggles to get free. In either case, but especially with the first, the animal must be very careful not to use its biting capacities. In other tussle maneuvers the human may pin the animal and must be careful not to use his superior weight to injure or hurt it. In tussling there is maximum body contact between person and animal. Touching is frequently mixed with petting or branches from petting into a continuation of the tussle. The contact includes pats; fur ruffles; clasping the dog between the person's hands or legs; keeping the chest, groin, and face in contact with the dog's body and turning the dog over to end the tussle with a good scratch or tickle. If the tussle ends in a scratch, the dog stops struggling and just makes ecstatic scratching movements of its legs. Tussle may also develop from petting games in which the animal becomes too insistent on licking the owner with its tongue, climbing on his lap, and starting a game of its own called spray saliva. Tussle becomes a way of keeping the animal from too actively licking the owner and changes the petting into a more active game.

Chase is a game usually more popular with children than adults. The children chase the animal within an enclosed space, and rapidity in making turns becomes the skill of the game. When the game is played on a slick surface, the animal's skidding becomes the fun of the game. When the animal is caught, the game branches into tussle or petting. When the dog catches the child, the game may branch into tug, with the child's clothing becoming the object tugged, much to the distress of the parent.

In all these games there is much talking and shouting and barking. All the games usually involve a lot of touch. In tussle the touching is obvious, but in fetch the dog is usually rewarded for the catch by being petted when it returns the object, and in tug the dog is petted when the object is returned to it to renew the tug, or it can branch to tussle.

An extraterrestrial ethologist watching humans and dogs playing together might wonder if they are, in fact, one species, but with furry young that have a drastically different appearance from the adults. To all appearances, they make up a family, with shared games and a shared hierarchy.

Nine

The Dog as a Therapeutic
Clown and Id on Four Legs

IN THE FREUDIAN mythology our minds are controlled by
three elements of enormously different temperaments: the
moralistic superego, which tries to make us live like a saint;
the id, which desires everything; and the beleaguered ego,
which tries to get through life by engineering compromises
between the other two. None of these three is better known
than the id: the furnace for our impulses, desires, and drives.
The id is part of the unconscious and is visible only in the
shadow play of dreams and poetry. Nonetheless, its wishes
and impulses are well understood: greed, lust, excremental
play, rage, jealousy, whimpering dependence, absolute domination, slobbering, sucking, gluttony, and, above all, continuous sexual excitement. Yet most popular accounts of the id
leave out one of its essential characteristics—the desires of
the id are represented in images, not words.

Animals also affect us in primarily visual ways. Our delight in dogs and cats would not be much impoverished if they uttered no sound; it might even be improved. In fact, the dog can be thought of as a mime, a comic psychotherapist who represents to us in pictures the content of our unconscious urges and the contradictions between those urges and our civilized way of life, a function performed by traditional clowns from medieval court jesters to the San Diego Chicken. The following pages explore the ways in which we permit dogs to personify many of the forbidden images of the human id.

THE JAWS THAT BITE,
THE CLAWS THAT CATCH

Civilized human beings are not expected to settle disputes with their teeth. They may use fists, feet, clubs, knives, guns, bombs, and atomic devices, but they may not bite. Even children who are permitted to fight are absolutely forbidden to bite, and very young children may be expelled from nursery school if they persist in doing so. Women, who are traditionally defined by men as being less civilized and more animalistic, are expected to fight "tooth and nail," like cats.

At the same time we are fascinated by the use of teeth to destroy and devour. Fewer parts of the zoo are more crowded than the building housing the large cats at feeding time. Despite the invasion of creatures from outer space into our imagination, vampires, cat people, and werewolves still hold a fascination for us. The movie *Jaws* captured the imagination and swept clear the beaches of the world. When children daydream about being animals, they transform themselves into lions, tigers, leopards, panthers, and wolves, and their night dreams are filled with dangerous animals with forbidding teeth.

The dog is descended from a predator and has teeth that can be effectively used for attack and predation. But when the dog bites, we often find humor in the act and laugh at cartoons of someone fleeing with a dog attached to the seat of his pants or a postman with a dog hanging from a pants leg. Perpetuating the humor, dogs can even be given treats shaped like a mailman!

Not only is a dog's biting humorous, it is tolerated and forgiven. Most bites that occur within the family go unreported, even when blood is drawn. There is no other person in the family who is permitted to injure kin in that way and not be severely punished for it. While an abusive human being is blamed for his fault, an animal who bites is usually presumed to be innocent. The large problem of dogs biting small children (most commonly, victims of dog bite are between five and ten years of age) is often dismissed by saying that the child in some way provoked the dog.

Not all biting is tolerated, and many dogs are turned in to shelters because of it. But people do not act effectively to control the problem, perhaps because at some level biting dogs act out our own aggressive urges, albeit in a comic fashion. In some instances, though, the comedy can have a tragic ending for the dog.

CAVIAR AND GARBAGE

"You are what you eat" is an expression that also embodies a social truth. The rules we establish to dictate what we can or cannot eat help define our social and moral positions. Muslims, Catholics, Jews, Hindus, Buddhists, and Jains must all refrain from eating certain foods, and for the most part humans take dietary taboos very seriously. The same is not true for our pets, however.

Dogs and cats, unlike other animals, regularly eat cooked food. Their diet is part of *our* culture. We prepare and choose their food, offering our pets dried dog food, semimoist food, canned food, food for a low-residue diet (less to scoop), food for the proper time in life, and special foods for large dogs. Dog-food companies pay for the services of veterinary nutritionists who test dog foods and perform solemn research on their nutritional content. Owners mix the food they purchase with food from their own tables and may even specially prepare dishes that contain fresh fish, beef tenderloin, eggs, and cream. Earlier we described the French restaurants that offer special menus for pets. Making the right choice of foods for their pets is an almost universal concern of pet owners.

Whatever our choices for dogs, they have their own ways, eating caviar, lobster, smoked salmon, and tenderloin and with equal or greater relish devouring vomit, excrement, garbage, decayed meat, old bones, fat-soaked paper, and long-dead birds out of the garden. Dogs will drink vintage wine and lap water from the toilet bowl. They will eat what is good for them and what can kill them. There is nothing forbidden or taboo to the dog; all things are permitted. In this sense the dog is like a very young child who has to be continually protected because it will put anything in its mouth.

The dog also violates our conventions about how to eat by eating, like the youngest infant, directly with its mouth or with its paws and mouth. For humans, drooling is a fall from social grace that is scarcely less serious than a lapse in toilet training. Even mothers do not like to be drooled upon by their infants and wipe off the saliva spilled in a child's kiss with some distaste. Yet dogs spill saliva all the time and are permitted to coat their owners with it. In the popular 1980s *Preppy Handbook*, the dog is acknowledged as a mechanism for the display of forbidden behaviors, and the singular role of saliva is acknowledged as well:

> It is allowed to contradict in its behavior every established rule and value of the Prep household. While the Prep adult and child are impeccably well behaved, the pet is not. All the affection that the Prep family holds back from each other is lavished upon the dog (or dogs)—therefore it is hideously spoiled. It leaps, it froths, it paws—it eats steak. Any eccentricity of character is indulged, no matter how extreme dogs that pee on the Sheraton sofa, or attack anyone outside the immediate family, or regularly disperse the contents of the neighborhood trash cans will be accommodated for years.

Labradors that think they're lap dogs, Great Danes that eat off the table. Golden retrievers, smiling foolishly, dig huge holes in the rose garden and basset hounds sunbathe on highways.

The proper dog should also be absolutely filthy. . . .

English or Irish setter. English is perhaps preferred. A nervous breed and therefore particularly difficult to control. Maintains a high level of saliva production, making it all the more desirable.

Newfoundland. Massive size and saliva output make this breed almost uncontrollable.

DOGGIE DO BUT HUMAN DON'T

The dog's behavior also flouts our conventions about defecation. Like children, dogs are toilet trained—or, more properly, housebroken—yet they may do what human beings must never do under any circumstances: they defecate in full view of strangers and in public places. Proper behavior for dogs violates the best-enforced social convention about human excremental behavior, and unlike wild animals, dogs are trained to do it that way; their behavior is part of our culture. Dog feces become, for us, the only acceptable way to represent shit. We can talk about it, debate about it, and joke about it. It can even appear in motion pictures and be talked about on television. Dogs permit us to bring the whole act of defecation into social space.

In our society there is nothing more humiliating than forced contact with human feces. There is no act of nursing more difficult than dealing with incontinent adult patients. The only kind of excrement exempt from this extreme distaste is that of babies. Infants, who know no better, will smear, handle, and even eat feces, an act that would call for us to label any other person insane. After toilet training, children are fascinated with defecation, and dogs, like children, are intensely curious about the substance, stopping to smell each pile on sidewalks. Their curiosity also extends to urine and to the anal areas of other dogs. Given the chance, dogs will, of course, show the same interest in toilet bowls and human excrement.

Just as dog waste is more socially acceptable than the human product, it is, like the excrement of babies, less contaminating. We can talk about dog waste on our shoes, comment on its odor. The relatively high rate of compliance with the scoop laws in New York City indicates that people are willing to handle the substance, just as cat owners have always been willing to handle cat excrement. Perhaps the best illustration of how contact with excrement does not contaminate pets as it would humans is in our willingness to permit dogs or cats that have just been licking their own anal areas to lick us.

PUREBRED AND MONGREL:
THE LADY CHATTERLY PROBLEM

Perhaps the dog best illustrates our conflict between the preservation of the purity of our lineage and the free expression of sexuality. Most Americans are human mongrels; immigrants have married outside of their linguistic, religious, social, and racial barriers. One element of the American Dream is the ability to marry outside of one's class—Horatio Alger's newsboys become captains of industry and marry their benefactors' daughters, and the little girl from a mining town in the West marries a rich and titled Englishman. Marrying up the social ladder is almost as meritorious as earning your way up. Yet with all this mobility and mingling, there is considerable anxiety that the universality of lust will erode all distinctions among people and there will be no identity that survives beyond a single generation.

We still cling to tokens of identity that span generations. The English royal family is a living symbol to millions of Americans, and the wedding of Charles and Diana and the birth of the new prince were almost as important in Peoria as they were in London. People with bloodlines of any kind excite the curiosity and admiration of Americans. For similar reasons the preservation of ethnic neighborhoods has become an issue to millions of Americans who do not live in ethnic neighborhoods; they symbolize resistance to the homogenization of the American melting pot.

Americans also search for and buy objects with a past to obtain some concrete, tangible expression of historical survival. The rich buy polished antiques, the middle class collects crude country furniture, and the less affluent search flea markets for bits of the past scarcely older than their parents: Depression glass, china, cut glass, stereopticon cards, old posters and old comic books, bits of lace, and costume jewelry of fifty years ago.

Another alternative for those in quest of historical identity or racial purity is the purchase of a pedigree dog. With as little as a hundred dollars, people who do not know the names of their great-grandparents can purchase animals with ancestors recorded for five to ten generations and related to the peerage of their breeds: those animals who have been grand champions. The purchaser can hope that the animal will become the founder of a new line of peers stretching into the future.

The pedigree dog, however, has one fatal flaw. It is ignorant of its breeding and does not recognize the differences among breeds. The brains and penises of all dogs, from Chihuahuas to Great Danes, are about the same size. To the dwarf poodle male, a female Great Dane in heat is an acrobatic challenge but not a different kind of animal. Left to their own devices, dogs would annihilate all distinctions among breeds within a few generations and create one race of mongrels. Thus all the breeds of dogs are dependent upon human intervention—social control—for their continued existence. The sexuality of the dog, like the sexuality of human beings, is always at war with social distinctions. The dog is a living satire of the perennial human conflict between unrestrained sexual urges and the cultural necessity of preserving distinctions among people.

It is interesting to note that this pattern of indiscriminate mating is not characteristic of wild animals—they do not exhibit the social destructiveness of unrestrained sex. Wolves, for example, carefully regulate mating. Only the dominant female and the dominant male mate, and the social order of the pack is never threatened. Thus the use of wild animals as totem animals, symbols of the careful regulation of sexuality to preserve social distinctions, is well deserved.

Is Beauty in the Eye or Nose of the Beholder?

The sexual lives of dogs and cats are ruled by odor—form is irrelevant. Males are attracted to females in heat by the odor of their secretions, and the female's acceptance of the male is not dependent on looks, either. Thus the dog's sexual behavior stands in opposition to our own ideas of sexual attractiveness, which are completely dependent upon visual stimuli. Women are supposed to look sexy and attractive, and their ability to arouse men is often thought to be dependent upon appearance. Needless to say, female odors, if they are a natural consequence of body function, are never thought to be sexually attractive. Smells are unattractive by definition and must be removed or replaced by unnatural odors. Our idea of beauty emphasizes small differences among members of the same species, but sexual attraction based upon odor tends to emphasize similarities because the odors of different individuals are basically the same. People do not look equally attractive, but dogs in heat smell equally attractive!

Heat

The sexuality of dogs is a symbol of the chaotic influence of desire and the ability of sex to disrupt orderly social action. A graphic representation of that loss of control is the familiar image of a crowd of male dogs around a bitch in heat. The noise of the dogs and their lack of obedience, order, and direction seem to signal chaos. Children can be reduced to fascinated giggling by this display. A standard memory from school days is of the class being disrupted by a pack of mating dogs in the schoolyard—everyone turns toward the window, whispering and laughing; one boy runs to the window to see better, and the teacher, slightly red-faced, restores order by pulling down the blinds. The disruptive urgings of the dog's sexuality were used by François Rabelais in his account of Panurge's revenge on the aristocratic lady who spurned his love.

> Panurge looked everywhere and finally, he found a bitch in heat, which he led to his room, and fed her very well during that day and night. In the morning he killed her and removed what the monks know well, chopped it into the tiniest possible pieces, hid them well and took them with him to church. There he waited for the lady who was to follow the procession, as it was the custom on that feast day. . . .
>
> And as she was opening the paper to see what it was, Panurge quickly poured the paste on her in several places, both in the fold of her sleeves and on her dress. He then said to her, "My lady, unfortunate lovers are not always happy. As for me, I hope that the bad nights, the pains, and the worries which are the result of my love for you, will be deducted from my pains in Purgatory. At least, pray God that he give me patience to bear my pain." Panurge had hardly talked when all of the dogs that were in the church came to the lady attracted by the smell of the paste: short and tall, big and small, they all came and smelled and pissed all over her. Panurge chased them a little and took his leave of her. He went into a chapel to see the rest. All those wicked dogs were pissing on all of her clothes, and a very big hound even pissed on her head and collar from behind. The others soaked the sleeves and the behind and the smallest ones fouled the shoes. . . .
>
> But the best happened during the procession: for here were over six hundred dogs around her, and wherever she was going, the newcomers would follow the scent, pissing on the ground the dress had touched. Everyone stopped at the sight, gazing at the behavior of those dogs. . . .
>
> When she entered her house and closed the door behind her, all the dogs rushed there from a half a league away, and they pissed at the door of her house so that they made a stream with their urine in which the ducks could have swum.

Caught in the Act

Our belief that sexual intercourse is punishable unless it is performed in secret is comically illustrated by the image of male and female dogs locked together. The darkest meaning of that image can be seen in the account of a Polish peasant's rape of a Jewish girl in Jerzy Kosinski's *The Painted Bird:*

> He tried again to detach himself from her crotch, but seemed unable to do so. He was held fast by some strange force inside her, just as a hare or fox is caught in a snare. . . .
>
> I had often seen the same thing happen to dogs. Sometimes when they coupled violently, starved for release, they could not break loose again. They struggled with the painful tie, turning more and more away from each other, finally joined only at their rear ends. They seemed to be one body with two heads, and two tails growing in the same place. From man's friend they became nature's practical joke. They howled, yelped, and shook all over. Their blood shot eyes, begging for help, gaped with unspeakable agony at the people hitting them with rakes and sticks. Rolling in the dust and bleeding under the blows, they redoubled their efforts to break apart. People laughed, kicked the dogs, threw screeching cats and rocks at them.

Here Kosinski makes the explicit connection between an illicit sexual encounter and the fate of being tied together and then exposed. The tie always ensures embarrassment, exposure, and punishment by society.

In Front of the Children

While the sexuality of pets is used as a metaphor for sexual license and disorder, the actual sexuality of pets is not considered evil. Quite the reverse, it is commonly thought to be good for children to learn about life by watching animals, and many parents believe that the miracle of birth is best demonstrated by watching a dog or a cat give birth.

Animal sex is the only kind of sexuality that is permitted to leak through the repression of the respectable living room.

When Aaron Katcher was a child, he was taken at least twice a year to a farmhouse in New Jersey to visit one of his father's former high-school teachers. She was a proper Presbyterian spinster who lived with her father and mother and her widowed sister. Her father was once on the faculty of Princeton Theological Seminary. It seemed that almost all the visits were made in late fall and early spring, so it was always raining, and Katcher had to endure the adult conversation, which was always about morality and religion. There were only two sources of relief in the whole day. Grandmother was senile and would at random interrupt the conversation with some completely irrelevant question or remark. The best entertainment, however, was the family Great Dane. He would spend most of the time lying by the fire licking his genitals, and Katcher would happily glance from the religious debaters to the dog. No one ever commented on the dog's behavior or on the contrast between the elevated discussion and the basic sexual action. Instead, the dog acted as a comic but socially invisible id.

Dogs and cats licking their genitals is a public demonstration of what must be a very private act: masturbation. The animal is allowed to do what most human beings have difficulty talking about. People having intercourse in public are assumed to be reprehensible and flouting convention, but people masturbating in public are assumed to be insane. Moreover, in adolescents' jokes and tales, the sexual activity of dogs is equated with human sexual behavior. The earliest one we remember concerns a woman whose husband had had an implant of dog testicle for treatment of impotence. A friend inquiring about the success of the treatment was told that the man was dead. When the widow was asked what happened, she replied, "We were lying in bed together. He turned to lick his balls, fell off the bed, and broke his neck." The latest one was told by an eight-year-old French child and translates as follows: "Two Belgians were watching a large dog lick his 'zizzi.' One said, 'I wish I could do that.' The other said, 'You should pet him first.'"

Not only can animals play with their own genitals, they

can engage human beings, both children and adults, in their sexual excitement. Cats in heat rub against people with their spine in obvious arousal. Dogs put their noses under dresses, and they hump people—with children, who are less dominant than adults, being their favorite targets. Such acts may be greeted with embarrassment, but they are tolerated and not considered dangerous for the child to witness, unlike similar human acts.

The dog is like a child, but human sex is not dangerous for it, and it is permitted in the family bedroom when children are excluded. Dogs and cats are permitted to sleep in the parental bedroom and even stay on the bed during adult sexual activity. Sometimes the animal's response leads to problems, as we discussed in chapter 3, when one partner objects to its presence, but most frequently the animal is tolerated. Dog trainer Pat Widmer insists that the dog must sleep in the bedroom if it is to be housebroken effectively, and she recommends tying the dog to the bedpost if it becomes excited by human sexual activity and insists on participating. Even dogs who take no notice of the sexual activity itself will take note of the sexual secretions that remain on the genitals the morning after and attempt to investigate, sniff, and lick the genital area. Some owners are embarrassed by this curiosity, but in describing the event there is no horror and even a hint that there is something amusing and stimulating about the animal's interest. The pet permits adult human beings to be exhibitionistic about their sexual activity, but they have the safety of a dumb witness. Some people use the animal to work out exhibitionist fantasies in two ways—by letting the animal exhibit its own sexual arousal within the home, and by making the animal an observer and a partial participant in their own sexual activity. Since the pet is, at a symbolic level, both mother and child, the presence of the pet permits the acting out of two forbidden themes—flaunting of sexuality before the family and curiosity about parental sexuality.

In all these ways dogs help us handle our repressed impulses by exhibiting them in comic form. Their sexuality, gluttonous appetite, and public display of excrement are all seen as comic commentaries on our social conventions. The dog is a living illustration of the contradictions between our id impulses and the rules of society. The animal has human conventions, which are completely irrelevant to it, forced upon it by its human owners, and is capable of complying with those conventions (by breeding with the proper dog or eating the proper food) or of violating them at any time (by eating garbage or escaping to mate with any other dog). The behavior of our dogs permits us to get around our social repressions without violating any taboos. This insight is not at all new. The word "cynic" is derived from the Greek word for "doglike," *kynikos*. Diogenes and the other Cynic philosophers devoted themselves to breaking the conventions of the Greek social order in order to demonstrate their futile and arbitrary nature. They likened themselves to dogs because, as the Greek biographer Plutarch said, like the dog, they "make a cult of shamelessness, eat and make love in public, go barefoot, and sleep in tubs at crossroads."

Ten

Breaking the Bond

MR. G. WAS brought to the office of a psychiatrist associated with a western veterinary school by his daughter, who said only, "I'm sorry, we can't do anything with him." Although Mr. G. was a retired real-estate broker with children, grand-children, friends, an established position in his church con-gregation, and a garden he cared for, there was now only one significant activity in his life: seeking redress for the death of his beloved dog at the veterinary school clinic. He only agreed to talk to the psychiatrist because he was on the fac-ulty of the medical school and he wanted the rest of the uni-versity to know "the horrible conditions in the veterinary school." He spoke slowly but with some vehemence and shed tears whenever he talked about his pet, Kikki.

Kikki, a nine-year-old miniature schnauzer, had been list-less for three or four days and was not even tempted by one of her special dishes, steak tartare with two raw egg yolks and a crumbled strip of crisp bacon. When Mr. G. noted that she was dragging one of her hind legs when she walked, he took her to their regular veterinarian, who said that the limp was due to pressure on a spinal nerve root and also mentioned that he had found a large tumor in her abdomen. Mr. G. was then referred to the veterinary school.

Unfortunately, the local veterinarian had made the referral without discussing the meaning of the abdominal tumor, saying only that "it should be looked at by a specialist." At the veterinary school the dog was examined by students and the hospital staff, and an abdominal X ray was taken. The tumor was malignant and had spread throughout the abdomen. However, the dog's symptoms were due to dehydration and fluid in the abdominal cavity—conditions that could be treated. This was all explained to Mr. G., as was the possibility of chemotherapy for the tumor.

Initially Mr. G. showed very little emotion. However, this stoicism was actually blind, uncomprehending shock at being told for the first time that his Kikki had cancer. With apparent indifference he agreed to place his dog in the hospital for treatment with intravenous fluids and abdominal drainage and to permit a doctor from the tumor clinic to see the animal. Numbly he went through the admissions procedures and went home.

There he watched some television and suddenly became panic-stricken. He called the hospital and discovered that Kikki was now listed as being in critical condition. He then talked to the staff officer in charge about taking his dog out of the hospital so that "Kikki could die at home among family." The resident on call that night said that Mr. G. could take his dog out of the hospital if he wished but encouraged him to leave the dog and give the treatment time to work. Mr. G. could not make any decision on the telephone but insisted on coming in to see Kikki. The resident agreed to allow him to see his pet, although visiting was usually not permitted.

When Mr. G. arrived at the hospital and was taken to see Kikki, the dog, obviously weak, became quite agitated. Fearing that the dog's agitation would make its condition worse, the resident asked Mr. G. to leave, and he did so with some reluctance. He sat in the waiting room with his daughter and finally agreed to be taken home. He would return for Kikki in the morning and was assured by the student on call that he would be notified of any change in Kikki's condition. On arriving at the hospital the next morning, Mr. G. was told that Kikki was dead. The dog had been alive at 3 A.M. but was found dead by the student who came on duty with the day shift at 7 A.M. Mr. G. exploded in rage, demanding to know why he had not been called, why they had not known that Kikki's condition was worsening, why no one checked the critically ill animal between 3 and 7 A.M. Demanding to see the doctor in charge that day, he was told that the doctor was in "experimental surgery." Mr. G. waited for four hours to see him, refusing to leave the waiting room, although his daughter begged him to come home. When the chief of clinic did arrive, Mr. G. listened to his explanation, but when he requested an autopsy, Mr. G. accused him of experimenting on Kikki, neglecting the animals in his care, not caring about people or animals, and wanting the autopsy to "cover up" what had been done to Kikki. Mr. G. then broke down, started crying uncontrollably, and was taken home by his daughter. She returned the next day to pick up Kikki's body for burial.

For the next six months Mr. G. spent much of every day seeking some retribution for the death of his dog. During the first two weeks he called the hospital daily, speaking either to the student, the resident, or the chief of the clinic. They all explained again and again that a dog weakened by a cancerous tumor could die at any moment. They apologized for the failure to call him immediately when the dog was found dead and admitted that Kikki should have been seen between 3 and 7 A.M., although little could have been done to change the outcome.

These explanations did not help Mr. G. He still asserted

that his Kikki had been mistreated, neglected, and experimented upon and that the hospital was concealing the negligence of its staff. Eventually the staff stopped responding to his calls, and he called the dean, who referred him to the head of the department. After careful consideration Mr. G. was sent to a psychiatrist at the medical school who was interested in the therapeutic use of animals.

The psychiatrist saw Mr. G. one month after Kikki's death. He was still visibly depressed, always looking at the floor, talking slowly—except when he worked up a renewal of his anger—and crying every time he talked about his dog. He described his routine with Kikki—the three daily walks, the evening walk to purchase Kikki's supper, the weekly trips to the groomer, and the monthly trips to the veterinarian. He told how the whole neighborhood knew and loved Kikki and how twenty-five people came to the funeral.

Mr. G.'s daughter said that Mr. G. now spent most of his time at home. He refused to cook meals, visit friends, or even go to church. He would talk only to her or make phone calls about Kikki. Nothing that the psychiatrist said could dissuade Mr. G. from his belief that his dog had been harmed in the hospital. When treatment for depression was suggested, Mr. G.'s daughter said she could not interfere in his life and would do only what her father wanted her to do. This obsessive concern with his dog's death continued until Mr. G.'s family was forced to hospitalize him. He had lost thirty pounds, was no longer able to sleep, and was talking about killing himself—after first killing the doctors who had abused Kikki. He was diagnosed as having a major depressive disorder and treated appropriately with medication.

Mr. G.'s response to losing his dog is unusual in its intensity and in the psychotic elaboration of the grief, but severe grief after the loss of a pet has always been part of the spectrum of reactions to that kind of a loss. Other cases reveal how the family pet, originally adopted for children, becomes the parents' "last child" when their own children have grown up. The loss of such a companion can be truly devastating. As

Judith Wax described in the *New York Times* of April 22, 1979,

I had Alfie killed not long ago. "Put to sleep" is the comforting term, of course, but you can't pet a euphemism. . . .
Well, children are a shifty lot; they'll grow up, move out, and guess who's left holding the leash? Yet although my husband and I groused about being tied down to him, the truth was that Alfie had become a sort of midlife balm . . . a skewed version of the change-of-life child. So if flesh of our flesh no longer greeted our return from anywhere, we settled for the kid in the fun fur who whirled in ecstatic circles at the very sight of us (and we never had to worry whether he was flunking algebra or smoking funny stuff). I know that dogs are sometimes scorned for sycophantic corruptibility, but what can I do? To be uncritically adored and blindly worshiped happens to be my idea of a good time.
. . . And when the vet phoned at last to say the lab report confirmed that the only thing in Alfie's future was more anguish, I wailed like Medea, but I knew what had to be done.
I attached the leash at that fluffy neck for the millionth and final time, and the voice in my head accused, "You're leading the lamb to slaughter." As the vet had promised on the phone, he ushered us in immediately. He also complied with my other request, that I be allowed to hold Alfie in my arms while the shot took effect. Cuddled close, Alf took that injection quietly; a few seconds later, he sagged out of his life and out of ours. The doctor asked me if I wanted his collar and tags, but I didn't. I don't want to see his blue plastic bowl again, either, or even the ragged towel we used to wipe his feet on.
Another veterinarian I know told me that after he and an elderly client agreed that the man's ancient collie deserved a humane death, the old gentleman watched the procedure, then rolled up his sleeve. "Now give me the shot, too, doc," he said. "That dog was the only thing left for me to care about."
I think I could do worse someday than to die like our old dog did.

Such histories raise several questions. How frequently and how intensely do people mourn animals? Does the mourning after the loss of a pet resemble the grief after the loss of a human family member? What makes a person vulnerable to the loss of a pet?

The experience that makes the death of a pet unique is the rational discussion of euthanasia. If there is one time when the veterinary profession and the client both demonstrate an essential commitment to decency and courage, it is during the decision to terminate the life of a pet who is both loved and in pain.

THE MOURNING PERIOD

Suicide, giving up and dying, severe psychotic depression, such as in the case of Mr. G., and intense, prolonged sadness have all been reported after the loss of a pet. Such grief has been with us for a long time. The Egyptians shaved their eyebrows after the death of a cat, and Caligula built a tomb for his horse. Plutarch, trying to refute the belief that philosophers should not marry, wrote:

> For the soul, having a principle of kindness in itself, and being born to love, as well as perceive, think, or remember, inclines and fixes upon some stranger, when a man has none of his own to embrace. And alien or illegitimate objects insinuate themselves into his affections, as into some estate that lacks lawful heirs; and with affection come anxiety and care; insomuch that you may see men that use the strongest language against the marriage-bed and the fruit of it, when some servant's or concubine's child is sick or dies, almost killed with grief, and abjectly lamenting. Some have given way to shameful and desperate sorrow at the loss of a dog or a horse.

How many people mourn their animal in the same way that they mourn the loss of a human family member? It is difficult to make any statement about the frequency of such mourning because the phenomenon has been so poorly studied. James Harris, a sensitive veterinary practitioner in

California, sees many clients who are closely bonded to their pets. He studied seventy-three patients who had lost a pet, and thirty-seven of them (51 percent) exhibited overt grief in the veterinary office. The most common reaction was crying (thirty clients), but only one client was so grief-stricken that she was described as hysterical.

Jamie Quackenbush, a social worker formerly attached to the clinics of the University of Pennsylvania Veterinary School, saw clients referred by the clinic veterinarians because of "excessive" grief either at the time that a decision about euthanasia has to be made or after the animal's death. Quackenbush saw only 3 percent of those clients whose animals died at the clinic. This estimate of the number of people experiencing severe grief after the loss of an animal has been confirmed by two studies of clients who have lost their animals at a veterinary hospital. In a study of more than one hundred randomly selected clients at the University of Pennsylvania Veterinary Hospital, Kathleen Dunn and Katcher found that fewer than 3 percent of the subjects had to take medication or seek medical help. In a larger study of clients at a general practice and a veterinary-school hospital, Judith Stutts tested more than two hundred clients who had lost their pet in the previous year with the Beck depression inventory. Only three patients (1 percent) were severely depressed, and 6 percent moderately depressed. However, it should be said that more than 90 percent of all clients in both studies had symptoms of grief, sometimes severe, on the day of the pet's death, and for most the symptoms persisted for the first week after death.

Most people remember grieving over an animal at some time in their lives. In Michael Robin's study of pet ownership, more than half of the five hundred normal and delinquent youths (see chapter 3) had lost their "special pet," and only two children did not report significant grief at the animal's death. Mary Stewart, a Scottish veterinarian, surveyed 135 schoolchildren in central Scotland, and 62 (44 percent) wrote about an animal's death; two-thirds of these children told of their grief at that loss. There is little equivalent data for adults. However, a survey by the pet industry indicated that 23 percent of former owners said that grief over the loss of a pet was the reason they no longer had one.

There are no social conventions regulating our grief at the death of an animal, so that any response is socially permissible. People are free to mourn intensely or not at all. You can throw your cat's body in the garbage can or bury it in a bronze casket with a marble headstone. It is quite a different situation after the loss of a close family member, when some sort of mourning is required to prove your humanity. In Albert Camus's *The Stranger*, the hero of the book feels that he was convicted of murder not because he killed an Arab but because his inhumanity was demonstrated to the jury by his failure to grieve after his mother's death. Camus contrasts the hero's detachment from his mother's death with the grief of the old man Salamano after his dog is lost.

In general, there is a notion that grief after the loss of an animal is appropriate for children but not adults. In children it is said to provide a useful "rehearsal" for the death of human family members, but because mourning a pet is not considered necessary or appropriate for adults, there is a lack of social support for the mature person working through such grief.

The very large number of animals surrendered annually to shelters seems to indicate that many Americans can give up their animals with very little grief at all. Recent estimates indicate that between 4 and 6 million animals were given up to shelters annually in the United States, and more than half of these animals were killed in the shelters. In three cities— New York, Baltimore, and St. Louis—nearly 20 percent of the estimated dog population, brought in by owners or animal control officers, ended their lives in animal shelters.

The data also indicate that there is a large turnover of young animals within the pet-owning population. For example, a California survey of many years ago enumerated animal ownership in two different counties. One year later a survey of the same households found that 40 percent of all dogs and 30 percent of all cats had been given away by their owners. Approximately 35 percent of dogs that were less than one year old were no longer in the household by the end of the first year. The same tendency to give away young animals was reported in New York, where 36 percent of dogs surrendered to a shelter were puppies and 46 percent of cats were kittens. Some of these animals were unwanted offspring of family pets, but many were recently acquired animals that had failed to establish a place for themselves in the household. Either there were problems controlling the animal's behavior or the family conditions had changed, a move from one house to another being a frequent reason for surrendering a pet.

More recent studies, conducted by Dr. Gary Patronek at Purdue University, identified some of the patterns associated with relinquishing a dog to an animal shelter. What is often not appreciated by the general public is that older animals— more than one year of age—are more likely to be surrendered to shelters, not puppies. Older and mixed-breed dogs are more likely to be surrendered. Patronek found in his doctoral studies that people who had more contact with veterinarians and obedience classes were less likely to give away their pet, perhaps indicating that the bond is reinforced by social facilitation from others and by building a relationship with the animal. Without facilitating the bonding, breaking the bond is easier and, therefore, more common.

Stewart has provided us with a detailed comparison between the kinds of sorrow experienced after the death of a pet and of a child, based on personal experience and on a survey of Scottish adults. Her account agrees with a study of grief after the loss of an animal made by Katcher and Dr. Marc Rosenberg, a veterinarian in private practice. Although there are similarities between the two experiences—as there are among all forms of grief—the differences illuminate the nature of the relationship with the animal.

The initial reaction of both adults and children after the death of an animal is usually a flood of tears. It is not unusual for people to say that they cried more over the death of a pet than they did at the death of a close relative, at which time the person is frequently so shocked that there are no tears, just a numb, inert awareness of final loss.

People are freer to mourn an animal unaffectedly, at least in private, because, as Sigmund Freud noted, they are not as ambivalent about animals as they are about human family members. The grief is simple, lacking the complexity of our feelings toward parents and children. Also the loss of the animal does not threaten the social world in the way that a family death does. The mourner does not face the dissolution of self that is felt after losing a family member, and grief does not have to be suppressed to hold yourself or others together. With the death of a close family member, it seems necessary to guard against excessive grief lest we descend too far too fast.

After the loss of a pet, the sorrow may be intense but brief, and the stages of grief—denial, sense of loss, numbness, anger—are run through rapidly, like a film speeded up. Any disturbances in eating, sleeping, or working last only a few days at most, except in extreme cases.

The social response to the two events is also quite different. The mourner who has lost a close relative is rarely left alone—family, friends, and local groups mobilize to help the mourner work through the sorrow, everyone making themselves available and helping, if only by acknowledging the loss. Rarely are people as sensitive to the loss of a pet. Frequently the mourner feels that he or she has to conceal the grief from the outside world. At the very least, normal activity is expected to continue.

Loss of a spouse or a child can disorganize the survivor's life completely. So much of the activity of living may have been sustained by the deceased person that the survivor literally does not know what to do. Friends and relatives will all respond to the survivor in a different way—sometimes for the better, sometimes for the worse. With a pet's death, there is rarely a change in the mourner's social life, the exceptions being those owners who centered their lives around the animal and those who related to others through the animal.

The validity of a person's grief at a pet's death is, however, gaining more social recognition and a more sympathetic response. In part, this has been due to the excellent media coverage of the growing body of information about the existence of this kind of grief. The veterinary profession has also made an effort to educate veterinarians about grief. Some progressive schools, such as the University of Pennsylvania, Purdue University, the University of California at Davis, and Colorado State University, employ social workers and publish research on the impact of client grief. In New York City the Animal Medical Center has supported the research of Susan Cohen, who was instrumental in promoting the value of pet-loss support groups.

When someone loses a pet, there may be very little resolution of the sorrow with time. The initial grief is resolved rapidly, but the lingering sorrow persists for years. People are incredibly faithful in visiting graves at pet cemeteries. One reason for the persistence of mourning is the pet's ability to serve as a bridge to other people, a bridge that is ultimately severed at the death of the pet. Veterinarians have described the phenomenon of *double death*. For example, a wife inherited her dead husband's dog, and when the dog died, she mourned the animal and mourned her husband a second time because she had lost the last connection to him. One woman we interviewed was still, after six months, grieving for her Great Dane. The dog had been purchased after her child died of Tay-Sachs disease. The large, healthy animal was a replacement for her frail child, with whom she had never been able to roughhouse and play. Sadly, the animal went blind, just as her son had gone blind shortly before his death. She had to have her pet put to sleep, but after its death, she mourned both for the pet and for the child it represented.

People who mourn their pets for a prolonged period of time still find it difficult to recruit support and comfort nowadays. In Dunn and Katcher's study almost no one consulted a psychiatrist or physician, and when directly asked about support, fewer than 6 percent sought it from their clergy. Neither clergy nor psychotherapists seem to be sensitive to people's distress at losing a pet. At the University of Pennsylvania Veterinary School, Katcher had to call many psychiatrists and psychologists to inform them that their client had lost a pet and was in need of special help during the mourning period. Almost always, the therapist seemed to be ignorant of the importance of the animal in the person's life and was surprised at the patient's grief. In questioning the owner, Katcher determined that people who were happy with their pets, and frequently highly dependent upon them, almost never talked about the animal in psychotherapy. The animal was a source of comfort, not a problem, and thus never entered into the therapeutic discussion. Because of the insensitivity of the helping professions, people who were distressed when a pet died had few places they could find help. Most, according to the survey data, found their comfort from the veterinarian and from friends who owned pets. Pet-owning friends were a more important part of support than family, which prompted Cohen to form the first pet-loss support group in 1983. This form of help was soon widely discussed at the meetings of the Delta Society.

Many of the studies of how people mourn pets have attempted to determine who is most vulnerable to such a loss. Harris grouped his clients according to the closeness of their attachment to their pets. Not surprisingly, 74 percent of the clients who were closely bonded exhibited grief at the deaths of their animals, while only 40 percent of the less closely attached owners grieved. All other studies have confirmed this intuitively obvious finding; the more closely people are bonded to their pet, the more they grieve. Unfortunately, we do not know very much more about which people will mourn their animals intensely. In some studies, but not all, grief was more intense in older owners who lived only with other adults. The perception of support from friends and family has a small and inconsistent effect in decreasing the probability of mourning. Having other pets does not seem to help. People seem to feel that their animals are individuals, and one cannot replace another. Poor health and environmental stress seem to increase mourning, but not consistently. Taking all the data into consideration, it seems that mourning is determined by the circumstances of the owner's particular relationship with the pet, and not by the external factors.

EUTHANASIA

In one very important way, veterinary medicine is a more rational system than human medicine. It can consider the humane termination of life as well as its sustenance. Only in the past twenty years has human medicine begun to cope with the problems faced by a patient in managing his or her own death. It is still difficult to discuss the passive termination of life to meet the wishes of patient or family, and the active termination of life to spare pain or suffering—euthanasia—is still a crime.

One of the great gifts that veterinarians give to their clients is helping them make the rational decision to gently terminate the life of a beloved animal. Katcher was first made aware of the meaning of this experience when he was interviewing a husband and wife about the death of their pet. Rosenberg, their veterinarian, was also present. In the middle of the discussion, the husband turned to his wife and said, "I wish, if the time ever comes, that you could give me as fine a death as we gave Pirate." Wax's description of her pet's death, which we quoted above, reflects the same sentiment. The termination of a pet's life in consultation with a veterinarian is one of the few times when people can act sanely, positively, and gently in the face of death.

As described in chapter 4, the pet can stand for the self and reflect love back at the self. Some owners have a kind of symbiotic bond with their pet. An owner's whole life may be centered around the animal; as one young man said, "That dog was just like my right arm." Another woman, who arrived in Katcher's office carrying her dog in a sling designed for babies, could not distinguish between her pet's heart disease and her own heart disease. Her health and the animal's health were one in her mind. When asked what would happen if the animal died, she screamed loud enough to bring a concerned colleague into Katcher's office. She could not consider the possibility of the animal's death.

Such owners find it very difficult to make a decision about euthanasia. They can see only their own pain at the loss of something that is part of themselves, and they have little perception of the animal's situation. It is the veterinarian's difficult task to separate them from their pets so that they can see the animal's situation and make the decision to terminate its pain.

A SUCCESSION OF PETS

A pet can be loved without being made part of the self or an artificial person. We can, even in grief, recognize the identity of the animal with its own species. We can appreciate the animal's own reality and see it both as part of our lives and as part of nature. This is the kind of relationship with animals that is shared by farmers and even hunters, who witness a succession of living things that are loved, reared, sacrificed, and replaced. We have lost the notion that it is possible to love animals and see them die or sacrifice them in their time. John Berger, in a very insightful essay, "Looking at Animals," reminds us of the coupling of love and sacrifice:

> Animals came from over the horizon. They belonged there and here. Likewise they were mortal and immortal. An animal's blood flowed like human blood, but its species was undying and each lion was Lion, each ox was Ox. This—maybe the first existential dualism—was reflected in the treatment of animals. They were subjected and worshipped, bred and sacrificed.

Eleven

Why Lassie Is a Bitch

THE DOG MAKES an admirable companion, as we have seen in chapter 9 and in much of the rest of this book, but dogs are not completely flawless in their relationships with humans. Some of the problems stem from the dog's own immutable nature as the descendant of a predator, while many other problems originate with the human end of the partnership, for example, overpopulation and strays. Our examination of dog and human would not be complete without considering these problems.

PREDATOR AS PET

So common is the problem of animal bite that almost everyone knows the quote of John B. Bogart, city editor of the New York *Sun:* "When a dog bites a man, that is not news, because it happens so often. But if a man bites a dog, that is news."

Case one: The four-day-old Jones baby was resting in his bassinet, being watched by other members of the family—Mr. and Mrs. Jones, their six-year-old child, and the husky they had owned for three years. The dog was well socialized and behaved appropriately with the older child. The parents were well versed in the proper care of the animal and permitted carefully supervised interactions with the new baby. With all members of the family nearby, the dog lifted the baby out of the bassinet by the head. Because of the animal's jaw size, the act of holding the baby for just a split second caused a massive intracerebral hemorrhage, and the child died. Behavioral studies made later found the dog to be inquisitive, with slight predatory tendencies, but not vicious.

Case two: Following a stroke, eighty-one-year-old Mrs. Ryan needed a caretaker, and her son moved in, bringing his five small dogs—beagles, dachshunds, a terrier, and their crosses. A sixth dog was born afterward. The son had few friends and cared most for his dogs. His mother shared his affection for the pets in only a peripheral way; she played with one or two of them but had little feeling for the others. The dogs were locked into a separate room when her son left to work or shop.

One day they had a visitor, the first in many months, an old friend. The two men left to buy some beer after first locking away the dogs. When they returned less than forty-five minutes later, the dogs had apparently escaped from their room, and the mother lay in a pool of blood on the floor. All her clothes had been torn away, her arms had been eaten down to the bone, and portions of her scalp were missing. She was still alive but died of severe hemorrhage in the hospital.

Members of the humane society described the dogs as "nice little pets" and expressed displeasure at having to destroy such animals if, in fact, they were not the culprits. Public response was similar; anonymous phone callers made such statements as "Maybe the woman died, and the dogs were just investigating or eating her body out of hunger," "Maybe the son killed his mother and is blaming the dogs," and "Maybe some intruder was really to blame." It is true that animals are sometimes blamed when found near a corpse, but that was not the case here.

Testing showed that individually the dogs were as gentle as described, but together they attacked a well-padded handler who was part of the study team. He carried a four-foot-high doll, which the dogs pulled down, chewing the head and arms. The doll was attacked in ways that would have left wounds similar to those suffered by the real victim.

Case three: A group of young boys was playing in an open, sandy field, surrounded by woods, when they were chased and treed by eleven dogs. The dogs left, and after several minutes the boys returned to their games. The dogs again emerged from the woods, and the boys ran. One child tripped and fell, and the dogs ignored him, jumping over him to reach his eleven-year-old friend. In less than five minutes they had ripped off all the boy's clothing and removed chunks of muscle from his back. He would certainly have been killed if it hadn't been for a teenager in a nearby car, who realized what was happening and chased the dogs away, then placed the injured boy in the car. Even so, the dogs kept up their attack, trying in vain to reach the boy. By this time the victim's young companion was able to run for help, bringing the victim's father. The dogs were kept away long enough to carry the boy to a police car.

The victim's injuries were described as "dirty, ragged lacerations all over the face, ears, neck, axilla, arms, trunk, groin, thighs and back, the left axilla revealed arteries and veins exposed, the skin showed multiple ragged lacerations, the right trunk and left trunk were ragged, down to the fascia." The boy was not simply bitten, he had been attacked with an attempt to be eaten.

Through extensive interviews it was discovered that a motorcycle had passed shortly before the incident. The dogs, whose home was a property used for the storage of large machinery that also had some trailer residents, were routinely permitted to roam, had often been observed to hunt, and had a history of chasing and threatening people. Individually they were found to be easy to handle. In behavioral tests a professional dog trainer in a padded bite unit approached them with no problems. Then they were released in an open but fenced schoolyard, and as luck would have it, a motorcycle went by outside the fence. The dogs gave chase until the cycle disappeared from view, then turned their attention to the trainer. In their aroused state they pursued him and would have pulled him down had he not been skilled at handling aggressive dogs. He was rescued before he was injured, but the dogs had demonstrated their willingness to attack once the preliminary behavior of chasing was initiated for a hunt.

These three studies are unusual only in their severity. (They also illustrate specific types of bite behavior, which we will analyze a bit later.) That dogs bite comes as no surprise; but what may be surprising is that they account for the majority of animal bites that are reported in the United States. Cats are in second place; third are humans (yes, they're animals, too); and much, much farther down the list is a variety of rats and mice, livestock, and other small pets. The 1977 breakdown of bites reported to the New York City Department of Health makes this clear:

Reported bites, New York City, 1977

Animal	Number of reports	Total
Dogs	22,076	89.1
Cats	1,152	4.6
Humans	892	3.6
Rodents	548	2.2
Rabbits	40	0.2
Small mammals[1]	32	0.1
Horses	18	0.1
Reptiles	17	0.1
Birds	8	0.03
Large mammals[2]	7	0.03

1. Includes 21 monkeys, 4 raccoons, 3 ferrets, 1 weasel, 1 coatimundi, 1 skunk, and 1 goat.
2. Includes 3 lions, 1 ocelot, 1 leopard, 1 polar bear, and 1 anteater.

In spite of these figures, many people still wrongly assume that wild animals are responsible for the greater number of animal bites. To obtain a better picture of the scope of the dog-bite problem, Alan Beck and Randall Lockwood studied dog-bite patterns in St. Louis, reviewing all the reported cases of dog bite for a three-year period. They found, as we already know, that dog bite is not rare. Some 350 to 450 people per 100,000 in the population are bitten annually—that is, 1 person in 250. However, dog bite does not affect everyone equally. Children from five to nine years old are overwhelmingly the primary victims; more than 5 percent (1 in 50) of that age group receive a reported bite every year—more than the combined annual reports of measles, mumps, chicken pox, and whooping cough. In other words, although children in this age category comprise less than 9 percent of the population, they are the victims of nearly 30 percent of the bites from dogs. Children from nine to fourteen years old are the group with the next most bites.

As startling as these figures are, we should also remember that only a small percentage of bites are reported. There are several reasons for this. For one, the report rate decreases when there are cuts in public-health budgets—there are too few people to handle the bite reports. Dog owners who tolerate and even encourage biting behavior in the family dog seldom report bites when they occur. For the most part, such bites are minor injuries, requiring only family-provided first aid, and only 5 to 10 percent of the bites are reported. Yet every animal obedience trainer and behaviorist who handles behavior problems reports that animal bite and aggression are the major reasons that their services are sought.

Also, in spite of the figures, officialdom tends to view dog bites as a minor problem. The United States Public Health Service's Centers for Disease Control in Atlanta maintains records of all reportable diseases for the whole country. However, dog bite is reported by states on an optional basis. Although only twenty or so states report, they list more than a million bites annually. Studies made by Drs. David Harris and Pascal Imperato, deputy commissioners of New York City's Department of Health, showed that private physicians reported fewer than 9.4 percent of all bites, and Beck later showed that even fewer cases were reported by veterinarians, despite the legal requirement that members of both professions do so. The vast majority of all official reports come from hospital emergency rooms, which must be considered only the tip of the iceberg.

A truer picture of the problem was obtained by veterinarian Thomas Hanna, who reviewed the bite-report records on Air Force bases, where there is free medical care and regulations are strictly enforced, thus promoting better reporting. Hanna determined that the dog and human populations were roughly comparable to those in the civilian world, although there were fewer single and elderly people and slightly fewer dogs. The ages of the victims and the dog breeds involved were also similar to those in the civilian world. Nevertheless, the bite rate reported was approximately twice the civilian rate. This was not because the situation encouraged more biting but because there was better reporting. The total was probably more accurate than that reported for the civilian world.

In another study Dr. Barbara Jones, at the University of Pennsylvania School of Veterinary Medicine, queried some 3,200 youngsters, ranging from ages four to eighteen years, in schools in rural Pennsylvania. More than 45 percent of this population reported being bitten during their lives; 15.5 percent reported being bitten in 1980, giving a more accurate insight into the actual rate. As with other studies, children from seven to twelve years of age were seen to receive the vast majority of bite injuries. Jones found that in 1980 more than 32 percent of the schoolchildren in the group had been bitten seriously enough to seek medical attention. In the order of frequency, dogs bite legs, the right arm, and the head. Children, however, are bitten much more often on the face, a source of concern and trauma regardless of the severity of the bite.

Dog bites are an economic problem as well. In the 1970s Drs. David Berzon and John De Hoff of the Baltimore City Health Department found that actual costs to the victim for the treatment of dog bites average nearly fifty dollars, ranging from a seven-dollar tetanus shot to the multithousand-dollar reconstruction of a child's face. In addition, taxpayers subsidize the system—and pay nearly an additional fifty dollars per bite, not including the costs associated with observing or testing the animal for rabies.

If rabies is suspected, the costs become staggering. From 1976 to 1977, in Laredo, Texas (population 77,000), an outbreak of rabies was controlled in three and a half months by intensified stray-animal control, a mass immunization program, and increased surveillance activities. The cost? Out of pocket, it was $137,651, and there was a conservatively estimated $1.8 million in lost revenue because of decreased tourism alone.

The country is now experiencing an increase in raccoon rabies. While rabid raccoons do not routinely bite people, they can conceivably transmit the disease to the pet dogs and cats that roam the suburban areas they inhabit, and there is real concern that rabies will return to our cities. Raccoon rabies has spread from the southeastern United States up the East Coast and is now reported in New York City, New Jersey, and Connecticut for the first time in years. To date, no human fatalities have been associated with raccoon bites, but a great deal of money and concern is expended on tracking down victims, vaccinating those bitten, and trying to get both dogs and cats vaccinated for rabies. The majority of people receiving rabies treatments were bitten by raccoons; they feared that the animals might have rabies.

We may soon see tax-supported vaccination clinics, along with demands for the hunting of raccoons. The most likely way that rabies from raccoons will reach us is through our pets, and owners should seriously consider vaccinating all pets that roam or are penned outside the home. In general, millions of dollars of tax money are spent each year for rabies surveillance, laboratory testing, and the vaccination of approximately thirty thousand people annually.

Considerable economic loss is also incurred when dogs attack livestock, with sheep being frequent targets. And farmers are just as quick to blame wild animals for the damage as most people are to blame these same creatures for biting humans.

In a similar misconception, many people attribute the greatest number of dog bites to stray or feral dogs rather than to family dogs. Wrong again. Reported bites from stray dogs are never more than 15 percent of the total of all dog bites. Even this number is undoubtedly an overestimate, as any loose dog is considered a stray, and few people will claim ownership of a dog who has bitten somebody. The Air Force base study, where reporting was far more representative of the actual problem, found that only 9.5 percent of the bites could be attributed to stray animals. Jones's study found that while nearly 16 percent of the respondents had been bitten by dogs in 1980, only slightly more than one-tenth had been bitten by dogs for which no owner could be found; family dogs accounted for 31.5 percent of the bites, and the dogs of neighbors accounted for 48.9 percent.

Stray dogs behave like other wild animals—aloof, wary of human contact, and fearful of human interaction. When Beck was studying stray dogs in Baltimore and St. Louis, he found that they invariably tried to escape or hide, cowering and quivering in fear when they were confronted. They would do anything to avoid contact with humans, even leaping through a closed window in one case. Humans are formidable adversaries against a thirty-pound animal. Even the feral dogs of rural America are secretive; most of the damage to livestock in these areas is caused by loose pets.

Why then all the furor about strays? Perhaps it is because they are associated with the threat of rabies, or because they roam in packs more frequently than pets do, and pack behavior is considered threatening—although fewer than 1 percent of all reported cases of dog bite involve more than one dog. Strays may also be blamed automatically for bite cases because it takes the heat off the real culprit: to blame strays is not to blame pets or their owners. How convenient to assume that dog bite was the product of wild fury rather than the bad breeding or training of beloved pets or the irresponsibility of the owner!

Perhaps one of the most insidious myths that prevails about dog bite is that it occurs as a result of the victim's wrong attitude or behavior, a cultural prejudice somewhat analogous to the assertion that the rape victim somehow "asked for it." Some dogs bite because they are trained to do so. In New York City we estimated from surveys associated with the rabies surveillance program that approximately 7 to 14 percent of biting dogs were considered guard dogs by their owners—from the three-thousand-dollar trained animal to the "mean" dog.

However, the so-called guard dog is not the usual culprit. In Beck's St. Louis dog-bite study, nearly 75 percent of the victims had no encounter with the dog prior to the bite incident. These are only reported bite cases; we suspect that many of the unreported bites that take place within the dog's own family do involve some interaction. However, the most common behavior associated with being bitten by someone else's dog is simply entering the dog's territory when the dog is running loose. Nearly half of all bites occur on the street, sidewalk, or alley adjacent to the dog owner's property. It is that simple! Deliberate or unintentional provocation—touching a dog's puppies, untangling fighting dogs, or even playing with the dog—sometimes precedes bites, but in relatively low frequency compared to just being there when the animal decides that its perceived territory needs protecting.

In part this explains why nearly 30 percent of letter carriers are bitten during their careers and why meter readers experience nearly a 200-percent bite rate annually. The post office has training films on how to behave when confronted by dogs, and letter carriers can refuse to deliver mail to families who do not confine their dog during delivery hours.

Being bitten by a dog is not random; victims tend to be

young and near where a dog lives. It appears that the dogs involved are also not random. Drs. Kenneth Gershman and Jeffrey Sacks of the Centers for Disease Control and John Wright of Mercer University studied reported bites epidemiologically by comparing the characteristics of dogs that bite people and those of dogs in the same area that had no bite history—that is, a case-control approach. Biting dogs were more likely to be German shepherds, chow chows, collies, and Akitas, while the golden retriever and poodle were significantly less likely to bite. Male dogs, especially unneutered ones chained outside, showed a greater tendency to bite.

How to Avoid Dog Bite

Children learn in school how to turn in fire alarms, how to cross the street safely, and how to observe safety regulations in the school shop, for example. Never are they instructed in avoiding what we now know is a common danger—dog bite. Because most dog bites occur as the dog guards its territory, the following guidelines might help to avoid the most likely occasions of being bitten.

Avoid going onto private property unless specifically invited.

Do not run when confronted with a threatening dog. Running only stimulates the dog to increase its aggression.

Do hold your ground and demonstrate moderate dominance by telling the dog firmly to go home, which usually works wonders. Firmly saying "no" and "sit" may also work.

Avoid direct eye contact, which the dog interprets as a challenge. Instead, appear nonchalant, as if you do not care.

When the dog begins to back away, slowly retreat also, keeping the dog in view without paying too much attention to it. If the dog begins to come back, stop and wait until it moves off again.

Do not try to outdistance the dog on a bicycle. Stop, dismount, and stand with the bicycle between you and the dog. Without something to chase, the dog may lose interest.

Do not try to pet a strange, free-roaming dog.
Do not be embarrassed to jump on a car, climb a tree, or call for help if you are threatened.

As a last resort, throw or pretend to throw an object at an aggressive dog.

Do not be embarrassed to ask a dog owner to restrain the dog until it clearly recognizes you as a friend.

Avoid any encounters with guard-trained dogs. Find out if any are patrolling before you walk in a new area.

If you are threatened by a guard-trained dog and it is about to go into a bite sequence, take off your jacket or hat or something handy and give it to the dog to bite or pull. This might spare your own flesh.

If you cannot deflect the attack, roll up into a ball, protecting your face and ears with clenched fists, and wait for help or until the dog calms down. You may be able then to get away very slowly.

Report all aggressive loose dogs or incidents of actual bites. Dog owners should have their dogs leashed, supervised, or confined. Dogs should not be allowed to run free in heavily populated areas, and dogs with behavior problems should be treated by a behaviorist or trainer. Pets not intended for showing should be neutered; they tend to make better pets, have fewer health problems, and be less aggressive.

Fatal Dog Bite

The problem of the fatal dog bite has received little scientific or public attention. Because it involves the worst aspect of dogs and most often the death of children or the elderly, it challenges our social sensitivities, defying objective discussion. We cannot rationalize such death, and we hide behind any of the shields that are applied to dog bite in general. The dogs that kill are not strays and are rarely, if ever, rabid, as the cases described earlier revealed.

Drs. Lee Pinchney and Leslie Kennedy are two radiologists who became interested in the problem through their radiographic studies of skulls of children bitten by dogs. When they realized the paucity of information in the medical journals, they wrote to 245 major newspapers requesting stories about deaths caused by dogs during a five-year period from May 1, 1975, to April 30, 1980. Many newspapers did not keep such indexed files; many others would not release them or had incomplete files. The reporting was uncertain. Some newspapers recalled no such attacks, whereas other papers in the same vicinity had reports to offer. In spite of these obstacles, the doctors received valid reports of forty-nine fatal attacks during the period and added two more from the medical literature, for a total of fifty-one in five years, about ten per year. They eventually found a total of seventy-four by extending their time frame. While this number clearly does not represent every case, it is enough to allow for a general epidemiological analysis.

Many who read the report were surprised to learn that not a single case involved an unowned or rabid dog. The geographic distribution of attacks was roughly the same as for all bite cases: areas with more people, therefore more dogs, experience more bites and more fatal attacks. More than half of all fatal bite incidents involve dogs owned by the victim's family, and most of the other cases involve dogs of neighbors, friends, baby-sitters, or other acquaintances, meaning the animal is known to the victim. The vast majority of dogs were described as family dogs without a history of viciousness, and most of the incidents occurred in or around the home of the victim. Fatal-bite victims are usually younger or older than those who are bitten less severely, and there is a slight tendency for the involvement of more dogs, although pack attacks as described in cases two and three are relatively rare.

A more representative sample was studied by Sacks and his associates, using the National Center for Health Statistics and a computerized searching of news stories. They identified 157 dog-related fatalities from 1979 to 1988, and 70 percent of the victims were under ten years of age. The neonatal mortality rate, 294.9 deaths per 100 million people each year, was nearly 370 times greater than the rate for adults of

30–49 years, 0.8 percent. More than 50 percent of all deaths were of children under age four, and 70 percent were under age ten. Pit bulls accounted for 41.6 percent of all fatal bites where dog breed was reported, and pit bulls were implicated more than twice as often when the attack was caused by loose dogs. As in other studies, deaths of infants were mainly caused by single animals in the home. The breeds implicated during 1979 through 1988 are listed below, taken from the September 1989 article that appeared in the *Journal of the American Medical Association:*

Breeds of Dogs Involved in Dog Bite-Related Fatalities, 1979–88

Purebred

Pit bull	37
German shepherd	9
Husky	7
Malamute	6
Doberman pinscher	5
Rottweiler	5
Great Dane	4
Saint Bernard	4
English bulldog	2
Hound	2
Other[1]	9
Total	90

Crossbred dogs by bloodline

Pit bull	6
German shepherd	6
Husky	5
Wolf hybrid	5
Total	22
Total of all dogs	112

1. Boxer, chow chow, cocker spaniel, dingo, English sheepdog, Japanese hunting dog, Labrador retriever, unspecified retriever, and Rhodesian Ridgeback accounted for one fatality each.

As with bites in general, the larger breeds, which are more capable of inflicting injury, are more commonly represented.

But even smaller breeds and breeds popularly touted as being very friendly are on the list.

One of the major questions remaining is whether fatal bite is just one end of the spectrum of the bite problem—from the trivial nip to the bite that kills—or the result of a special set of circumstances. The epidemiological information indicated that at least in some cases, victim vulnerability by virtue of age turned what might have otherwise been simple bites into fatal ones.

To study the problem firsthand, Beck joined a multidisciplinary task force that also included Lockwood, Victoria Voith, and Dr. Peter Borchelt. This team studied, among others, the three cases cited earlier, and found that they illustrate different circumstances under which dogs will inflict severe bites or even kill.

Case one was a classic freak accident. The husky who killed the four-day-old Jones baby was displaying the normal, inquisitive behavior that the breed shows toward smaller creatures, but owing to the victim's vulnerability, the bite led to a tragic end. The child's parents in this case were careful, responsible dog owners. Many such accidents occur because dogs are well-armed predators who often communicate by mouthing and even face-biting a subordinate member of the pack. When they are face-biting another dog, however, the canine teeth soon encounter the hard, bony snout, and this resistance probably triggers the dog to inhibit its bite; the point of establishing dominance has probably been made. The soft tissues of a baby's face and skull do not offer such resistance, and serious injury, even death, can unwittingly be inflicted through the pack animal's instinctive display of dominance. No matter what the dog's size, it should never be left alone with a baby.

The tragedy of case two could have been foretold. Mrs. Ryan's son had lived alone with his dogs, raising them in virtual isolation from people. Even when they all moved in with Mrs. Ryan, they remained isolated. Then a visitor arrived and they were aroused to an unusually excited state. The dogs were then confined while the son and guest went off to the store, and the dogs' heightened emotional state motivated intense scratching, which led to breaching of the partition that confined them. They encountered Mrs. Ryan, a vulnerable victim, who was probably frightened by their unusual energy but was incapable of restraining them. She probably fell, and the bites on the outer portions of her arms indicate that she tried to shoo them away. Also, she was relatively unfamiliar to them, and the biting was probably even stimulated by her attempts to resist.

In case three we see the dangers of permitting dogs to live as free-roaming predators in the human environment. The dogs had learned to chase and hunt. Once aroused by the motorcycle or any moving stimulus, they were not inhibited from redirecting their predatory tendencies to another prey species, and they attacked the small boy. Interestingly, the boy who fell—thus providing no additional stimulus for a chase—was left untouched, which is not unlike what has been reported by people pursued by sharks and bears. This supports the hypothesis that standing perfectly still often saves a potential victim from continued attack. Incidentally, the owners of these dogs were found guilty of criminal neglect.

The team was able to identify the behavior of these otherwise gentle dogs as aspects of pack behavior traceable to the dog's ancestry as a predatory pack animal. In observations made at the Behavior Clinic at the University of Pennsylvania's School of Veterinary Medicine, syndromes and patterns of behavior that predispose an animal to biting were also identified. The most common cause is that the animal, not the owner, is the dominant animal in the family "pack" and displays dominance aggression, which sometimes results in a serious bite. Voith, who works at the clinic, diagnoses behavior problems while assessing the client's ability to modify an animal's behavior. The vast majority of animals that are brought to the clinic are aggressive toward people. Proper diagnosis is crucial; error could lead to serious, if not fatal, bites.

In one case a two-year-old 120-pound unneutered male Doberman pinscher, Duke, was brought to the clinic by his twenty-four-year-old male owner, Jim. Because of Duke's aggressiveness, Jim had already used the services of a professional obedience trainer, who considered the dog extremely aggressive and had used pulleys to hoist it off the floor just to get control of it. Duke was friendly to all strangers, especially to Jim's girlfriend. One day Duke refused to get out of the car, became increasingly threatening, growled, snarled, and even challenged Jim, whose knowledge of kung fu and use of a Whiffle-ball bat kept him from being bitten. Duke still treated strangers well, however.

In the clinic the dog was alert, almost never blinking, with his ears held stiffly erect. While sitting for the reward of cheese, he was on the verge of attacking. Voith had to look away in order to defuse the situation. Her diagnosis was "dominance-aggression" with a poor prognosis. While euthanasia would be the safest course to follow, Jim wanted to try to save the animal. He was instructed on how to reshape the animal's behavior by acting as the alpha animal himself and by using positive rewards to reinforce the behaviors he desired or at least could live with. Duke was given synthetic progesterone to lessen his desire to be dominant; a slight shifting of the male-female ratio of sex hormones would favor feminization.

A two-week follow-up visit found the dog progressing well; he had not growled, even when he was being disciplined. Duke actually appeared more friendly, with ears less erect and with less intense staring at people; he was even blinking. Then some six weeks later, Voith received a phone call from Jim, from his hospital bed! Jim told her that Duke was completely trained and off his medication. He did want us to know of one incident; he had wrongly punished the dog for running into the street, and the dog, in frustration, had snapped in the air. Duke had learned to inhibit or ritualize his aggression, and in this case the bite was purposely misdirected so as to cause no injury. We all thought that was great, but Voith asked, "Why are you in the hospital?" "Had a car accident, nothing to do with the dog," said Jim, adding, "Now I feel dominant!" Between a person and a dog, that is the way it is supposed to be.

Another owner, Sally, reported that she arrived home to find that her eight-year-old female poodle had been torn apart by her eight-month-old female German shepherd. Sally was upset, needless to say, about the poodle; but she was also concerned for the safety of her five-year-old son. Was the dog too vicious to keep in the home with a young child, who naturally loved the dog? An interview revealed that the dogs were routinely kept together when left alone, even though they had had several growling matches. Actual fighting was never observed. The shepherd was from a good breeder known to have healthy and normally behaving dogs. The day after the attack the shepherd came into estrus (heat). Because she was always a good family pet that was appropriately obedient to all people, Sally decided to keep her but to have no other female pets. A three-month follow-up found them all living together happily.

In another case study the Lawtons came to the clinic when their Old English sheepdog became increasingly threatening toward Brian, their adopted two-year-old retarded child. When they found the dog standing over Brian, growling, they thought it was time for help. The child's age and mental state made it impossible to teach him not to tease the animal or even to leave the animal alone, and the dog was clearly asserting dominance without receiving the proper cues to inhibit its behavior. The dog's behavior was dangerously close to going beyond ritualization and becoming a full attack. The dog had been a member of the family before Brian arrived, and its dominant propensities had never been discouraged. Voith and her colleagues felt that the situation was too dangerous to attempt the long process of reshaping the animal's behavior to accept a subordinate role in the family. Getting rid of the dog was suggested, but the Lawtons could not bear the thought and never returned.

These three cases are very different, but all illustrate how dogs can establish dominance with humans and other dogs. Duke, the Doberman, was attempting to establish his dominance over his male owner, using the gestures of growl and threat postures. Jim was accepting the challenges and even winning by using kung fu and baseball bats, but he was not asserting his own dominance. Such challenges would have continued because the roles of dog and owner were not clearly defined. Who was to be the "leader of the pack"? The hormone therapy and certain food rewards permitted Jim safely to assert his rightful dominance by standing over Duke while the dog sat and making Duke lie down for food. By being trained to assume the postures of a subordinate animal, the dog perceived himself to be subordinate. Eventually Jim would even be able to hold the dog's mouth closed, mimicking the alpha animal's muzzle bite. The challenges ended once Jim's true dominance was established. When the members of the pack know their place, there can be peace and everyone is happier.

The second example illustrates a totally different reason for biting—interdog aggression. The German shepherd knew her place in the family and probably enjoyed it. But once she became a mature female, she could not tolerate the presence of another adult female dog. As we discussed in the previous chapter, in canines the dominance hierarchy is linear within each sex. Perhaps if the two dogs had been able to escape each other's company, the distance might have defused the altercation. In contrast to the popular notion that all of nature is good except for humans, dogs and even wolves do kill each other.

The last case study is particularly sad. The Lawtons' first child, the Old English sheepdog, had enjoyed its position but now had to be relegated to a lower position in the pack. The new arrival, the retarded child, could not give the appropriate signals to assert his human dominance and would probably lose a dominance battle with the dog. The parents' inability to recognize the need for appropriate hierarchy or to disband the "pack" by disposing of the dog indicates that the dog had some dominance over them as well. Permitting Brian to be placed in such a dangerous situation may also demonstrate some ambivalence toward him or their family structure. These cases give some idea of the kinds of pack problems that arise when a clear hierarchy is not established. As we have described in earlier chapters, the well-socialized dog that knows its subordinate position within the human family is a healthy animal and a joy to be around.

The Outcasts

Stray, ownerless dogs—the outcasts—present a different kind of problem from biting dogs. It is a moral dilemma, and one that affects us all. By domesticating the dog, man assumed responsibility for its survival, and like other domestic animals, the dog does not do well without the intervention of humans. Abdicating that responsibility is, simply put, morally wrong. Abandoning dogs or passively allowing dogs to languish and die—usually under the wheels of a car—is one way in which our humanity is lessened. It contributes to a pervasively careless attitude toward life. Despite the presence of free-roaming and ownerless stray dogs in all societies, they have not been as widely studied as their wild ancestors.

There is no official census of the pet, let alone the feral, dog population. Likewise, there is no data on how many pets are abandoned to the streets to be added to the stray population, although methods exist for those interested in animal control or public health. Since the urban stray population comes mostly from pets, we assume that the feral population is decreasing, as is the population of pets.

Not all free-roaming dogs are true strays—dogs that are unowned while they roam loose (strays are often referred to as feral dogs if they breed more of their own kind). Some are pets that roam continually or sporadically during the day without their owners' direct supervision. In New York City, where Beck and his assistant, Hildy Rubin, conducted a study of strays, they found that several dogs they had isolated were actually pets. One morning they arrived in the study area at 4 A.M. and saw the dogs leaving their owners' backyards for a morning tour of the garbage cans. Following the fieldwork portion of the study, they interviewed the owners, many of whom did not know of their dogs' "double" lives as strays.

In all studies the young born to urban strays never survived long enough to mature and contribute more dogs to the population. The stray population is actually maintained by the continued abandonment or escape of dogs that spent at least part of their early lives in the protection of a home environment. This means that the average age of the stray population is young. Younger animals are more susceptible to such diseases as rabies, leptospirosis, and worms, all of which have implications for human health as well. Moreover, animals that are less than two years old bite more often than older ones.

In rural areas where there is enough small game for food and freedom from human intervention, some breeding stray populations apparently exist. The dogs tend to evolve toward a medium size, with dark brown fur, resembling German shepherds (somewhat wolflike), which is apparently the best-adapted form for the situation.

There is a general impression that unowned stray and feral dogs are more common than they actually are. Most urban and even rural uncontrolled dogs are really straying pets. Surveys of animal-control personnel taken from 1952 to 1965 requesting estimates of the dog population in their areas revealed a wide range in the ratio of unowned to owned dogs; the results ranged from 1 unowned to every 2.6 owned dogs in Atlanta to 1 to 40 in Denver (both in the city and the county). Interestingly, animal-control officers perceived a greater stray problem in a large city, such as Atlanta, compared with the more rural area of Denver, where there is even greater dog ownership. It may be that people are more used to dogs in Colorado and perceive the problem as being less important.

Much of what is known of the behavior and life of the stray dog stems from Beck's work with urban strays in Baltimore, which was summarized in his book *The Ecology of Stray Dogs* and subsequent articles. In his field studies Beck made no attempt to distinguish loose pets from truly ownerless strays but only to estimate the dog population that was unsupervised on the streets. Using the methods of estimating wildlife population, he determined that there were approximately 450 dogs per square mile, for a total city population of approximately 43,000. But Baltimore probably has more dogs on the streets than most cities because many more people live in row houses than in large apartment houses. Row houses have direct access to the streets, so that dogs can be conveniently let outside; homes in high-rise buildings do not have the same ease of access.

Urban stray dogs are active in the early morning and late afternoon and sporadically throughout the night. Owned but loose dogs appear on the streets later in the morning and well before sunset, as if owners were letting their dogs out before and after their own nine-to-five jobs. The flush of dogs on the streets just before 8 A.M. and after 5 P.M. is the very population that does the most social damage—bites, trash disruption, and car accidents (while people drive to and from work)—and it is this population that would best benefit from being captured by the animal-control agency. However, animal control agencies are not active until after 10 A.M. and close by 4 P.M. Recognizing this inefficiency, many municipalities are now beginning to send their trucks out earlier, at 6 A.M.

During their morning activity, pets and strays interact most. In the afternoon, which is often too early for true strays, loose pets and some strays have the most opportunity to interact with pedestrians, especially children returning from school. Although dog bites are reported for every hour of the day and night, more than 50 percent of all bites occur between 2 and 7 P.M., when loose pets have the greatest human population to meet and perhaps to bite. The proportion of the population that is bitten by strays often reflects the occurrence of loose pets on the streets; the bite rate on Staten Island, where there are many private homes, is four times the number reported from the borough of Manhattan, with its many apartment houses.

Each stray usually has a home range, not unlike the wolf, although the dog's territory will be much smaller, its size depending on how easy it is to find food, water, and shelter. The better the habitat, the smaller the range. Free-roaming pets have a home range of 0.02 to 0.1 square kilometers, or around 0.05 square miles. Urban ownerless strays have ranges from 0.25 to 0.61 square kilometers, or 0.1–0.24 square miles. Rural strays may wander as much as 28.5 square kilometers, or 11 square miles.

Strays use whatever is available for concealment; in cities they inhabit vacant buildings and garages as well as construction sites. Large open spaces, such as wooded lots, landfills, and dumps, are frequently used by true strays because they encounter few humans there and few people complain about their presence. Strays will even occupy the hallways and common areas of occupied buildings. One true stray in Baltimore used an occupied brownstone for a while. By pushing the front door open he gained entry, and by waiting for someone to leave he would be let out. Each person assumed the dog belonged to someone else in the building and politely let it out. While it was in the building, the dog slept, fed, and even "marked" in the area under the back stairway. This latter behavior was his undoing. Eventually the odor got so bad that he was chased out by the superintendent, forcing him to join another stray, which used the shrubbery around an office building for cover.

In rural areas strays find many of the same shelters that urban dogs do, with the addition of such rural features as natural caves. Of course, most rural strays are really pets and spend their evenings in the farmhouses of their owners.

Being tolerant of human proximity, dogs can use parked cars and discarded mattresses for shade and comfort in full view of people. Except at times of extreme adversity or when they cause trouble, stray dogs go virtually unnoticed. Apparently, one adaptation of unowned stray dogs in an urban environment is to behave like socialized pet dogs. In this way they are indistinguishable from owned stray dogs and are tolerated as loose pets—a form of "cultural camouflage." There are differences between owned and unowned stray dogs, which are not easily observed without extensive study.

The Urban Stray Dog

	Owned Dog	Unowned Dog
Origin	offspring of owned dog or from breeders	released or escaped pets
Abundance	approx. $\frac{1}{3}$ of owned population	approx. $\frac{1}{40}$ of stray population
Distribution	high human density, low and high socioeconomic urban area	low human density, low socioeconomic urban and rural areas
Home range	0.04–0.08 sq. mile	0.1–0.24 sq. mile
Activity period	before and after human activity	twilight and night (crepuscular)
Food source	from owner, garbage	from garbage, some hunting
Social behavior	solitary or human companionship	in groups of 2–3
Behavior with people	friendly or aggressive	wary, secretive
Causes of death	owner rejection, old age, injury, disease, dogcatcher	injury, disease, dogcatcher
Dog bite problem	very serious	less serious
Dog waste problem	increasing social and health problem	less serious, unknown
Noise problem	serious	less serious
Control	owner responsibility	self-limiting

Strays scavenge for food in human trash but are occasionally fed by people. When he was exploring the back alleys of Baltimore, Beck sometimes found deposits of dog food that had been clearly left for the strays. Nearly 20 percent of the people interviewed in a low-income area observed people putting food out for dogs or had done so themselves; the phenomenon was less commonly reported in a middle-class neighborhood. In one case two strays regularly waited in front of a building at about 8 A.M. Before long a woman appeared at a second-floor window and dropped hot dogs to one and chopped meat to the other.

Because they scatter garbage in their search for edibles and increase the cost of trash collection, strays have a negative impact on the environment, and their habits help rats find food as well. Beck found that rats were more common in areas that were heavily used by dogs; in fact, stray dogs could probably be used to indicate rat problems—more dogs probably mean there is a more serious rat problem.

Actual predation—that is, hunting for food—appears to be extremely rare in the urban environment. In St. Louis a group of three strays that frequented a park to scavenge trash would often wait for and watch squirrels after their feeding period. They would sit, each looking over the other's shoulder, an apparently ingenious strategy. In this way they could see each other while watching for squirrels and could respond to each other's orientation and gestures if a squirrel was spotted. The first to see a squirrel would dash off instantly. The dogs would simply tree the squirrel, which would in time leap to the ground, apparently in a panic, and be chased up another tree. A capture was never observed; they seemed to enjoy the chase for its own sake.

Some dogs do get into zoos and kill, but they do not eat the prey and may be engaged in play rather than hunting, perhaps motivated by some ancestral drives. Dogs in more rural areas are often reported to chase and kill snowbound deer and livestock, again without eating the animals.

Urban strays drink water from puddles in gutters and on sidewalks. They routinely use park streams and fountains and eat snow during the winter. They have been observed feeding and drinking from containers that have clearly been left out for the benefit of pets in backyards and on porches. Just as people feed strays, they also put water out for them. Rats too have been observed to use the same sources for food and water.

Anyone who has walked urban streets will report seeing

sick dogs, although truly emaciated ones are very rare in most parts of the United States. Extremely thin and starving dogs are seen in countries where the human standard of living is significantly lower; there are reports of such dogs from the Middle East, Mexico, Puerto Rico, and Africa. In the United States, even in the poorest sections of our cities, there appears to be enough residual protein to be found to support our outcast dogs.

Strays form social groups of usually no more than three members unless there is particularly good eating or a female in heat. Beck's morning surveys of a quarter-mile area in Baltimore revealed the following group sizes (twenty-eight surveys in all):

Group size	No. of groups observed	No. of dogs involved	% of dogs involved
1	270	270	50.6
2	69	138	25.9
3	29	87	16.3
4	7	28	5.3
5	2	10	1.9
6 or more	extremely rare (except about a receptive female)		

Although half of all dogs are seen alone, these are usually free-roaming pets who remain solitary because their "pack" loyalty is to their human families. That true strays seem to prefer a single companion, traveling most often in pairs, was unexpected. The pair usually consisted of two males or a male and a female, but never of two females. Large groups are very rare and seem to be of short duration, formed while a female is in heat.

Within the social groupings, stray dogs communicate in ways that are roughly reminiscent of wolves, although perhaps because they have lost some skills during domestication, there is more fighting than among wolves. The communications are similar to what is seen between a dog and its owner. The greeting displays and play bows upon remeeting after a separation and the solicitous crouching before the alpha animal (or human owner) are routinely observed behaviors.

Nothing distinguishes strays from pets more than their

deaths—they die younger and with less dignity. Death comes from other dogs, disease, and injury but is most often from automobiles. When they are surprised by a rapidly approaching car, many dogs reflexively assume a submissive posture, crouching or rolling over on one side, which, of course, is fatal. Yet to the dog, it is the posture that would ordinarily save its life by turning off the aggression if the dominant aggressor were another dog or wolf. Most cities maintain trucks that work year-round to clear roadways of dog carcasses. Nearly half the dogs brought into the emergency room at the Veterinary Hospital of the University of Pennsylvania have been hit by cars when running free.

Of course, stray dogs are also killed intentionally by people. And animal-control agents (dogcatchers) capture and bring loose dogs to shelters. Only some 6 to 10 percent of captured pets are ever reclaimed by their owners, and more than 90 percent of all dogs brought to shelters are put to death. No city shelter can hold animals for more than a few days; there simply is neither the space nor the money to do so.

In New York City some eight thousand to fifteen thousand stray dogs are collected from the streets yearly. This number, as large as it may appear, pales by comparison to the more than eighty thousand pet dogs that are brought in to shelters each year by owners who no longer want them. This situation is not often discussed or appreciated; it is too painful for most people even to consider the problem. Keep in mind, when you are reading about the 2 to 6 million animals that are killed every year in animal shelters, that the vast majority were put there by their owners (this is more true of cats than dogs; there is still a good portion of dogs collected from the streets and therefore listed as unowned). And the figure does not include dogs turned over to private veterinarians for disposal.

Nevertheless, stray dogs continue to have little impact on human public health, be it from animal bites or rabies. The major threat facing strays remains humans; the dogs are killed by cars or collected by animal control. For some people, ownerless dogs are part of the urban scene, living out their lives as wild canids; for others, they are animals that must be captured as pests or removed from life on the streets, after which they are usually killed; some are adopted and become owned pets.

We are often deflected from thinking about this tragedy by the media, which are fed stories about the plight of strays and laboratory animals, both of which comprise very small populations in comparison to surrendered pets. The loss of pets occurs at a great social and financial cost to cities, which are already suffering from insufficient funds for human-health and educational programs.

Sadly, there are many similarities between outcast dogs and homeless people. They both use the same kinds of shelter, depend largely on trash or handouts for food, and reject most of their own kind, especially those of mainstream society. They belong to self-limiting populations and function within the framework of the culture without being part of it. We know that outcast dogs have a significantly shorter life span, and we can only assume that this similarity also exists for outcast people. Very young and very old street dwellers are almost never seen.

The outcasts, both dogs and people, survive, but society tolerates their existence without any real commitment to improve the quality of their lives. Most people will admit that our treatment of homeless people lacks humanity, but they are much less likely to admit the same of our treatment of outcast dogs. Yet, to repeat, stray dogs come from our pet population and they interact with it. Ultimately, if we have a responsibility to dogs in general, that responsibility must include the outcasts.

AMBIVALENCE

The same aspects of our relationship with dogs that give us the feeling of overflowing love and loyalty also make the idea of being a dog horrifying and cause us to identify people with dogs when we want to express disgust and contempt. Dogs are loved and cursed for essentially the same traits. They are loved for their loyalty, for their ability to pour out affection on demand, for their constant attentiveness, for their willingness to please, and for their loving obedience. Yet we call people "son of a bitch," "cur," "dog," "shit-eating dog," "bootlicking dog," "fawning cur," and "running dog lackey." These terms of abuse reflect our ambivalence about voluntary submission to authority. Our desire to give and receive unconditional love is always in conflict with the belief that self-esteem is vitally dependent upon gaining or at least maintaining reciprocity in the exchange of love or affection.

A human being who loves with the devotion of the dog can be admirable or despicable. If the loved object is God, then it is admirable to love without measure. But when the object of the love and obedience is an unjust master and the source a slave, our feelings turn about. It becomes despicable. To love a master who abuses, hurts, or humiliates you is to be cowardly, less than male, less than human. It is a posture traditionally assigned to traitors, cowards, and women in love.

This ambivalence seems to be a predominantly male problem: the idea of passivity or submission—especially when it spills over into the sexual realm—touches the core of American male anxiety. In a research project conducted by Aaron Katcher and Harold Frank, American graduate students were asked to rate an ideal leader, a peer, and a subordinate. All three ideal types invariably scored equally high on dominance because the students could not tolerate the idea of a submissive subordinate. Our relationship with dogs permits men to express polar feelings about submission with little psychic pain.

Our ambivalence about the submissive nature of dogs was enshrined in biological theory by Konrad Lorenz, the founder of modern ethology. He let his own feelings about aggression and submission dominate his scientific thinking. Lorenz postulated the existence of two descent lines for dogs: one from the wolf, the other from the jackal. The wolflike dogs (*Lupus* dogs), such as chows or malamutes, were loyal only to one person, and even then were never completely obedient. The jackal race of dogs (*Aureus* dogs), of which dachshunds would be a good example, were obedient to anyone, totally submissive, and obnoxiously friendly. Lest you think we are exaggerating Lorenz's feelings, here they are in his own words (emphasis added):

> The reticent exclusiveness and the mutual defence at any price are properties of the wolf which influence favourably the character of all strongly wolf-blooded dog breeds and distinguish them to their advantage from Aureus dogs, which are mostly "hail-fellow-well-met" with every man and will follow any one who holds the other end of the lead in his hand. A Lupus dog, on the contrary, who has once sworn allegiance to a certain man, is forever a one-man dog and no stranger can win from him so much as a single wag of his busy tail. *Nobody who has once possessed the one-man love of a Lupus dog will ever be content with one of pure Aureus blood.* . . .
>
> Besides this, a predominantly Lupus blooded dog is, in spite of his boundless loyalty and affection, never quite sufficiently submissive. He is ready to die for you but not to obey you. . . . Not so the Aureus dog; in him, as a result of his age-old domestication, that *infantile affection* has persisted which makes him a manageable and tractable companion. *Instead of the proud, manly loyalty of the Lupus dog* which is far removed from obedience, the Aureus dog will grant you that *servitude* which, day and night, by the hour and by the minute, awaits your command and even your slightest wish. . . .
>
> Such *big babies* (Aureus dogs) are often correspondingly trustful and importunate toward everybody. Like many *spoiled human children* who call every grown-up "uncle," they pester people and animals alike with overtures to play. . . . The worst part of it lies in the literally *"dog-like submission"* that these animals, who see in every man an "uncle," show toward anyone who treats them with the least sign of severity; the playful storm of affection is immediately transformed into a *cringing state of humility.*

We have quoted Lorenz at such great length because his

values illustrate the ambivalence we have been describing. Since writing the preceding, Lorenz has recognized that there is only one descent line for the domestic dog. To our knowledge, however, he has not reevaluated his opinion of overly friendly dogs.

The desire for intense loyalty and the distaste for indiscriminate loving submission have had a strong influence on individual choice of dogs. Large, relatively aggressive dogs, such as malamutes, German shepherds, and Dobermans, are often thought of as "one-man" dogs and are very popular breeds. In this regard, however, their popularity is unfounded. There is no evidence that any one kind of dog is more or less loyal to a single person than another. And the observations that have been made about animal behavior suggest that dogs are more promiscuous than faithful in their choice of masters. No matter what the correspondence between truth and reality, the myth may have a critical social function. The belief that some large, aggressive dogs are "one-man" (never one-woman) dogs permits men to accept their affection without anxiety and without feeling any overt contempt.

The fact that men identify with their large male dogs comes into sharp focus when they bring their pets in for treatment of overly aggressive behavior. There are three forms of treatment that can be used alone or in combination: castration, treatment with synthetic progesterone, and behavioral therapy. When castration is suggested, there is a uniformly negative reaction from male owners. Sometimes the response is angry and immediate: the owner jackknifes forward in his chair, crosses his legs, and rejects the suggestion. Frequently owners would rather have the dog killed than "mutilate" him. Even the temporary treatment with synthetic progesterone is viewed with distaste. The maleness of the animal is important in a way that the femaleness of a bitch is not. There is much less resistance to spaying of females. The male identification with the sexuality of male dogs was demonstrated in a hoax by a New York City wag, who took out advertisements for a dog "brothel." The project was not identified as a joke until the prankster was brought into court for alleged cruelty to animals. The humane societies, the animal control officials, and the courts apparently felt it was quite natural for owners of male dogs to want them to have regular sexual experience.

Having large, aggressive male dogs permits men to enjoy the submissive love offered by the pet without feeling that love to be contemptible. They identify with the dog and feel that the love and submission are directed toward them only and that it is thus permissible. Nevertheless, the identification is never quite good enough—some fear of the feminizing properties of submission and affection remains, and so the terms "dog" and especially "bitch" remain words of contempt.

Dr. Mark Hollander, a psychiatrist, has written perceptively about the differences between male and female attitudes toward sexuality and affection. In brief, his argument can be stated by saying that men will be affectionate to get sex and women will give sex to get affection. In less stark terms, women seem to need affection more than men and sometimes trade off sex in order to get it. There is, however, a complementary feeling among men that affection is feminine and that men should be sexual without being affectionate. The tendency to define men as phallic and dominant and women as sensuous and submissive creates a conflict for men because the display of tenderness through touch and submission to another's needs become feminine traits and must be repudiated or denied. That repudiation requires that a man's natural needs for touch, passivity, and expressing love by giving in to another be labeled as demeaning. We contemptuously call those needs feminine, homosexual, or doglike.

One of the fortunate changes in society accompanying the change in the social role of women has been in the male image. Men are now permitted to be more tender, more affectionate, less dominating and phallic. They can hold babies, change diapers, cook, and nurture others. They can even be the submissive member of a marriage. However, these changes are not consistent throughout our society. Books like *Real Men*

Don't Eat Quiche are still published and read. There is still enormous anger directed against women who are wage earners and have a life outside of the home. This persistence of the traditional male image means that men will still go on denying their own needs for a tender kind of loving. As long as men feel that way, dogs will have a special role in their lives. They are the male's child—the one being that a man can love tenderly and touch as women touch. The dog's capacity to inflict harm with his teeth guarantees that this tenderness and affection will not contaminate their male nature.

Twelve

Animals in the City

ACCORDING TO THE American Veterinary Medical Association, in 1991 Americans owned more than 52.5 million dogs, 57 million cats, 11.7 million caged birds, 4.9 million horses, 125 million small mammals and reptiles, and over a billion fish, totaling more than 1.2 billion (1,251,000,000) pet creatures. Almost three-quarters of all these companion animals live in cities and their suburbs, where most people live. Perhaps the frequency with which companion animals share our homes is easier to comprehend than the number of animals: in 1991, 36.5 percent of American households owned dogs, 30.9 percent cats, 5.7 percent birds, 2.0 percent horses, 6.7 percent other pets. Dog owners have an average of 1.52 dogs per household, while cat owners have 1.92 cats per household; hence, although there are more dog-owning households than cat-owning ones, there are more cats in the United

States than dogs. Those households with cats have more animals.

The dog population has varied over the years, apparently in response to the health of the economy; it increased during the early sixties, leveled off toward the end of the decade, and decreased coming into the 1990s. The fact that the numbers of cats in people's homes now exceeds dogs is probably because of changes in ownership patterns, not animal-population policy. We believe people want to have household pets and find cats easier to maintain if they have a busy schedule, travel, or live in smaller living quarters. In spite of—or perhaps because of—most Americans' hectic lifestyles, more than 58 percent of urban and suburban families have a companion animal; rural families have even greater rates of ownership.

In the modern city pets and houseplants can be the rare link between people and the natural world that urbanization has not paved over or built upon. Some relief has also been provided by city planners, who have traditionally included parks with grass and open spaces that attract birds, streets with trees and plantings, and zoological and botanical gardens with a variety of exotic animals and flowers for all to view.

A 1974 survey by the National League of Cities found that complaints about animals and animal control problems ranked highest among 60 percent of city mayors—before complaints about crime, drugs, taxes, and health care. Com-panion animals are potentially a source of disease, bite injury, environmental degradation, and nuisance. These problems are more common in cities because of the concentration of animals and people.

Here we will not discuss the many benefits that urbanites derive from pet ownership, for they are not that different from those received by any pet owner. However, the relationship between pet and person in the smaller space of a city apartment may be even closer and more intense for many people.

Cities and animals form an uneasy alliance. Conflicts arise

between owners and nonowners, and as we saw in the last chapter, loose owned and unowned animals do not fare well in the urban environment, where they are likely to be hit by cars or be captured by animal control. Because of the constraints of city life, responsible pet ownership is very important, and most of the problems stem from owners' carelessness or thoughtlessness. Many of these problems concern dogs, the most highly visible city animal.

DOGS, CATS, AND DISEASE

With the exception of rabies, diseases that can be transmitted by pets are often overlooked. Yet they do exist and should be of more concern than they are. Dog waste, a perennial nuisance in cities, is more than just an aesthetic problem. It is a breeding ground for flies and a source of bacteria and parasite eggs that cause illness in humans; as with dog bite, children are the most common victims. A survey in Savannah, Georgia, showed that a single canine fecal deposit produced an average of 144 house flies. The percentage of dog stools breeding flies was higher in economically better neighborhoods, presumably because garbage was less available to the flies. Although we devote much energy to keeping flies out of our homes, we pay little attention to their breeding places, where control would be more effective. Among the many bacteria that are passed by dogs directly or with the help of the flies that breed in feces are salmonella and campylobacter, both of which have been implicated in diarrheal diseases of children. More than 10 percent of dogs pass forms of salmonella that infect children, and campylobacter forms are rapidly surpassing salmonella infections and may soon become a serious problem associated with animal ownership.

Probably no dog parasite has received more attention than the worm *Toxocara canis*. Not only is it very common but it has been associated with human illness. There are other species of worms that have caused disease in humans, but less often. Virtually all dogs are infected with *Toxocara* when they are born. They shed eggs of the worm in their feces unless they are dewormed. Pups are infected while still in utero if the bitch was ever infected. Pregnancy reactivates even dormant larvae, and dewormed females may still reinfect their puppies. There are numerous studies documenting the frequency of worms in dogs: for example, 20 percent of the dogs tested in Philadelphia, 58.1 percent of those in New Jersey, and 31.8 percent in Saskatchewan were infected. Nearly 10 percent of soil samples from parks in Philadelphia were contaminated with *Toxocara*, more than 20 percent of samples from Kansas City, Missouri, and 24.4 percent of samples from Great Britain.

Puppies and young dogs shed copious amounts of microscopic eggs in their feces. The parasite eggs can survive many months throughout the winter in the soil. When the eggs are ingested by people, mostly by children, who play in the soil long after any trace of dog feces is gone, they can hatch. The larvae of the worm will migrate throughout the body tissues, causing *visceral larval migrans* (VLM). Depending on where the larvae migrate in the body, the human victim will exhibit a variety of symptoms: coughing or wheezing if in the lungs, epilepticlike convulsions if in the brain or spine, and vision problems if in the eye. Usually the larvae settle in the liver or become encapsulated in the body's tissues, causing only transient symptoms. The symptoms can be extremely general, making a definitive diagnosis difficult. Within the last few years a test for blood antibodies indicating previous infection has been developed, and serum surveys are being conducted. A study by the New York City Health Department found that more than 4 percent of five-year-olds had blood antibodies indicative of previous VLM infection, but few had any long-lasting symptoms.

Invasion of the eye by VLM has been most studied, for there larvae can be seen without dissection or biopsy and a definitive diagnosis can be made. In addition, the clinical symptoms are generally more pronounced and serious, ranging from a partial loss of vision to complete blindness, which can only be called a social tragedy. There are many reasons why VLM is not better understood: it is relatively new, being first described in 1952; it is difficult to diagnose; its effects are usually transient; it is too rare for a comparative study of many cases but too common for the publication of individual case reports; and perhaps, like dog bite, it reminds us of the problems of dogs as pets, which is not a popular notion. Nevertheless, VLM is being recognized and diagnosed. New York consumer advocate Fran Lee, who headed a campaign called "Children before Dogs," recognized not only that the problem mainly involves children but also that dogs are perceived as people and at times are put in competition with them. Unfortunately, the many heated debates that followed degenerated when participants accused each other of being either pro- or anti-dog and never addressed the real issues of responsible animal ownership and common courtesy.

Cats, too, have been subjects of concern; house cats feeding on the raw flesh of rats, mice, and birds can be infected with *Toxoplasma gondii*, a protozoan (a microscopic single-celled organism). An infective stage of the parasite, the oocyst, can be shed in the feces of the cat, after a four- to five-day incubation period, for from nine to twenty days, averaging twelve days. After this period the cat develops antibody defenses and it is no longer a source of infection. Cats rarely show any specific symptoms besides a loss of appetite for two to three days and soft or watery stools. Relatively large concentrations of the parasite are required to produce noticeable infections.

People can get toxoplasmosis from eating uncooked meats or from handling cat waste or contaminated soil and ingesting the oocysts. A new infection of a woman in the earliest stages of pregnancy can infect the fetus via the umbilical vein, causing retardation, blindness, or miscarriage. The pathological responses in the infant are basically similar to those seen in adults, but because of the immunologic immaturity of the newborn, the damage is more severe. The problem is not that common because many women have developed immunities from earlier encounters with *Toxoplasma* and cats shed the oocysts for no more than three weeks after their initial infection. But the potential for serious problems exists, and many health departments have public-information programs warning of the dangers. Avoiding freshly passed cat waste and washing hands thoroughly after working in the garden are recommended for women in the early stages of pregnancy. Letting other people clean the litter box and not taking in any new outside cats during this time are also suggested.

Cat scratch disease (CDS), believed to be caused by *Rochalimaea henselae*, is the most common cause of chronic swollen or infected lymph nodes (lymphadenopathy), and these swellings are often at the site of a cat scratch; other symptoms include fever, fatigue, headache, and loss of appetite. While CDS is often thought of as a disease of children and adolescents, nearly 45 percent of cases occur in adults. Dr. Cynthia Pérez studied the role of cats in families where a member had CDS and compared the findings with matched cat-owning families without CDS. She confirmed that the disease was more common from September to February and also identified newer insights. The disease was significantly associated with the owning of intact (non-neutered) cats, cats that had fleas, cats that scratched, and cats that used indoor litter boxes. Declawing the cats or trimming their claws appeared to decrease transmission. The association with fleas and litter boxes may indicate that the bacteria may also occur in the blood and urine of cats, as well as the saliva. Improved diagnostic tests are helping people distinguish the disease from others that have similar symptoms, though there is still no specific treatment other than alleviating the varied symptoms.

THE URBAN DOG

It has been our experience that when people track dog waste onto a new shag carpet, they are not concerned about salmonella or even *Toxocara;* they get angry because of the filth. The ecology movement has raised our consciousness about waste and pollution and respect for one's habitat. Living in cities need not be punishment; it is the natural habitat for most Americans. Much of the impetus for the canine-waste laws—the so-called scoop laws—was the nuisance and aesthetic insult caused by the accumulation of dog feces in public places and only secondarily the public-health implications of fecal contamination of the environment.

On August 1, 1978, Public Health Law 1310 went into effect in New York City, requiring all owners of dogs to clean up after their animals in city streets and parks. Contrary to all expectations, it was a resounding success, partly because it was strenuously enforced. Other cities—Boston, Philadelphia, and Chicago, for example—have similar laws, but there is no official encouragement for compliance or enforcement.

Enforcement was only part of the reason for the law's success. Many dog owners had long felt that they should clean up after their pets but were embarrassed to do so. The law took embarrassment out of the act. Also, contrary to expectations, there was no real increase in the number of animals turned in to the shelters; neither was there a significant drop in the number of adoptions. Because of this the ASPCA and other humane organizations have become supporters of clean-up laws.

Fouling is not the only way dogs have an impact on the environment; free-roaming animals disrupt and scatter trash, bark, and kill trees and plants with their digging and urine. Disrupted trash attracts rats and greatly increases the cost of trash collection. Complaints about barking are often handled by the agency that is responsible for air quality because it is viewed as an air pollutant. The urine of dogs is so salty that it is one of the major reasons young trees fail to thrive in the urban environment. Dogs do have an impact on the environment, although it is subtle and far less documented or appreciated than their many other roles.

Addressing these problems, most large metropolitan areas have laws that restrict the activity of animals, especially dogs, in public areas. Animals are completely banned, with few exceptions, from designated areas or must be restrained by leash in other areas. Most cities prohibit pets from entering restaurants or food stores or going on public transportation (except for contained animals or guide dogs leading the blind). Many cities now also exempt from these restrictions the orange-collared dogs that aid those with hearing or physical challenges.

A leash law in one form or another is a common way of reducing the many problems associated with dogs. The law should set some maximum length of a leash—about six feet, or else people will tether their dogs on ropes so long that the dogs will still be a public nuisance, and the long leads can endanger the animals. A dog jumping a fence with too long a leash can even be hanged. Smaller communities should require direct supervision, such as voice control, in lieu of an actual physical connection between the animal and the owner. Ideally the law should set some standard for the person at the other end of the leash, such as a minimum age, or at least specify that the person must be able to control the animal.

Some cities have experimented with designated dog runs, where dogs can be set free yet supervised by vocal and visual contact. These runs have not always been completely successful. In 1976, before the canine clean-up law was enacted, the New York City Health Department monitored an officially condoned dog run that was part of a large housing complex in Greenwich Village. Dog owners using the area were supposed to clean up after their animals. As an indicator of use, the investigators spray-painted every fecal deposit in the run and adjacent streets over a twenty-four-hour period so as to keep track of new deposits. (Needless to say, they had a lot of explaining to do to passersby.) The team found only 26 new deposits in the run, although 175 were found on the adjacent streets. Only 12.9 percent of the people who came to the street on which the run was located actually had their dogs use it. Interviews with people who preferred to use areas outside the run indicated that they were concerned that their dogs might get sick from the fecal deposits that were not cleaned up by previous users or by the puddling of fluids that accumulated in the run. However, the most common reason was the fear of dogfights caused by large dogs.

Obviously dog runs have to be planned. They should be located where they will not be a nuisance; they should be completely enclosed by a fence at least four feet high, with a double gate permitting entrance and exit without letting animals escape. The surface should be hard, nonporous, well maintained, and sloped to facilitate drainage and flushing with water, which should be available for this purpose. The area should be at least fifty feet from areas used by children or from occupied buildings. Local wind currents should be considered for odor control. Separate areas for smaller dogs would be useful if the run is large enough to be subdivided. Plastic or metal scoops and ample covered receptacles should be available to facilitate the collection and disposal of fecal material. If the dog run is adjacent to occupied dwellings, it should not be used between 11 P.M. and 7 A.M. An adequate maintenance program is essential. Properly designed runs on rooftops are a possibility, and some areas encourage their development and use to lessen the opportunity for crime and vandalism.

Even if planned runs are not immediately available, cities could designate other areas for dog use separate from parks and playgrounds. Many state-run picnic areas have separate areas for dogs away from where people will rest, eat, or exercise. If the areas are large enough, natural decaying processes will keep them usable.

Dogs and other animals are part of city life and should be anticipated, accepted, and included in urban design. Cleaning up after and leashing dogs are only part of responsible ownership. Registration is also essential. Not only is licensing a source of revenue for sadly underbudgeted health and animal management programs, but it also permits cities to identify the presence of animals and estimate their number in the event of a rabies outbreak or other disease that may enter the population. However, not all people license their dogs, and licensing is not particularly well enforced, so most cities have little notion as to the size of the dog population, making it difficult to plan for it.

Most of the animals that require retrieval from the streets are unlicensed, and while abandonment is illegal in many cities, there are no laws that would permit municipalities to recoup the expense for the service. Such laws do exist when a city has to collect an abandoned car. Registration should imply a full responsibility to the dog and the community.

The bite problem with urban dogs was fully discussed in chapter 11. Most metropolitan areas ban the ownership of wild or potentially dangerous animals (such as wolves, lions, and venomous snakes). Their potential for escape poses problems not only for the human population but also for the animals themselves. In New York City an illegally kept lion was killed when it jumped or fell from the apartment-house roof where it lived.

Attack-trained dogs pose some special problems in cities. They are less inhibited about biting, and their bites tend to be more serious. While many cities have regulations requiring that a notice be posted in areas where such dogs are in service, too many people fail to see the warnings before they encounter the animals. In addition, such laws do not address the problems of a potential victim's age or language. In New York City guard and attack-trained dogs have to be specially registered and must wear a conspicuous tag that has an imprint of a dog baring its teeth; this means the warning is on the dog itself, and it carries a nonverbal, easily understood message.

Choosing the right type and number of companion animals is especially important in crowded urban conditions.

Because exotic and wild animals pose special problems of bite, disease transmission, and proper humane care in crowded areas, such animals should not be permitted as companions of the general public. Providing special permits to individuals and institutions that are capable of safe and humane care must be considered, but as a general rule, the ownership of the following animals should be discouraged as pets: nondomesticated carnivores (wolves, lions, bobcats, and so forth), venomous spiders and reptiles, *all* monkeys and apes, raptorial birds (such as hawks and eagles), and all endangered species. However, it is better to develop a "clean" list of animals that are permitted (to which we can add species if necessary) rather than a "dirty" list of banned species, which might accidentally omit an inappropriate animal. It is a sad fact that most wild animals become unmanageable as adults and must be disposed of at public expense. Obviously, the animals pay the real price.

OWNERSHIP OUT OF CONTROL

One of the saddest problems of urban animal life is that of the multiple-animal owner. Alan Beck and Dooley Worth, an anthropologist at the New School for Social Research in New York, reviewed New York City Health Department cases of complaints about multiple-animal owners. They identified thirty-one different cases over a two-year period, not all of which were handled by the health department or the ASPCA. The list contained information on thirty-six people who owned an average of thirty-four cats or twenty-three dogs. In three cases other animals were involved, including full-grown alligators, large lizards, poisonous snakes, rabbits, turtles, turkeys, ducks, and tarantulas.

One case involved a woman who lured wild pigeons into her apartment by putting seed on the windowsills and then captured the birds. At the time of her arrest, she had more than fifty wild pigeons and other wild birds flying freely in her two-room apartment. Such ownership causes problems for other urban dwellers and is most assuredly cruel to the animals themselves. For one thing, an accumulation of birds and scattered birdseed attracts rats. Also, the pathogenic fungus *Cryptococcus neoformans* thrives on accumulated bird dung, and its spores fill the air, infecting people whose defenses are weakened by age or other diseases. The resulting disease, cryptococcosis, may infect the lungs or, more seriously with *cryptococcus meningitidis*, the linings of the brain.

In another case a large contingent of neighbors and a state legislator complained in person to the health department about an elderly woman who owned so many dogs that the odor was causing pedestrians on the street to gag. People were moving out of this middle-class neighborhood, and property values were falling. The woman was visited and interviewed. The house was a total shambles, and the dogs were too numerous to count. The woman and the animals appeared to be eating from common pans on the floor. She insisted in a screaming, whining tone that Jesus told her directly to take care of stray animals. She roamed the streets collecting them and the garbage on which all fed. Her way of life was indistinguishable from that of the stray dogs that shared her existence.

Neighborhood tensions mounted, and there was an attempt to burn down her home. To protect her as well as the neighbors and animals, she was ordered to appear in court. The judge did not doubt the charges, but, as he said: "What am I to do, throw an old lady in jail?" He ordered her to get rid of all but three dogs of the same sex. A New Jersey-based humane society collected some thirty-six dogs and began a fund-raising campaign for their support. Peace was restored.

Before long, though, the complaints began again. The ASPCA was sent to collect the new population and found more than fifty dogs, most of them very ill. The woman, in protest, hit a policeman and was arrested and brought to a city hospital for psychiatric evaluation. The overworked psychiatrist did not quite grasp the situation; he saw only a lonely woman and advised her to get a dog! Such cycling of cases is a common problem.

A similar case illustrates another kind of multiple-animal owner. Neighbors complained of intense odors coming from the home of a single man who lived with fourteen dogs. The dogs were never walked, and the floors were covered with layers of feces. Neighbors also complained that the man slept naked with the animals. He could be seen, although not easily, through windows clouded by feces, fur, and dirt. The bed, too, was covered with waste. The man, a retired attorney, defended himself in court, arriving in a perfectly respectable manner. This case, too, was never resolved and was only controlled by continual hearings, which temporarily lowered the animal population and its effects on the neighborhood.

These three cases are, unfortunately, not rare. The people involved are usually unmarried; most are female, especially those keeping large cat populations. Most express a strong affinity toward animals early in their lives, whether or not they actually had pets as children. In every case the animals began to accumulate after the person had left the parental home and established his or her own residence, most commonly in the late teens or middle twenties. Often the accumulation of animals was just part of a constellation of problems, as seen in the first two cases.

In other cases people kept the animals even after they had died. One apartment was filled with carcasses of dead dogs and another with dead cats. The cats had been put on the fire escape, and seeping fluids and flies had brought the situation to the attention of the health department. In two other cases dead people were also found in the residence. In cases also involving children, the parents paid more attention to the accumulated animals than to the children in the home, and a child-welfare agency had to intervene.

Another case illustrates some of the dangers that can be associated with inappropriate animals in an urban setting. Beck received a call from the Staten Island Zoo, which had just been given a dead snake by the ASPCA. The snake was identified as a spitting cobra, a very dangerous animal to have around people. It had been killed when it emerged from the bathroom piping in a city apartment. Together with two somewhat nervous health inspectors, Beck visited the landlord of the building in which the snake had been found. The snake's owner had already moved, but found in the bathtub of his apartment were two full-grown alligators, several snakes, including another cobra, some other smaller reptiles, a live dog, and a dead dog. How many other animals, like the cobra, had escaped or been released? Were others still in the building's walls? The heat was turned off for two days to drive the snakes out; every apartment was searched, especially under refrigerators, radiators, and other warm places. The tenants were alerted to notify the health department if any animals were spotted. Antivenin supplies at zoos and hospitals were checked for freshness.

The owner was eventually tracked down, and his new apartment was searched. Only a fourteen-foot python and smaller reptiles were found. He assured us that the cobra's escape in his old apartment had been an accident. He promised not to keep any more venomous snakes. It was decided not to file charges, since the courts are so overburdened that they must summarily issue a small fine, usually far less than the cost of bringing the charges in the first place. The second cobra died at the zoo, for it was not particularly healthy, but the alligators are still in residence and are now enjoyed by other people from the safety of a proper enclosure.

We do not understand all the motivations of those who own dangerous animals. Exotic animals do bring them needed attention and make them feel different, special. Perhaps, too, handling an animal that can kill brightens up an otherwise dull existence and supplies an extreme stimulation, like reckless driving or Russian roulette. Those accumulating large numbers of animals behave as if they are addicted, and Randall Lockwood has coined the term "animal addicts" for such people. Similarities between collecting animals and drug dependence include preoccupation with acquisition, denial, social isolation, neglect of personal and environmental conditions, and repetition of the acquisition behaviors. Other possible explanations for animal collecting include the "zoophilia model," whereby animals are real or even symbolic love objects; the "power model," whereby a person finds joy in the power and control that comes from managing dependent animals; and the "obsessive-compulsive disorder model," whereby collecting is a preoccupation without conscious thought.

Multiple-animal owners, as described here, may or may not be animal lovers, but they are a major nuisance in cities and add fuel to the fires of controversy surrounding animal ownership in our cities. It is difficult to determine what would constitute a manageable number of dogs and cats for any one owner. Some people can create a nuisance with one dog; others can keep an entire kennel with no undue problem for the community. New York City's law simply says that you cannot create a nuisance, as determined by an inspector and adjudicated in court. Baltimore permits the ownership of three adult cats and/or dogs before requiring a kennel license, with special zoning requirements. These are two differing approaches, each with merit. Surely some number should exist beyond which a mechanism would permit a city to take action. Perhaps owners with more than five adult animals should be required to have special licenses. The licensing procedure could include determination of the nature and location of the premises to see if the number of animals can be incorporated into the area without being a burden to neighbors or an act of cruelty to the animals.

When we consider that nearly half of all urban dwellers do not have animals; that owned animals do their share of biting, barking, and soiling the environment; that many of the diseases associated with animals are receiving more public attention; and that multiple-animal owners can cause havoc in living areas, it is not surprising that landlords and the general public support a trend to limit or even prohibit animal ownership in urban areas. To many observers who witness these problems, the animal owner in the city is often someone who does not like people or, at times, even animals. After all, when animals bite, bark, cause disease, or create a nuisance, it is they, not their masters, who are destroyed, even though the problems are not viewed as really being the animals' fault. It is time we started thinking about solutions to the very real problems associated with animal ownership in cities.

THE LAST RESORT: NO PETS ALLOWED

Unfortunately, the last resort—total banning of animals— often becomes the first or only solution to an animal problem.

A major housing complex on Roosevelt Island in New York City has a comprehensive no-pet policy. That the policy provoked little protest might be seen as an indication of wide public support of New Yorkers wanting another chance to have unspoiled parks. It might also indicate a severe housing shortage—people in need do not have much latitude.

The banning of animals stems primarily from the problems that urban dogs can create—noise, odor, and feces littering adjacent streets. But these aren't reason enough to prohibit all animals. Cats, birds, and even limited numbers of well-managed dogs do not create a nuisance. Many of those who suffer the most from such prohibitive laws are the elderly who live in city-subsidized housing, which almost invariably forbids pets. Yet as we have discussed, the elderly can benefit greatly from the companionship of animals. To be forced to give up their pets would be another loss in their lives at a time when loss is a particularly painful experience.

On September 23, 1980, a Philadelphia newspaper ran an article under the following headline: "No-Pet Rule a Killer? Elderly Woman Dies after Giving Up Terrier." The article reported that a seventy-seven-year-old woman died of a "broken heart" when housing officials forced her to give up her beloved pet. We do not know whether the woman actually deteriorated and died as a result of the loss of her dog, but the fact is she may have, and in any event, it was perceived that way.

Because there has been a long history of laws, regulations, and traditions that prohibit animals in general, it is necessary to change public expectations and codify legislation that would permit the restructuring of existing laws to help the elderly. At the White House Conference on Aging in 1981, a resolution was adopted encouraging federal, state, and municipal governments and health professionals to stop the forced separation of older persons from their companion animals upon entering housing projects for the elderly. The resolution stated that

> The companionship of animal pets is a source of security, helps to keep aged persons physically active and responsible through the caring for their pet, fulfills their need for giving and receiving affection, and has been proven to have measurable therapeutic effects on their physical and emotional health.

Humane societies have also taken up this cause, seeking to develop new laws and to amend and adapt old ones to meet the needs of the elderly pet owner. The State of Maryland passed legislation (House of Delegates 896 and 971) that took effect in July 1982 requiring the state health department to establish guidelines for keeping pet animals in nursing homes, addressing another problem facing many of the urban elderly. This law may not actually permit the animals, but it is the first step, for nursing homes often run into conflict with health regulations over animals.

Other laws being written and enacted in Maryland, California, Minnesota, New York, and elsewhere are attempting to protect the pet-owning rights of elderly tenants living on their own, as the vast majority of over-sixty-five-year-old Americans do. The laws aim to prevent landlords from charging higher rents to elderly pet owners, forcing them to move if their pet violates leases, or forcing them to give up their pets before they move in. Where no-pet regulations do exist, legislators are suggesting that they not be applied to elderly tenants. Denying the elderly the right to own a pet is part of a general pattern of injustice foisted on them by society, and although the first steps described above indicate a growing sensitivity to the needs of the elderly, much still remains to be accomplished.

HEALTH DEPARTMENTS
AND HUMANE SOCIETIES

The functions of health departments and humane societies are all the more essential in an urban environment. Health departments throughout the country spend considerable funds to investigate animal bites, keep track of animal diseases, and maintain laboratories to test for rabies and other animal-related diseases. Often serious consequences can be averted by proper reporting and appropriate intervention in anticipation of future occurrences. For example, a single case of rabies in animals or people is so out of the ordinary that health officials will initiate an investigation as to its source and take steps to prevent further spread of the problem. The reporting of bites also serves to keep a record of biting animals. The owners of these animals can be warned to exercise better supervision, and the animals themselves can be removed if necessary. These programs aid the whole society and permit animals to be incorporated into our lives with greater safety.

The presence of animals requires that a city provide control programs to capture stray animals and accept unwanted ones; and more than 40 percent of such programs are part of various cities' health departments. This public funding is justifiable because a vast majority of people benefit from the companionship of animals at one time or another in their lives.

Most cities also have some kind of humane society. The urban dweller's attitude toward animals is very different from those of his "country cousins." In fact, the first Societies for the Prevention of Cruelty to Animals (SPCA) were formed in urban centers—New York City (1866), Boston (1868), and Philadelphia (1869)—to protect horses from overwork; the agencies' corporate seals illustrate one man stopping another from beating a horse.

In Philadelphia, Caroline Earl White believed that humane societies had to address the problems of other domestic animals and in 1869 organized the Women's SPCA, entirely separate from the newly formed Pennsylvania SPCA, with a totally female board and its own animal shelter. To this day Philadelphia still has two totally separate functioning SPCAs, colloquially referred to as the Men's and Women's SPCAs, which vie each year for the city contract to provide animal-control services.

Often public attitudes about animals are different in cities, and this, too, shapes legislation; for instance, New York City bans the ownership of alligators or even the importing of products made from alligator hide, not because the citizenry fears attack but because they are concerned about the survival of this protected species in its natural habitat. (No, there are no alligators in that city's extensive sewer system; the system is often flooded and could not support air-breathing animals that require food in larger portions than are usually found in that particular habitat.) As a result, the modern humane society finds itself in the difficult position of being accountable to many factions. When humane societies are involved in policing a city's animal population, which is demanded by some sectors of society, they must constantly justify the need for, and the conduct of, such programs to those who afford humanlike status to cats and dogs. "I wouldn't let him be the dogcatcher" is an expression of social contempt. There are major federal and state pest-control programs (for rats or coyotes, for example), but there are no such programs for dog control except during rare rabies outbreaks.

The sad truth is that animal-control agencies are often charged with the task of killing dogs and cats. No city can afford to maintain the thousands of abandoned and homeless animals indefinitely. But humane societies are dependent on donations and volunteer help, so they must promote an image of saving animals. Of course they do do this to a certain extent through hospital work and adoption programs (such as pet-of-the-week campaigns in newspapers and on television), but only a small percentage of animals find new homes. Many are in the shelter in the first place because they were problems for their owners. They are usually not well trained or well socialized, and chances are good that adopted animals will wind up either back on the streets or back in the shelter—another sad irony concerning the humane societies.

Humane societies also try to improve their image by fostering the perception that their primary purpose is to capture stray dogs that threaten the public with bites and rabies, which also spares the animals from starvation and disease. In reality, real strays have little impact on human public health, be it from animal bites or rabies, and can compete, like any wild canid in many areas, especially if away from human activity. The unpleasant fact is that the primary function of humane societies is to serve as a depository for unwanted pets.

Within society there are often deep conflicts about the best method to kill the thousands of animals that must be disposed of. Obviously it is cost-efficient to kill many animals at once, but the techniques that accomplish this appear to be acutely uncomfortable for the animals. These methods are systematically being banned and replaced by the individual intravenous injection of barbituric acid derivative, such as sodium pentobarbital. This is the most expensive method because each animal must be handled individually by a veterinarian. It cost the ASPCA in New York an additional $100,000 annually when they replaced their "high altitude chambers" with injection euthanasia—money that would have supported another ambulance to aid injured animals on the streets.

Once an animal has been killed, disposal of the body is another area of controversy. Most urbanites have little experience with fat-rendering plants, which recycle dead farm animals. Rendering is a process whereby entire animals are cooked under pressure and the oils are extracted; the powdery residue is utilized as a chicken and hog food supplement and as fertilizer, and the grease is used in low-phosphate soaps. To some people this fate is unacceptable for pets. Most humane societies in larger metropolitan areas do send their animals to rural rendering plants, but they must keep this a secret.

The pet status afforded dogs and cats does not let them be killed or disposed of in ways usually used for other animals. The distinction between pets and animals also makes using animals in scientific or medical research a socially sensitive issue. Few people deny the need for such research; in fact, it is often expected—but not on our pets or on animals that are given some human status. Therefore, there is a growing trend to prohibit "pound seizure," which allows animal shelters to register dogs for research. Dogs are now bred specifically for research purposes; since they are never people's pets, they are more acceptable for experimentation. There is little protest about the plight of rats and mice, which are used in much greater numbers. However, all such research should be carefully evaluated to determine its necessity and to minimize the use of animals.

There is a long-standing social belief that there is a dog overpopulation, and that is why so many animals die in animal shelters every year. Gary Patronek conducted one of the most sophisticated analyses of the dynamics of the pet population. It appears that the wildly touted estimates that 12 to 18 million dogs die in the nation's animal shelters yearly is not accurate, reflecting faulty methodology. This exaggerated figure may be motivated by a need to encourage financial support for humane groups. Patronek and his colleagues estimate that at most 6 million animals (2 million dogs and 4 million cats) are killed annually. In reality, it is not clear if there is an overpopulation in general; perhaps there are local imbalances. Some communities actually have to import animals for sale or adoption as pets, and dog breeders are raising mixed-breed animals because of local shortages.

Many humane societies have focused on spay/neuter (sterilization) programs, as if that would totally solve the problem of having to kill animals in shelters. Simple, identifiable solutions make good press and a focus for fund-raising but serve to distract attention from the real problems and real solutions. That is probably why the spay/neuter solution has been with us for more than fifty years with little impact. To be sure, the numbers of animals killed in shelters, although less than originally believed, is sad. But not all the animals killed were "surplus" or "unwanted"; many were old or had untreatable medical or behavioral problems (see chapter 10). Many of the cats at shelters were feral—that is, collected from the streets—and sterilizing clinics have little to do with the problem.

Much of this chapter may make it seem that pets, especially dogs, are nothing but trouble in the city, sources of noise, odor, filth, and disease—in short, all-around pests. However, like people, animals make cities the wonderful places they are—environments that live and breathe almost in direct contradiction to the steel and stone with which they are constructed. The picture would be brighter if city-dwelling pet owners and nonowners alike better understood the needs of urban animals and people.

The first step is to educate the public on the value of animals and to realistically address the problems that arise in cities. For example, contrary to the beliefs of many owners, their animals are better off neutered. The myths that animals need to have offspring or that sterilization should not be done until after the first litter or that the home breeding of dogs and cats can be lucrative must be dispelled. None of these notions is true. Sterile animals appear to adjust to city life much better and are more tractable and less likely to bite and roam. They are also spared many of the diseases associated with reproductive organs in old age. There is no evidence that a dog or cat is better off having at least one litter. Owners may believe they can make money from their animals' offspring, but ask anyone who has tried to make money by breeding animals at home about the financial value of such a venture.

Public-school programs include remarkably little information about how to avoid animal bite or how to care for animals. Teaching about animals is a marvelous vehicle for instilling sound civic attitudes and useful biological lessons. Is it better to teach anatomy by dissection of dead animals in a laboratory when it could be taught from models, or to teach social behavior by observing living pets at home or on the streets? The ultimate usefulness of the information and the universally accepted value of having respect for life make social behavior a more logical choice of subject.

Schools should teach the realities of animal behavior to dispel the myths presented by movies and television. Such education must be an appreciation of the marvelous and necessary bond between pets and people, with a sincere understanding and respect for its consequences for all participants.

Animals are all around us—pigeons and squirrels in parks, birds on power wires or at feeders. We must learn to take advantage of the opportunities for watching city animals to form special, if transient, relationships with animals where we can. Is the person feeding the pigeons any different from those who put out food for dogs? We do not know. The point is that we share the earth—including cities—with many interesting creatures, and enjoying them and learning more about them will help us learn a bit more about ourselves. For each of us, we are our own ultimate companion.

The dog views the human family as a pack, which can be a source of danger for young children and babies.
Photo courtesy of Pet Food Institute.

The owned urban stray presents an increasingly serious social problem. *Photo by Alan Beck.*

Stray dogs scatter garbage, which increases the cost of trash collection and encourages rat populations.
Photos by Alan Beck.

True urban strays often live together in small packs.
Photo by Alan Beck.

Only 6 to 10 percent of pet dogs captured by animal-control
agents are reclaimed by their owners. *Photo by Alan Beck.*

Thirteen

Being a Pet

THE GIFTS THAT pets give us are too important to be exchanged only between animals and people. People can learn how to substitute for pets in certain emergency situations and take over their functions in others, as pets sometimes substitute for people. The earlier chapters of this book describe some of the ways that pets do this—for example, as comic actors displaying our unconscious wishes and conflicts to us. They have been acting their roles for a long time.

Perhaps we should begin to emulate them. How much anyone should take over some of a pet's role is not for us to say. Throughout this book we have implied ways in which we can be more like our animals. There are, however, some specific, important ways to treat other people like pets: to listen without using words, to talk with gentle touch, and to come to terms with the need to be subservient in love. Men especially can discover the joys of affection and tenderness.

Parents can emulate the parenting of animals, being physically close to their small babies, raising their children with living things, and training them much as wolves train their young: with firm physical correction and control so that children learn to obey and parents continue to dominate their household. When children are obedient without question, parents can love them more, be more affectionate, and use less verbal abuse.

LISTENING WITH INTIMACY

To listen like animals means to focus full attention on the person speaking and, if one is giving comfort, to hold or be held silently. If words are used, they should be a kind of music, meaning only, "Continue, I am listening." Learn to listen without asking for clarification, without offering advice, without cheering the speaker up, without telling him his feelings are incorrect or unfair. Just listen and indicate that the feelings are understood and that your attention is still there and that the speaker can continue if he wants to. This is active listening. It takes time and must be reserved for those times of the day when calm and attention are possible and where two people can sit side by side, touching naturally.

Between people and pets the best time is often at the end of the day, when the owner returns home. Being greeted by a beloved pet at the door seems to be the most compressed moment of joy. For some, another important moment is on awakening in the morning. Ann Cain noted that being greeted by an animal at either time was preferable to meeting the human members of the family. This is hardly surprising. While young children greet others more as animals do—right there when you come home, always eager to be picked up, and always smiling—as they get older, their greetings become more like human greetings. First, they may no longer be there consistently. They become involved in other things, and parents face the prospect of walking into the home and having to find their children to announce their presence, sometimes to the backs of heads watching television. Perhaps if you move close and pat a head, the face might lift up to be kissed. Alternatively you may be greeted with the troubles of the day: "Paul broke my truck and you have to go out and get me another one right now! You promised!" Then, if you are fortunate, your spouse may chime in with his or her litany of daily problems. Instead of complaints, there should be some ceremonial greeting like the animal's, that permits the returning person to feel safe, to feel that home is a sanctuary that gives peace after the efforts of the day. People should give each other a constant, dependable greeting of welcome.

As responsive as they are, animals cannot replace human companions. Although we tend to overvalue words, they are necessary for sharing what is unique about human existence. Words are used to cleanse the troubles of the day. Many people do this by reenacting the day's trials and angers. In doing so they often use the same angry tones, gestures, and expressions that were used or thought and suppressed and thus inflict all the tensions and anxieties of the original incident on their loved ones. Instead, think about how people confide in their pets. Problems are not reenacted; that would only frighten the animal out of the room. The entire narrative is presented in a kind of filtered replay, stripped of the garish emotional paint, leaving only outlines that are indicated by words rather than feelings. We use this same technique to confide in children—it is a narrative cadence employing a stylized representation of emotion, recognizing it and not inhibiting it. We need to be able to talk to people that way, both venting our feelings and calming them at the same time. To do so requires only faith that the other person understands.

SERVING

In some real sense our pets are subservient to us in a way that human beings no longer are. There was a time, perhaps, when the wife and children were absolutely subservient to the man in the household, but those days are gone forever.

If men and women no longer wish to be that servile to

other people, how can they experience the comforts of submission to an enveloping love that protects and dominates? Earlier we said that pets, particularly dogs, can stand for both mother, child, and self. In the love of their dogs, owners feel their own potential servility without bending a knee to any human being. Yet between human beings servility is a perversion; the lack of an acceptable outlet for obedience fuels perverse sadomasochism.

Yet there is a being that demands the same kind of loving submission that we receive from our pets. The Old Testament commands believers to love and fear God. Some modern members of the clergy have problems with the submission demanded by that command. They prefer a friendlier, arm-around-the-shoulder God. Yet the God of the Old Testament was not a friendly being. He was a loving being who demanded submission to his will as a necessary part of his love. Submission was not the price; it was the action that made the feeling of being loved and protected possible. A loving worship of God should be fulfilling for people who want to have comfort from submissive, obedient love. Perhaps the dog is fulfilling a religious vacuum.

Perhaps one great need in our aggressive, individualistic society is some means of actually feeling—in word, thought, and action—the submission demanded by God. Unfortunately, there are few places in society where people can withdraw to feel that love. There are few retreats where, for the entire day and night, all our actions can reflect submission to the orders and will of a supreme being. The comfort that some find in retreats is the comfort of making the actions of the day consistent with a submissive and loving orientation to a loving God.

PARENTING

It is in raising our children that we can perhaps benefit most from the lessons that pets teach. This is true right from the moment of birth. Thanks to the pioneering efforts of Dr. Frederick Leboyer, a Swiss obstetrician, more "animallike" childbirth is being practiced in many hospitals. Babies no longer must come into the world under bright lights, with a ritualistic slap and a wail of protest. Leboyer believes, as do many psychiatrists, that birth, especially a hospital delivery, must be traumatic. The infant leaves a world of total satisfaction, peace, weightless support, and complete comfort, is expelled by hard muscular contractions, and then has to cope with totally unfamiliar activities, such as breathing and maintaining poise against gravity. Leboyer tried to do what he could to ease this trauma. He turned down the lights in the delivery room to ease the passage from dark to light. He then floated the baby face upward in a body-temperature bath so that the infant would still be supported, as it was in the womb. After the bath the child was given to its mother to be held against her belly or nursed. The child was not scrubbed, banded like a chicken, fingerprinted, weighed, and measured as in a regular American hospital.

Leboyer was impressed by the influence of this gentler passage on the demeanor of the infant. The child was relaxed and attentive, responding to the mother's gaze by fixing his eyes on hers and even smiling. Leboyer commented that the children born without anesthesia in this gentler fashion were calmer; they looked more serene than children born into the bright, dry, busy, mechanical environment of a conventional delivery room. They did not have that infantile frown that usually characterizes newborns. Leboyer went on to develop his concern with the comfort of the infant by using massage to soothe and relax the infant in those troublesome first few days of life. The massage was meant to augment, not replace, nearly constant contact with the mother's body.

Leboyer's ideas scandalized the American obstetrical profession in a perfectly predictable way: American doctors were worried about being unable to perform heroic feats of surgery in the dark, about germs in the bath, about germs from the mother. Yet having bent to permit natural childbirth, husbands in the delivery room, and rooming in, they bent again, and portions of Leboyer's method are being tried at most urban medical centers in the United States. Thus we may be returning to a more animallike way of raising our children, providing them with the comfort of living touch, the feel, warmth, odor, motion, and rhythm of life from the first moments.

The reality, however, does not yet live up to that ideal picture. For example, most babies are relegated to lifeless cribs, and most parents never think of giving the infant the same privilege as the family cat or dog: a warm spot in the family bed. This is just what we are suggesting—sleep with your baby. Pediatric practice makes no official pronouncement on this subject; most professionals never even discuss it, in the literature or elsewhere. It is usually assumed that the child will be out of the maternal bedroom within weeks or months after its arrival. Most mothers recoil from sleeping with very young infants, as if they think of themselves as sows and fear crushing their children. They seem to forget the millions of years that mothers and infants always slept together and the billions of mothers who still do sleep with their infants elsewhere in this world.

American parents have an additional concern. They have been taught to feel that a child in the bedroom will interfere with sleep and inhibit sexual activity—or, far worse, the child will be injured by witnessing the dread "primal scene," the relatively ordinary sight of two people making love. In the theories of essentially Victorian psychoanalysts, it became a dream phantom that indelibly marked the mind of the child. Accidental viewing of the primal scene has been blamed for phobias, compulsions, and, most horribly, frigidity. However, there is no scientific evidence that the chance sight of parental intercourse is more damaging than the sights and sounds of any other activity that is mystifying to the child. If children were really harmed by the "primal scene," then frigidity, phobias, and compulsive neuroses would be more common in children born in efficiency apartments, and separate bedrooms for children would be a preventive mental health measure paid for by health insurance.

One must avoid misinterpreting this idea of sleeping with

one's baby. There are many analysts who would say that we (the authors) are trying to live vicariously through little children. We are not suggesting that anyone perform to the admiring cheers and crib rattlings of a two- or even one-year-old child, but we do think it is a good idea to sleep with an infant for the first six or seven months, especially when it is sick or fussy. It might be easier on the infant and mother if the child is nursed in bed, so that less sleep is lost. When couples wish to make love, the little dickens can be picked up and carried to the crib. I think that infants are in more danger from parental rage at the continual disruption of sleep than from the rare chance of their noticing some noise or motion under the covers.

Mothers and fathers occasionally do discover the joys of sleeping with children. Mothers who breast-feed discover this pleasure rapidly when they let the child fall asleep on its stomach after feeding. The child sleeps after being sated, and the mother sleeps with emptied breasts and without a disrupting trip back to the crib. Many parents have unpleasant experiences sleeping with their children because they sleep together too rarely. Sleep is as social a time as our waking hours. People who sleep together synchronize their periods of dreaming and their moments of restless flailing about and rearranging of position. When children sleep with their parents, they learn how to synchronize their sleep with that of the adults, so the parents' sleep is not disturbed by the children's motions. When a child has not ever slept with his or her parents, the initial experience is likely to be mildly exciting, making the child restless. The parents conclude that it is impossible to sleep with the child and return the baby to the crib, not realizing that the child might need only one or two more nights to become adjusted.

Another missed opportunity for developing closeness is the bath. Most babies are bathed alone, in their own baths. Why not with a parent? Many mothers discover the delights of bathing with the baby instead of just bathing it, but some, under social pressure, continue to wash the child in a

Bathinette the way they wash dishes in a sink. Even this type of bathing is has its merits: it is one of the few times when the child's bare body remains in contact with the mother's bare arm, as she must support the child to keep his nose and mouth out of water.

Baby apes have an advantage over our own children, who cannot hold onto their mothers. Most human infants are moved in carriages and strollers, missing the warmth, feel, motion, and smell of their mothers as they go about their business. Now, however, there are many different kinds of carriers that permit one to hold small babies close, freeing the hands. And strapping a fussy, colicky child to back or breast can comfort both child and parents. Children learn about the world from the safe proximity of a parent's body.

Just as moving the baby has been assigned to objects like carriages, feeding the baby is also done in a material context. The child is strapped in a chair as soon as he can sit up and be fed with a spoon. We have seen mothers who love to feed their dogs from their fingers or have trained their birds to feed from their mouths yet are horrified at the suggestion that they treat their infants to the same kind of sensuous eating.

We suggest that you play pet games with your child, the same kinds of games described chapter 8. No score is kept: the object is just to keep the game going. Games flow into each other with action and interaction, touch and tussle. Parent and child reverse roles, first one, then the other being chased or chasing, being caught or catching. When objects are used, parent and child use them to build, to unbuild, to play with, and to play side by side. In these games, as in much later learning, the child should be held, touched, and talked to. The talk should not be instructive except when it is necessary, but it should be the kind of overflowing, playful speech you share with pets. When children are taught how to play with parents without keeping score, they are one big step along the way to working with their parents, not for reward but just to keep the work going.

Brothers and sisters must seem like islands of life in a

plastic and cloth desert. Unfortunately, there are fewer and fewer brothers and sisters because most families have either one or two children, and many children are raised alone. Even where there are two or more children in a family, they are close together in age because today's parents like to "get the kids out of diapers" rapidly. The older ones are too little to take care of the infants and are more like natural antagonists than additional parents.

The situation is repeated at school, where such children find themselves with other children who lack the same experience. Since schools are rigidly segregated by age, the child finds himself with others of the same age, natural competitors rather than comforters. Studies of nursery schools reveal that contact with children is most frequently antagonistic, occurring in disputes over objects. Physical contact without fighting occurs during games, but there is relatively little physical comforting among the children. They comfort themselves by sucking their thumbs or twisting a strand of hair or seek comfort from the teachers. They are not able to comfort each other. If classrooms could be more open, so that older children could help and comfort younger ones, schools could offer an experience in nurturance that would compensate for an important missing element in small families.

As children grow up, they begin to withdraw from their parents. Boys, especially, are likely to deny themselves the need for touch because being kissed, petted, and held by parents is defined as girlish, childish, and "sissy." Boys confuse affection with subordination and reject the affection in an attempt to reject the obvious tokens of subordination. They are selectively trained to be less dependent upon touch, to look upon touch as subordination, and to touch less with affection. With girls, the training to avoid parental comfort and intimacy begins after puberty. In general they are permitted to seek and receive more affection than boys, both from their mothers and their fathers.

The easiest way for parents to integrate touch as the child grows up is to have it be an integral part of ongoing routine activity. Such touch is started as an almost unconscious event—the kind of touch that arises within an action but is not part of an action; the touch that occurs in play, accentuated at the end of games, a signal that the game is terminated; the touch that occurs when two people watch television, maintaining a kind of unfocused contact with each other. Homework sessions would profit from touch because it lowers the tension of the situation as the child tries to avoid failure and the parent tries to avoid frustration and anger at the child's failure. Touching a child and letting a child touch you as you work together is a means of mutual reward. The child is calm and motivated to continue, even though he may not be succeeding too well at the task. When parents and children do not touch in situations in which the child is being trained, verbal reward tends to be meted out in proportion to success or failure at the task at hand.

When parents are willing to be affectionate in public, to touch and hold each other as part of the visible activities of family life, they set a model for the children. By making it visible and casual, they also separate the affection from sexuality. Of course it is impossible to separate affection and sexuality completely, but by making one part of the public life, a distinction can be indicated, and a realm of affection that can be shared by children and parents is created. Cultural changes—the increase in affectionate touching among athletes, the willingness of more men to assume the role of nurturers of children, the greater acceptability of affection between men—all contribute to a child being more willing to continue accepting affection from parents.

To say that we have to be a pet to our children—that is, that we must touch them more—will shock no one. It inflicts a little guilt, because busy parents are prone to feeling guilty about giving enough to their children, and the book-reading audiences like a little guilt. It makes up for not going to church or synagogue. To say, however, that children should be disciplined as wolves discipline pups and subordinate members of the band or as people discipline their pets will outrage some parents and professionals. For the past fifty years psychologists and teachers have agreed that physical punishment is bad for little children. They should be shaped by rewards and should be given alternative behaviors that will substitute for the forbidden ones. The professional advice-givers suggest that children's unacceptable behavior be corrected by redirection of attention, explanation, and reinforcement of acceptable alternative behaviors: "No, Gerald! Please do not touch the hot stove! Come here and play in the sink instead! You can spray water around and water does not hurt the way fire does. Mommy gets upset when you touch the stove and get burned. It makes her a little angry and frightened." Now, if little Gerald goes into a rage because he cannot touch the red and glowing stove, the best advice, they say, is to let him stamp, scream, scowl, threaten, wave his fists about, and perhaps beat Mommy a little on the thigh. He must not learn to repress his feelings, as this might lead to the worst forms of physical and mental disease.

We feel that it is just this sort of advice that is perhaps at the root of a major problem with today's discipline—child abuse. It seems odd to say that advice against punishment is bad and causes people to beat children excessively, yet this kind of advice is part of the problem behind the explosive anger of some parents. Moreover, the children who are severely beaten are a small fraction of those who suffer when a parent is unable or unwilling to use direct, immediate, and temperate control: more children are traumatized by the continual use of angry words, which have more potential for harm than most beatings. Far too few parents recognize that uninhibited yelling teaches a child how to yell without inhibition and to ignore signals of anger. Yelling brings about what it was used to prevent; it demonstrates lack of control and encourages the child to pitch his anger at the same level. The better solution is to punish rapidly with minimally effective gestures, such as restraining the child tightly and sitting him on a chair, administering an attention-getting slap to the thigh, or holding the child's chin in your cupped hand to bring his face up to your gaze.

Elements of animal obedience training can be used to

teach children. For example, dogs are taught to be subordinate through control of their movements in space and by firm, but not very painful, physical signals when they are not paying attention. They are also given a great deal of reward and praise when they do the right thing. The best example of this kind of control is the "sit-stay" lesson. The dog is firmly controlled with the leash so that he learns to sit when the owner says "sit" and to stay when the owner says "stay." The punishment for failure to respond is a quick jerk of the leash; the rewards are praise, a pat, and perhaps a treat.

With children, the use of controlled force will make them conform. If the child's movements are controlled by the parents immediately and without question, then proper subordination is established. The child "knows his place." Sometimes when the child explodes with rage, actual physical restraint is necessary to control the flailing movements, but usually the discipline can just be an enforced change in the child's physical position or movement. The child is put in another room, for example, or told to sit in a certain chair.

If the child can be made to alter his movements at the parent's request, either by light physical punishment, such as a slap on the hand or thigh, or by actual physical control, discipline is rapidly effected. But it is more than discipline, and it does more than change a specific kind of behavior. The parent is training obedience and effective subordination. Children must be subordinate to their parents in order to fit into social groups effectively. Such subordination will not make the child grow up to be a submissive person. Instead, the parents are showing the child how to be subordinate when required and, by their behavior, how to be dominant when required. Most important, the child will want to be like the powerful person who is controlling his or her activities. All young children learn by identification with their parents, but when parents allow the child to escape discipline and subordination, the child ceases to want to identify and no longer sees the parent as the true leader. Parents must be the leader of the pack.

Gerald, who raged at his mother when he was not permitted to touch the stove, was threatening his mother's dominance. Dominance is established by making threat gestures, which discourage other members of your band from threatening you. Children who are permitted to rage angrily at parents and are never made to turn off that anger are learning to break their parents' domination. No child should be permitted to threaten, yell at, scowl at, or angrily attack a parent without the parent terminating the display rapidly and indicating strong disapproval. Inhibiting rage will not turn a child into a repressed neurotic. Feelings become repressed when they cannot be controlled. By asserting dominance the parent is actually helping the child exhibit controlled anger, which is not threatening. No child likes the idea of being angry and dangerous.

Parents have a great deal of difficulty coming to terms with the idea that they must effectively dominate a child. They often withdraw affection and are stern in the way that generals and other disciplinarians are stern. Instead, if discipline is administered rapidly, without using hurtful words and without parental anger building up, then parent and child can be affectionate as soon as the child complies, the same way one can discipline a dog one minute and love it the next minute. There is no need to withdraw love—the animal never carries a grudge, neither does the person. Why should it be different with children?

Another way to view physical punishment is to see how children punish themselves when they want to learn some ultimately important activity. Learning to walk, run, skip, skate, ski, ride a bike, or use a skateboard inevitably involves falls—mistakes that are severely and painfully punished. Yet children all delight in gaining these skills. The pain of sports—of football, karate, wrestling, training for all manner of activities—rarely deters children from playing. The kind of punishment we have proposed for young children—control of their movements and greatly inhibited physical correction—is the same order of punishment inflicted by the natural universe when the child learns to operate against gravity and much less than the punishment administered by opponent players in sports. And the socializing benefits are eventually just as enjoyable to the individual as are the games. Good sports and team players are always liked.

We have reviewed the ways in which people can learn how to be better friends, lovers, and parents by learning from the way we love and raise our pets. The reader will be the ultimate judge of how valuable those lessons are. The psychology that our pets teach us is there for everyone and taught with love. There is, however, more to pets—to all animals—than a reflection of our love. Animals are part of nature, and we have a responsibility to nature that goes beyond the care of our pets. Our pets should be part of the order of things in nature, because we must tend nature the way we tend our pets. We must assume responsibility for it, a function that was formerly left to God. In some sense, if we are going to care for the world, we must find some love that is greater than ourselves so that we are protected and feel that there is something constant in our changing universe. We can use animals to experience some of that feeling, but the animal, in reality, is frailer than we are and lives a shorter life. How can we conquer the universe and act as the guardians of the world and at the same time feel love for a power that can protect us? That is one of the problems of our age. Animals only provide a momentary comic diversion that gives us an intimation of this feeling and distracts us from the search for an answer. In the end we must go beyond the animal in our search for love and constancy—for the sake of our animals and the sake of ourselves.

Sources

BOOKS AND ARTICLES

Overviews

Anderson, Robert K.; Benjamin L. Hart; and Lynette A. Hart, eds. *The Pet Connection: Its Influence on Our Health and Quality of Life.* Minneapolis: University of Minnesota, 1984.

Anderson, R. S., ed. *Pet Animals and Society: A BSAVA Symposium.* London: Baillière Tindall, 1975.

Beaver, Bonnie. *Veterinary Aspects of Feline Behavior.* St. Louis, Mo.: C. V. Mosby Co., 1980.

Bustad, Leo K. *Animals, Aging, and the Aged.* Minneapolis: University of Minnesota Press, 1980.

Clutton-Brock, Juliet. *Domesticated Animals from Early Times.* Austin: University of Texas Press, 1981.

Fogle, Bruce, ed. *Interrelations between People and Pets.* Springfield, Ill.: Charles C. Thomas, 1981.

Hediger, Heini. *Man and Animal in the Zoo.* New York: Delacorte Press, 1969.

Houpt, Katherine A.; and Theodore R. Wolski. *Domestic Animal Behavior for Veterinarians and Animal Scientists.* Ames: Iowa State University Press, 1982.

Katcher, Aaron H.; and Alan M. Beck, eds. *New Perspectives on Our Lives with Companion Animals.* Philadelphia: University of Pennsylvania Press, 1983.

Kay, William J.; Susan P. Cohen; Carole E. Fuden; Austin H. Kutscher; Herbert A. Nieburg; Ross E. Grey; and Mohamed M. Osman, eds. *Euthanasia of the Companion Animal.* Philadelphia, Pa.: Charles Press, 1988.

Levinson, Boris M. *Pet-oriented Child Psychotherapy.* Springfield, Ill.: Charles C. Thomas, 1969.

———. *Pets and Human Development.* Springfield, Ill.: Charles C. Thomas, 1972.

McCullough, Laurence B.; and James Polk Morris, III, eds. *Implications of History and Ethics to Medicine—Veterinary and Human*. College Station: Texas A&M University, 1978.

Messent, Peter. *Understanding Your Dog*. London: Macdonald and Jane's Publishers, Ltd., 1979.

Messent, Peter, ed. *All the World's Animals: Pets and Companion Animals*. New York: Torstar, 1986.

Quackenbush, James; and Victoria L. Voith. *The Veterinary Clinics of North America: Small Animal Practice, Symposium on the Human-Companion Animal Bond* 15, no. 2. Philadelphia, Pa.: W. B. Saunders, 1985.

Rowan, Andrew N., ed. *Animals and People Sharing the World*. Hanover, N.H.: University Press of New England, 1988.

Serpell, James. *In the Company of Animals: A Study of Human-Animal Relationships*. Oxford: Basil Blackwell Ltd., 1986.

Tannenbaum, Jerrold. *Veterinary Ethics*. Baltimore, Md.: Williams and Wilkins, 1989.

Tuan, Yi-Fu. *Dominance and Affection*. New Haven: Yale University Press, 1984.

Human-Animal Interaction

Adell-Bath, Margit; Ann Charlotte Krook; Gunnel Sandquist; and Kerstin Shantze. *Do We Need Dogs? A Study of Dog's Social Significance to Man*. Gothenburg: University of Gothenburg, School of Social Work and Public Administration, 1978.

Allen, Robert D.; and William H. Westbrook, eds. *The Handbook of Animal Welfare*. New York: Garland STPM Press, 1979.

American Pet Products Manufacturers Association. *1994 National Pet Owners Survey*. Scarsdale, N.Y.: NFO Research, Inc., 1994.

American Veterinary Medical Association. *U.S. Pet Ownership and Demographic Sourcebook*. Schaumburg, Ill.: Center for Information Management, 1993.

Beck, Alan M. *The Ecology of Stray Dogs: A Study of Free-Ranging Urban Animals*. Baltimore, Md.: York Press, 1973.

Coppinger, L.; and R. Coppinger. "Live Stock-Guarding Dogs That Wear Sheep's Clothing." *Smithsonian* 13, no. 1 (April 1982): 64–73.

Coppinger, Raymond; and R. Schneider. "Evolution of Working Dogs." In *The Domestic Dog*, edited by J. Serpell, 22–47. Cambridge: Cambridge University Press, 1995.

Darwin, Charles. *The Expression of the Emotions in Man and the Animals*. Chicago, Ill.: University of Chicago Press, 1965.

————. *The Origin of the Species.* Harmondsworth: Penguin, 1968.

Davis, Hank; and Dianne Balfour, eds. *The Inevitable Bond: Examining Scientist-Animal Interactions.* Cambridge: Cambridge University Press, 1992.

Goffman, Erving. "Gender Advertisements." *Studies in the Anthropology of Visual Communication* 3 (1976): 69–154.

Gould, Stephen Jay. *Ontogeny and Phylogeny.* Cambridge, Mass.: Harvard University Press, 1977.

————. "This View of Life: Mickey Mouse Meets Konrad Lorenz." *Natural History* 88, no. 5 (May 1979): 30, 32, 34, 36.

Griffin, Donald R. *Animal Minds.* Chicago, Ill.: University of Chicago Press, 1992.

————. *Animal Thinking.* Cambridge, Mass.: Harvard University Press, 1984.

————. *The Question of Animal Awareness.* 2d ed. New York: Rockefeller University Press, 1981.

Harlow, Harold. "The Development of Affectional Patterns in Infant Monkeys." In *Determinants of Infant Behavior,* edited by B. M. Foss, 7:75–97. London: Methuen, 1961.

Hemsworth, P. H.; J. L. Barnett; and G. J. Coleman. "The Human-Animal Relationship in Agriculture and Its Consequences for the Animal." *Animal Welfare* 2 (1993): 33–51.

Hoage, R. J., ed. *Perceptions of Animals in American Culture.* Washington, D.C.: Smithsonian Institution Press, 1989.

Hoage, R. J.; and Larry Goldman, eds. *Animal Intelligence: Insights into the Animal Mind.* Washington, D.C.: Smithsonian Institution Press, 1986.

Hollender, Mark H. "The Wish to Be Held." *Archives of General Psychiatry* 22 (1970): 445–53.

Katcher, A. H.; and A. M. Beck. "Human-Animal Communication." In *International Encyclopedia of Communications,* edited by E. Barnow, 2:295–96. London: Oxford University Press, 1989.

Kellert, Stephen R.; and Edward O. Wilson, eds. *The Biophilia Hypothesis.* Washington, D.C.: Island Press, 1993.

Lacey, J. I.; J. B. Kagen; B. C. Lacey; and H. A. Moss. "The Visceral Level: Situational Determinants and Behavioral Correlates of Autonomic Response Patterns." In *The Expression of the Emotions in Man,* edited by P. H. Knapp, 161–96. New York: International University Press, 1963.

Manning, Aubrey; and James Serpell, eds. *Animals and Human Society: Changing Perspectives.* London: Routledge, 1994.

Pritchard, William R., ed. *Future Directions for Veterinary Medicine.* Durham, N.C.: Pew National Veterinary Education Program, 1988.

Robinson, Michael H.; and Tiger Lionel, eds. *Man and Beast Revisited.* Washington, D.C.: Smithsonian Institution Press, 1991.

Rollin, Bernard E. *The Unheeded Cry: Animal Consciousness, Animal Pain and Science.* Oxford: Oxford University Press, 1989.

Schenkel, R. "Expression Studies of Wolves." *Behaviour* 1 (1947): 81–129. [Translation from German by Agnes Klasson.]

———. "Submission: Its Features and Functions in the Wolf and Dog." *American Zoologist* 7 (1967): 319–30.

Shepard, Paul. *Thinking Animals.* New York: Viking Press, 1978.

Ulrich, R. S. "Biophilia, Biophobia, and Natural Landscapes." In *The Biophilia Hypothesis*, edited by S. R. Kellert and E. O. Wilson, 73–137. Washington, D.C.: Island Press, 1993.

Winnicott, D. W. "Transitional Objects and Transitional Phenomena." *International Journal of Psychoanalysis* 24 (1953): 88–97.

Animals and Human Health

Allen, K.; J. Blascovich; J. Tomaka; & R. Kelsey. "Presence of Human Friends and Pet Dogs as Moderators of Autonomic Responses to Stress in Women." *Journal of Personality and Social Psychology* 61 (1991): 582–89.

Anderson, S.; and W. H. Gantt. "The Effect of Person on Cardiac and Motor Responsivity to Shock in Dogs." *Conditional Reflex* 1 (1966): 181–89.

Anderson W.; C. Reid; & G. Jennings. "Pet Ownership and Risk Factors for Cardiovascular Disease." *The Medical Journal of Australia* 157 (1992): 298–301.

Baun, M. M.; N. Bergstrom; N. F. Langston; and L. Thoma. "Physiological Effects of Petting Dogs: Influences of Attachment." In *The Pet Connection*, edited by R. K. Anderson, B. L. Hart, and L. A. Hart, 162–70. Minneapolis: University of Minnesota, 1984.

Beck, A. M. "Animals and Society." In *The World Congress on Alternatives and Animal Use in Life Sciences: Education, Research, Testing*, edited by A. Goldberg and L. F. M. van Zutphen, 59–64. New York: Mary Ann Liebert, Inc., 1995.

Beck, A. M.; and A. H. Katcher. "Bird-Human Interaction." *Journal of the Association of Avian Veterinarians* 3, no. 3 (1989): 152–53.

Beck, A. M.; and A. N. Rowan. "The Health Benefits of Human-Animal Interactions." *Anthrozoös* 7, no. 2 (1994): 85–89.

CAST [The Coronary Arrhythmia Suppression Trial Investigators].
"Preliminary Report: Effect of Encainide and Flexainide on
Mortality in a Randomized Trial of Arrhythmia Suppression after
Myocardial Infarction." *New England Journal of Medicine* 321
(1989): 406–12.

CDC [Division of Violence Prevention, National Center for Injury
Prevention and Control, CDC]. "Suicide among Older Persons—
United States, 1980–1992." *Morbidity and Mortality Weekly Reports*
(*MMWR*) 45, no. 1 (Jan. 12, 1996): 3–6.

Friedmann, E.; A. H. Katcher; J. J. Lynch; and S. A. Thomas. "Animal
Companions and One-year Survival of Patients after Discharge
from a Coronary Care Unit." *Public Health Reports* 95 (1980):
307–12.

Friedmann, E.; A. H. Katcher; S. A. Thomas; J. J. Lynch; and P. R.
Messent. "Social Interaction and Blood Pressure: Influence of
Animal Companions." *Journal of Nervous and Mental Diseases* 171
(1983): 461–65.

Friedmann, E.; S. A. Thomas; D. Kulick-Ciuffo; J. J. Lynch; and M.
Suginohara. "The Effects of Normal and Rapid Speech on Blood
Pressure." *Psychosomatic Medicine* 44 (1982): 545–53.

Friedmann, E.; B. Zuck; and R. Lockwood. "Perception of Animals and
Cardiovascular Responses during Verbalization with an Animal
Present." *Anthrozoös* 6, no. 2 (1993): 115–34.

House, J. S.; K. R. Landis; and D. Umberson. "Social Relationships and
Health." *Science* 241 (July 29, 1988): 540–45.

Katcher, A. H.; and A. M. Beck. "Dialogue with Animals." *Transactions
and Studies of the College of Physicians of Philadelphia* 8 (1986):
105–12.

———. "Health and Caring for Living Things." *Anthrozoös* 1 (1987):
175–83.

———. "Safety and Intimacy: Physiological and Behavioral Responses
to Interaction with Companion Animals." *The Human-Pet Relationship: Proceedings of the International Symposium on the Occasion
of the 80th Birthday of Nobel Prize Winner Prof. DDr. Konrad
Lorenz, October 27–28, 1983*, 122–28. Vienna: IEMT, 1985.

Katcher, A. H.; E. Friedmann; A. M. Beck; and J. J. Lynch. "Looking,
Talking, and Blood Pressure: The Physiological Consequences of
Interacting with the Living Environment." In *New Perspectives on
Our Lives with Companion Animals*, edited by A. H. Katcher and A.
M. Beck, 351–59. Philadelphia: University of Pennsylvania Press,
1983.

Katcher, A. H.; E. Friedmann; M. Goodman; and L. Goodman. "Men,

Women, and Dogs." *California Veterinarian* 3, no. 2 (February 1983): 14–17.

Lynch, J.; L. Faherty; C. Emrich; M. E. Mills; and A. Katcher. "Effects of Human Contact on the Heart Activity of Curarized Patients." *American Heart Journal* 88 (1974): 160–69.

Lynch, J.; and J. F. McCarthy. "Social Responding in Dogs: Heart Rate Changes to a Person." *Psychophysiology* 5 (1969): 389–93.

Lynch, J.; S. A. Thomas; M. E. Mills; K. Malinow; and A. Katcher. "The Effects of Human Contact on Cardiac Arrhythmia in Coronary Care Patients." *Journal of Nervous and Mental Diseases* 158 (1974): 88–89.

Lynch, J. J.; S. A. Thomas; D. A. Paskewitz; A. Katcher; and L. Weir. "Human Contact and Cardiac Arrhythmia in a Coronary Care Unit." *Psychosomatic Medicine* 39 (1977): 188–94.

Messent, P. R. "Social Facilitation of Contact with Other People by Pet Dogs." In *New Perspectives on Our Lives with Companion Animals*, edited by A. H. Katcher and A. M. Beck, 37–46. Philadelphia: University of Pennsylvania Press, 1983.

Moriyama, I. M.; D. E. Krueger; and J. Stamler. *Cardiovascular Diseases in the United States*. Cambridge, Mass.: Harvard University Press, 1971.

Robinson, I. *The Waltham Book of Human-Animal Interaction: Benefits and Responsibilities of Pet Ownership*. New York: Elsvier Science Inc., 1995.

Ross, L. "The Intuitive Psychologist and His Shortcomings: Distortions in the Attribution Process." In *Advances in Experimental Social Psychology*, edited by L. Berkowitz, 173–220. New York: Academic Press, 1977.

Ross, Lee; and Richard E. Nisbett. *The Person and the Situation*. Philadelphia, Pa.: Temple University Press, 1991.

Serpell, J. "Beneficial Effects of Pet Ownership on Some Aspects of Human Health and Behavior." *Journal of the Royal Society of Medicine* 84 (1991): 717–20.

Wax, J. *The New York Times Magazine*, April, 1979, 22.

Animal-Facilitated Therapy and Activities

Arkow, Phil. *Pet Therapy: A Study of the Use of Companion Animals in Selected Therapies*. Colorado Springs, Colo.: The Humane Society of the Pikes Peak Region, 1982.

Beck, A. M.; and L. T. Glickman. "Future Research on Pet Facilitated Therapy: A Plea for Comprehension before Intervention." *Health*

Benefits of Pets, NIII Technology Assessment Workshop, September 10–11, 1987.

Beck, A. M.; and A. H. Katcher. "A New Look at Pet-Facilitated Therapy." *Journal of the American Veterinary Medical Association* 184 (1984): 414–21.

Beck, A. M.; L. Seraydarian; and G. F. Hunter. "The Use of Animals in the Rehabilitation of Psychiatric Inpatients." *Psychological Reports* 8 (1986): 63–66.

Brickel, C. M. "The Therapeutic Roles of Cat Mascots with a Hospital-Based Geriatric Population: A Staff Survey." *The Gerontologist* 19, no. 4 (1979): 368–72.

Burch, Mary. *Volunteering with Your Pet.* New York: Howell Book House, 1996.

Corson, S. A.; E. O. Corson; P. H. Gwynne; and L. E. Arnold. "Pet Dogs as Nonverbal Communication Links in Hospital Psychiatry." *Comprehensive Psychiatry* 18, no. 1 (January/February 1977): 61–72.

Curtis, P. "Animals Are Good for the Handicapped, Perhaps All of Us." *Smithsonian* 12, no. 4 (July 1981): 49–57.

———. "Animal Shelters Struggle to Keep Up with Millions of Abandoned Pets." *Smithsonian* 13, no. 6 (September 1982): 40–49.

Eames, T.; and E. Eames. "Partners in Independence." *Dogworld*, Dec. 1992, 54–55, 84–87.

Eddy, J.; L. A. Hart; and R. P. Bolts. "The Effects of Service Dogs on Social Acknowledgements of People in Wheelchairs." *Journal of Psychology* 122, no. 1 (1988): 39–45.

Fredrickson, Maureen. *Handbook for Animal-Assisted Activities and Animal-Assisted Therapy.* Renton, Wash.: Delta Society, 1992.

Fudin, C. E.; and J. M. Harris. "Caring for Service Dogs." *Perspectives*, July/August 1994, 23–25.

Hart, L. A.; and B. L. Hart. "Socializing Effects of Service Dogs for People with Disabilities." *Anthrozoös* 1, no. 1 (1987): 41–44.

Iannuzzi, D.; and A. N. Rowan. "Ethical Issues in Animal-Assisted Therapy Programs." *Anthrozoös* 4, no. 3 (1991): 154–63.

Katcher, A. H.; A. M. Beck; and D. Levine. "Evaluation of a Pet Program in Prison: The Pal Project at Lorton." *Anthrozoös* 2, no. 3 (1989): 175–80.

Katcher, A. H.; E. Friedmann; M. Goodman; and L. Goodman. "Men, Woman, and Dogs." *California Veterinarian* 2 (1983): 14–16.

Katcher, A. H.; H. Segal; and A. M. Beck. "Comparison of Contemplation and Hypnosis for the Reduction of Anxiety and Discomfort during Dental Surgery." *American Journal of Clinical Hypnosis* 27 (1984): 14–21.

Lee, Ronal L.; Marie E. Zeglan; Terry Ryan; Clover B. Gowing; and Linda M. Hines. *Guidelines: Animals in Nursing Homes.* Revised edition. Renton, Wash.: The Delta Society, n.d.

Lee, Ronal L.; Marie E. Zeglan; Terry Ryan; and Linda M. Hines. "Guidelines: Animals in Nursing Homes." *California Veterinarian,* Suppl. 3 (1983): 1–42.

Levinson, B. M. "Interpersonal Relationships between Pets and Human Beings." In *Abnormal Behavior in Animals,* edited by Michael W. Fox, 504–22. Baltimore, Md.: Williams and Wilkins, 1975.

————. "Pets, Child Development and Mental Illness." *Journal of the American Veterinary Medical Association* 175 (1970): 1759–66.

Lockwood, R. "Pet-Facilitated Therapy Grows Up." *Humane Society News* (Spring 1986): 4–8.

Loney, J. "The Canine Therapist in a Residential Children's Setting: Qualifications, Recruitment, Training and Related Matters." *Journal of the American Academy of Child Psychiatry* 10, no. 3 (1971): 518–23.

McCulloch, M. J. "Companion Animals, Human Health, and the Veterinarian." In *Textbook of Veterinary Internal Medicine,* edited by Stephen J. Ettinger, 1:228–35. Philadelphia, Pa.: W. B. Saunders Co., 1983.

————. "The Pet as Prosthesis—Defining Criteria for the Adjunctive Use of Companion Animals in the Treatment of Medically Ill, Depressed Outpatients." In *Interrelations between People and Pets,* edited by B. Fogle, 101–23. Springfield, Ill.: Charles C. Thomas, 1981.

McCulloch, W. F.; A. O. Griffiths; M. L. Samuelson; and V. L. Voith. "AVMA Guidelines for Veterinarians: Animal-Facilitated Therapy Programs." *Journal of the American Veterinary Medical Association* 184, no. 2 (1984): 146–47.

Neer, C. A.; C. Dorn; and I. Grayson. "Dog Interaction with Persons Receiving Institutional Geriatric Care." *Journal of the American Veterinary Medical Association* 191 (1987): 300–304.

Reeves, David E.; William H. Reid; Doris M. Miller; and Brian T. Tankersley. *The People Pet Connection: 4-H Pet Facilitated Therapy Program.* Athens, Ga.: Cooperative Extension Service, University of Georgia, 1990.

Senter, S.; S. B. Ross, Jr.; and G. Mallon. *People and Animals: A Therapeutic Animal-Assisted Activities Manual.* Brewster, N.Y.: Green Chimneys, 1993.

Voelker, R. "Puppy Love Can Be Therapeutic, Too." *Journal of the American Medical Association* 274 (1995): 1897–99.

Warner, Rex J.; and Norman D. Long. *A Guide for 4-H Animal Care.* West Lafayette, Ind.: Purdue University Cooperative Extension Service, 1990.

Animals and Children

Cain, A. O. "A Study of Pets in the Family System." In *New Perspectives on Our Lives with Companion Animals,* edited by A. H. Katcher and A. M. Beck, 72–81. Philadelphia: University of Pennsylvania Press, 1983.

Davis, J. H. "Preadolescent Self-concept Development and Pet Ownership." *Anthrozoös* 1 (1987): 90–94.

Filiatre, J. C.; J. L. Millot; A. Montagner; A. Eckerlin; and A. C. Gagnon. "Advances in the Study of the Relationship between Children and Their Pet Dogs." *Anthrozoös* 2 (1988): 22–32.

Hunt, S. J.; L. A. Hart; and R. Gomulkiewicz. "The Role of Small Animals in Social Interactions between Strangers." *Journal of Social Psychology* 132, no. 2 (1992): 245–56.

Katcher, A. H.; and G. Wilkins. "Dialogue with Animals: Its Nature and Culture." In *The Biophilia Hypothesis,* edited by S. R. Kellert and E. O. Wilson, 173–97. Washington, D.C.: Island Press, 1993.

Levinson, Boris M. *Pet-Oriented Child Psychotherapy.* Springfield, Ill.: Charles C. Thomas, 1969.

———. *Pets and Human Development.* Springfield, Ill.: Charles C. Thomas, 1972.

Melson, G. F. "Availability of and Involvement with Pets by Children: Determinants and Correlates." *Anthrozoös* 2 (1988): 45–52.

———. "Studying Children's Attachment to Their Pets: A Conceptual and Methodological Review." *Anthrozoös* 4 (1990): 91–99.

Melson, G. F.; and A. Fogel. "Children's Ideas about Animal Young and Their Care: A Reassessment of Gender Differences in the Development of Nurturance." *Anthrozoös* 2 (1989): 265–73.

Nielsen, J. A.; and L. A. Delude. "Behavior of Young Children in the Presence of Different Kinds of Animals." *Anthrozoös* 3 (1989): 119–29.

Serpell, J. A. "Childhood Pets and Their Influence on Adults' Attitudes." *Psychological Reports* 49 (1981): 651–54.

Siegmund, R.; and K. Bierman. "Common Leisure Activities of Pets and Children." *Anthrozoös* 2 (1988): 53–57.

Stevens, L. T. "Attachment of Pets among Eighth Graders." *Anthrozoös* 3 (1990): 177–83.

ten Bensel, R. W. "The Importance of Animals and Children: Their Place in the Family and in the World." *Anthrozoös* 1 (1987): 137–39.

Animals and Older Adults

Ferraro, K. F.; and C. M. Albrecht-Jensen. "Does Religion Influence Adult Health?" *Journal of the Scientific Study of Religion* 30, no. 2 (1991): 193–202.

Gammonley, J.; and J. Yates. "Pet Projects: Animal Assisted Therapy in Nursing Homes." *Journal of Gerontological Nursing* 17, no. 1 (1991): 13–15.

Garrity, T. E.; L. Stallones; M. B. Marx; and T. P. Johnson. "Pet Ownership and Attachment as Supportive Factors in the Health of the Elderly." *Anthrozoös* 3 (1989): 35–44.

Goldmeier, J. "Pets or People: Another Research Note." *The Gerontologist.* 26 (1986): 203–6.

Kidd, A. H.; and B. M. Feldmann. "Pet Ownership and Self-perceptions of Older People." *Psychological Reports* 48 (1981): 867–75.

Kidd, A. H.; and R. M. Kidd. "Benefits and Liabilities of Pets for the Homeless." *Psychological Reports* 74 (1994): 715–22.

Neer, C. A.; C. R. Dorn; and I. Grayson. "Dog Interaction with Persons Receiving Institutional Geriatric Care." *Journal of the American Veterinary Medical Association* 191 (1987): 300–304.

Ory, M. G.; and E. L. Goldberg. "The Influence of Animals on Social Perception." In *New Perspectives on Our Lives with Companion Animals*, edited by A. H. Katcher and A. M. Beck, 303–17. Philadelphia: University of Pennsylvania Press, 1983.

Robb, S. S.; B. Michele; and C. L. A. Pristash. "Wine Bottle, Plant, and Puppy: Catalysts for Social Behavior." *Journal of Gerontological Nursing* 6, no. 12 (December 1980): 721–28.

Robb, S. S.; and C. E. Stegman. "Companion Animals and Elderly People: A Challenge for Evaluation of Social Support." *The Gerontologist* 23 (1983): 277–82.

Rosswurm, M. "Relocation and the Elderly." *Journal of Gerontological Nursing* 9 (1983): 632–37.

Siegel, J. M. "Companion Animals: In Sickness and in Health." *Journal of Social Issues* 49, no. 1 (1993): 157–67.

———. "Stressful Life Events and Use of Physican Services among the Elderly: The Moderating Role of Pet Ownership." *Journal of Personality and Social Psychology* 58, no. 6 (1990): 1081–86.

Smith, D. W.; C. S. Seibert; J. Jackson, III; and F. W. Snell. "Pet

Ownership by Elderly People: Two New Issues." *International Journal of Aging and Human Development* 34, no. 3 (1992): 175–84.

Stryler-Gordon, R.; N. Beall; and R. K. Anderson. "Facts and Fiction: Health Risks Associated with Pets in Nursing Homes." *Journal of the Delta Society* 2, no. 1 (1985): 73–74.

Wilson, C. C.; and F. E. Netting. "Companion Animals and the Elderly: A State-of-the-art Summary." *Journal of the American Veterinary Medical Association* 183 (1983): 1425–29.

Wilson, C. C.; F. E. Netting; and J. C. New. "Pet Ownership Characteristics of Community-Based Elderly Participants in a Pet Placement Program." *California Veterinarian* 39, no. 3 (1985): 26–28.

Zasloff, R. L.; and A. H. Kidd. "Loneliness and Pet Ownership among Single Women." *Pyschological Reports* 75 (1993): 747–52.

Breaking the Bond

Buttler, C.; and L. Lagoni. "Helping Clients in Crisis." *Perspectives*, January/February 1995, 18–26.

Edney, A. T. B. "The Management of Euthanasia in Small Animal Practice." *Journal of the American Hospital Association* 15 (1979): 645–49.

Gosse, G. H.; and M. J. Barnes. "Human Grief Resulting from Death of a Pet." *Anthrozoös* 7, no. 2 (1994): 103–12.

Greene, L. "Lawsuits and Pet Bereavement." *Intercom* (San Diego County Veterinary Medical Association), March, 1992, 5–6.

Katcher, A. H.; and M. A. Rosenberg. "Euthanasia and the Management of the Client's Grief." *The Compendium on Continuing Education for the Practicing Veterinarian* 1 (1979): 887–91.

Keddie, K. M. G. "Pathological Mourning after the Death of a Pet." *British Journal of Psychiatry* 131 (1977): 21–25.

Kübler-Ross, Elisabeth. *On Death and Dying.* New York: MacMillan, 1969.

Lagoni, Laurel; Carolyn Butler; and Suzanne Hetts. *The Human-Animal Bond and Grief.* Philadelphia, Pa.: W. B. Saunders Co., 1994.

Montgomery, Mary; and Herb Montgomery. *The Final Act of Caring.* Minneapolis, Minn: Montgomery Press, 1993.

———. *Good-bye My Friend.* Minneapolis, Minn.: Montgomery Press, 1991.

Nieburg, Herbert A.; and Arlene Fischer. *Pet Loss: A Thoughtful Guide for Adults and Children.* New York: Harper and Row, 1982.

Olson, D.; and L. Greene. "The Veterinarian as Counselor—Handling Pet Owner Grief." *Veterinary Reports* 1, no. 3 (1988): 10, 12.

Podberscek, A. L.; and J. K. Blackshaw. "The Attachment of Humans to Pets and Their Reactions to Pet Death." *Canine Practice* 19, no. 5 (1994): 16–19.

Quackenbush, Jamie; and Denise Graveline. *When Your Pet Dies: How to Cope with Your Feelings.* New York: Simon and Schuster, 1985.

Ryder, E. L.; and M. Romasco. "Social Work Service in a Veterinary Teaching Hospital." *The Compendium on Continuing Education for the Practicing Veterinarian* 2 (1980): 215–20.

Viorst, Judith. *The Tenth Good Thing about Barney.* New York: Aladdin Books, 1988.

Animals and Abuse

Arkow, P. "Child Abuse, Animal Abuse and the Veterinarian." *Journal of the American Veterinary Medical Association* 204, no. 7 (1994): 1004–7.

Ascione, F. R. "Enhancing Children's Attitudes about the Humane Treatment of Animals: Generalization to Human-Directed Empathy." *Anthrozoös* 5, no. 3 (1992): 176–91.

Felthous, A. R.; and S. R. Kellert. "Violence against Animals and People: Is Aggression against Living Creatures Generalized?" *Bulletin of the American Academy of Psychiatric Law* 14 (1986): 55–69.

Kellert, S.; and A. Felthouse. "Noncriminals and Criminals in Kansas and Connecticut." *The Human-Pet Relationship.* Proceedings of the International Symposium on the Occasion of the 80th Birthday of Nobel Prize Winner Prof. DDr. Konrad Lorenz, October 27–28, 1983, 72–81. Vienna: IEMT, 1985.

Worth, D.; and A. M. Beck. "Multiple Ownership of Animals in New York City." *Transactions and Studies of the College of Physicians of Philadelphia* 3, no. 4 (December 1981): 280–300.

Animals in Conflict with Human Heatlh

Baker, E. "A Veterinarian Looks at the Animal Allergy Problem." *Annals of Allergy* 43 (1979): 214–16.

Bancroft, R. L. "America's Mayor and Councilmen: Their Problems and Frustrations." *Nation's Cities* 12 (April 1974): 14–22, 24.

Beck, A. M. "The Companion Animal in Society (The John V. Lacroix Lecture)." In *Proceedings: 48th Annual Meeting, American Animal Hospital Association* (1981): 237–40.

———. "The Epidemiology of Animal Bite." *The Compendium on Continuing Education for the Practicing Veterinarian* 3, no. 3 (March 1981): 254–55, 257–58.

————. "Guidelines for Planning for Pets in Urban Areas." In *Interrelations between People and Pets*, edited by B. Fogle, 231–40. Springfield, Ill.: Charles C. Thomas, 1981.

————. "The Impact of the Canine Clean-up Law." *Environment* 21, no. 8 (October 1979): 28–31.

————. "The Life and Times of Shag, a Feral Dog in Baltimore." *Natural History* 80, no. 8 (October 1971): 58–65. Reprinted in *Ants, Indians and Little Dinosaurs*, edited by A. Ternes, 18–26. New York: Charles Scribner's Sons, 1975.

————. "The Public Health Implications of Urban Dogs." *American Journal of Public Health* 65 (December 1975): 1315–18.

Beck, A. M.; S. R. Felser; and L. T. Glickman. "An Epizootic of Rabies in Maryland, 1982–84." *American Journal of Public Health* 77 (1987): 42–44.

Beck, A. M.; H. Loring; and R. Lockwood. "The Ecology of Dog Bite Injury in St. Louis, Missouri." *Public Health Reports* 90 (May/June 1975): 262–67.

Beck, A. M.; and P. Marden. "Street Dwellers." *Natural History* 86, no. 9 (November 1977): 78–85.

Beck, A. M.; and M. N. Marshall. "The Pet Owner Experience. *New England and Regional Allergy Proceedings* 8, no. 3 (1987): 29–31.

Beckmann, Ed. *Love, Praise Reward*. New York: Coward, McCann and Geoghegan, Inc., 1979.

Berzon, D. R.; and J. De Hoff. "Medical Cost and Other Aspects of Dog Bites in Baltimore." *Public Health Reports* 89 (July/August 1974): 377–81.

Borchelt, P. L.; L. Lockwood; A. M. Beck; and V. L. Voith. "Attacks by Packs of Dogs Involving Predation on Human Beings." *Public Health Reports* 98, no. 1 (January/February 1983). 57–66.

Clifford, Donald H.; Kay Ann Green; and John Paul Scott. *Dos and Don'ts Concerning Vicious Dogs*. Chicago: AVMA Professional Liability Insurance Trust, 1993.

Diesch, S.; S. L. Hendricks; and R. W. Currier. "The Role of Cats in Human Rabies Exposures." *Journal of the American Veterinary Medical Association* 181, no. 12 (1982): 1510–12.

Dubin, S.; S. Segall; and J. Martindale. "Contamination of Soil in Two City Parks with Canine Nematode Ova Including *Toxocara canis:* A Preliminary Study." *American Journal of Public Health* 65 (November 1975): 1242–44.

Franti, C. E.; J. F. Kraus; and N. O. Borhani. "Pet Ownership in Suburban-Rural Area of California." *Public Health Reports* 89 (September/October 1974): 473–84.

Frenkel, J. K. Toxoplasma in and around Us. *Bio-Science* 23, no. 6 (June 1973): 343–52.

Gershman, K. A.; J. J. Sacks; and J. C. Wright. "Which Dogs Bite? A Case-Control Study of Risk Factors." *Pediatrics* 93, no. 6 (1994): 913–17.

Glickman, L. T.; and L. M. Domanski. "An Alternative to Laboratory Animal Experimentation for Human Health Risk Assessment: Epidemiological Studies of Pet Animals." *ATLA (Alternatives to Laboratory Animals)* 13 (1986): 267–85.

Glickman, L .T.; and P. M. Schantz. "Epidemiology and Pathogenesis of Zoonotic Toxocariasis." *Epidemiologic Reviews* 3 (1981): 230–50.

Glickman, L. T.; P. M. Schantz; and R. H. Cypess. "Canine and Human Toxocariasis: Review of Transmission, Pathogenesis, and Clinical Disease." *Journal of the American Veterinary Medical Association* 175, no. 12 (December 1979): 1265–69.

Greene, C. E.; R. Lockwood; and E. J. C. Goldstein. "Bite and Scratch Infections." In *Infectious Diseases of the Dog and Cat*, edited by Craig E. Greene, 614–18. Philadelphia, Pa.: W. B. Saunders, 1990.

Hafez, E. S. E., ed. *The Behaviour of Domestic Animals.* 3d ed. Baltimore, Md.: Williams and Wilkins Co., 1975.

Hanna, T. L.; and L. A. Selby. "Characteristics of the Human and Pet Population in Animal Bite Incidents Recorded at Two Air Force Bases." *Public Health Reports* 96, no. 6 (November/December 1981): 580–84.

Harris, D.; P. J. Imperato; and B. Oken. "Dog Bites—An Unrecognized Epidemic." *Bulletin of the New York Academy of Medicine* 50, no. 9 (October 1974): 981–1000.

Kelly, V. P.; J. L. Gonzalez; and K. A. Clark. "How Much Does Rabies Cost?" *Texas Veterinary Medical Journal* (June 1980): 6–7.

Lockwood, R. "Dangerous Dogs." *The HSUS News* (Fall 1992): 1–3.

———. "The Ethology and Epidemiology of Canine Aggression." In *The Domestic Dog*, edited by J. Serpell, 132–38. Cambridge: Cambridge University Press, 1995.

———. "The Influence of Animals on Social Perception." In *New Perspectives on Our Lives with Companion Animals*, edited by A. H. Katcher and A. M. Beck, 64–71. Philadelphia: University of Pennsylvania Press, 1983.

———. "Vicious Dogs." *The Humane Society News* (Winter 1986): 1–3.

Lockwood, R.; and A. M. Beck. "Dog Bites among Letter Carriers in St. Louis." *Public Health Reports* 90, no. 3 (May/June 1975): 267–69.

Lockwood, R.; and K. Rindy. "Are 'Pit-bulls' Different? An Analysis of the Pit Bull Terrier Controversy." *Anthrozoös* 1, no. 1 (1987): 2–8.

Marr, J. S.; and A. M. Beck. "Rabies in New York City, with Guidelines for Prophylaxis." *Bulletin of the New York Academy of Medicine* 52, no. 5 (June 1976): 605–16.

Marr, J. S.; A. M. Beck; and J. A. Lugo, Jr. "An Epidemiologic Study of the Human Bite." *Public Health Reports* 94, no. 6 (November/December 1979): 514–21.

Marx, M. B.; and M. L. Furcolow. "What Is the Dog Population?" *Archives of Environmental Health* 19 (1969): 217–19.

Monks of New Skete. *How to Be Your Dog's Best Friend.* Boston: Little, Brown and Co., 1978.

Nowell, Iris. *The Dog Crisis.* New York: St. Martin's Press, 1978.

Patronek, G. J. "Shelter Animals." *DVM Newsmagazine* 26, no. 12 (1995): 1s–2s, 11s–12s.

Patronek, G. J.; and L. T. Glickman. "Development of a Model for Estimating the Size of the Pet Dog Population." *Anthrozoös* 7, no. 1 (1994): 25 41.

————. "Pet Overpopulation." *Dog Fancy Magazine,* January 1995, 59–61.

————. "Pet Ownership Protects the Risks and Consequences of Coronary Heart Disease." *Medical Hypotheses* 40 (1993): 245–49.

Patronek, G. J.; L. T. Glickman; and Michael R. Moyer. "Population Dynamics and the Risk of Euthanasia for Dogs in an Animal Shelter." *Anthrozoös* 7, no. 1 (1995): 31–43.

Pet Food Institute. *US Pet Trends.* Washington, D.C., 1995.

Pinckney, L. E.; and L. A. Kennedy. "Traumatic Deaths from Dog Attacks in the United States." *Pediatrics* 69, no. 2 (1982): 193–96.

Purvis, M. J.; and D. M. Otto. "Household Demand for Pet Food and the Ownership of Cats and Dogs: An Analysis of a Neglected Component of US Food Use." *Staff Paper P,* 76-33. St. Paul: University of Minnesota, Department of Agriculture and Applied Economics, 1976.

Rice, Berkeley. *The Other End of the Leash.* Boston, Mass.: Little, Brown and Co., 1968.

Rubin, H.; and A. M. Beck. "Ecological Behavior of Free-Ranging Urban Dogs." *Applied Animal Ethology* 8 (1982):161–68.

Sacks, J. J.; R. W. Sattin; and S. E. Bonzo. "Dog Bite-Related Fatalities from 1979 through 1988." *Journal of the American Medical Association* 262 (1989): 1489–92.

Schneider, R. "Observations on Overpopulation of Dogs and Cats." *Journal of the American Veterinary Medical Association* 167, no. 4 (1975): 281–84.

Schneider, R.; and M. L. Vaida. "Survey of Canine and Feline Populations: Alameda and Contra Costa Counties, California, 1970." *Journal of the American Veterinary Medical Association* 166, no. 5 (1975): 481–86.

Selby, L.; J. D. Rhodes; J. E. Hewett; and J. A. Irwin. "A Survey of Attitudes toward Responsible Pet Ownership." *Public Health Reports* 94 (1979): 380–86.

Siegal, Mordecai; and Mathew Margolis. *Good Dog, Bad Dog.* New York: Holt, Rinehart and Winston, Inc., 1973.

Voith, V. L. "Behavioral Disorders." In *Textbook of Veterinary Internal Medicine,* edited by Stephen J. Ettinger, 1:208–27. Philadelphia, Pa.: W. B. Saunders Co., 1983.

Voith, V. L.; and P. L. Borchelt, eds. *Veterinary Clinics of North America: Small Animal Practice: Symposium on Animal Behavior* 12, no. 4 (November 1982).

Walthner-Toews, D. "Zoonotic Disease Concerns in Animal-Assisted Therapy and Animal Visitation Programs." *Canadian Veterinary Journal* 34 (1993): 549–51.

Winkler, W. G. "Human Deaths Induced by Dog Bites, United States, 1974–1975." *Public Health Reports* 92 (1977): 425–29.

Wright, J. C. "Severe Attacks by Dogs: Characteristics of the Dogs, the Victims, and the Attack Setting." *Public Health Reports* 100 (1985): 55–61.

Books of Related Interest

Bachelard, Gaston. *The Psychoanalysis of Fire.* Translated by Alan C. M. Ross. Boston, Mass.: Beacon Press, 1964.

Benson, Herbert. *The Relaxation Response.* New York: William Morrow and Co., 1975.

Berger, John. *Looking at Life.* New York: Pantheon, 1981.

Berkeley, Ellen Perry. *Maverick Cats.* New York: Walker and Co., 1982.

Birnbach, Lisa. *The Preppy Handbook.* New York: Workman Publishing, 1980.

Bond, Simon. *101 Uses for a Dead Cat.* New York: Clarkson N. Potter, Inc., 1981.

Camus, Albert. *The Stranger.* Translated by Matthew Ward. New York: Knopf, 1988.

Caras, Roger. *The Roger Caras Dog Book.* New York: Holt, Rinehart and Winston, 1980.

Connelly, Julie. "Special Report: The Great American Pet." *Money* 10, no. 12 (December 1982): 40–42, 44.

Cousins, Norman. *Anatomy of an Illness as Perceived by the Patient: Reflections on Healing and Regeneration.* New York: W.W. Norton and Co., 1979.

Daumier, Honoré. *Humours of Married Life.* Edited by Philippe Roberts-Jones. Paris: Andre Sauret, 1968.

Dennenberg, R. V.; and Eric Seidman. *Dog Catalog.* New York: Grosset and Dunlop, 1978.

Dolensek, Emil P.; and Barbara Burn. *A Practical Guide to Impractical Pets.* New York: The Viking Press, 1976.

Fagen, Robert. *Animal Play Behavior.* London: Oxford University Press, 1981.

Fox, Michael W. *Behavior of Wolves, Dogs and Related Canids.* New York: Harper and Row, 1971.

————. *Between Animal and Man.* New York: Coward, McCann and Geoghegan, Inc., 1976.

————. *The Dog: Its Domestication and Behavior.* New York: Garland STPM Press, 1978.

————. *Understanding Your Dog.* New York: Coward, McCann and Geoghegan, Inc., 1972.

————. *The Wild Canids.* New York: Van Nostrand Reinhold Co., 1975.

Fox, M. W.; A. M. Beck; and E. Blackman. "Behavior and Ecology of a Small Group of Urban Dogs (Canis familiaris)." *Applied Animal Ethology* 1 (1975): 119–37.

Frazier, Anitra; with Norma Eckroate. *The Natural Cat.* San Francisco, Calif.: Harbor Publishing, 1981.

Freidan, Betty. *The Fountain of Age.* New York: Simon and Schuster, 1993.

Gebhardt, Richard H.; Grace Pound; and Ivor Raleigh, eds. *A Standard Guide to Cat Breeds.* New York: McGraw-Hill Book Co., 1979.

Gerstenfeld, Sheldon L. *Taking Care of Your Cat.* Reading, Mass.: Addison-Wesley Publishing Co., 1979.

————. *Taking Care of Your Dog.* Reading, Mass.: Addison-Wesley Publishing Co., 1979.

Kinsey, Alfred C.; Wardell B. Pomeroy; and Clyde E. Martin. *Sexual Behavior in the Human Male.* Philadelphia, Pa.: W. B. Saunders Co., 1948.

Kinsey, Alfred C.; Wardell B. Pomeroy; Clyde E. Martin; and Paul H. Gebhard. *Sexual Behavior in the Human Female.* Philadelphia, Pa.: W. B. Saunders Co., 1953.

Kosinsky, Jerzy. *The Painted Bird.* New York: Bantam Books, 1972.

Leboyer, Frederick. *Birth without Violence.* New York: Alfred A. Knopf, 1975.

Lessing, Doris. "An Old Woman and Her Cat." In *Stories*, 429–44. New York: Alfred A. Knopf, 1978.

Leyhausen, Paul. *Cat Behavior: The Predatory and Social Behavior of Domestic and Wild Cats.* New York: Garland STPM Press, 1979.

Lorenz, Konrad Z. *King Solomon's Ring.* New York: Thomas Y. Crowell Co., 1961.

Lynch, James J. *The Broken Heart: The Medical Consequences of Loneliness.* New York: Basic Books, Inc., Harper Colophon Books, 1979.

Meares, Ainslie. *A System of Medical Hypnosis.* Philadelphia, Pa.: W. B. Saunders Co., 1961.

Mech, David L. *The Wolf.* New York: The Natural History Press, 1970.

Murie, Adolph. *The Wolves of Mt. McKinley.* Washington, D.C.: U.S. National Park Service, Fauna Series 5, U.S. Government Printing Office, 1944.

NRC [National Research Council, chair, L. T. Glickman]. *Animals as Sentinels of Environmental Health Hazards.* Washington, D.C.: National Academy Press, 1991.

Pringle, Laurence. *Feral: Tame Animals Gone Wild.* New York: Macmillan Publishing Co., 1983.

Proceedings of the National Conference on Dog and Cat Control: Denver, American Veterinary Medical Association, Feb. 3–5, 1976. Denver, Colo.: American Humane Association.

Proceedings of the National Conference on the Ecology of the Surplus Dog and Cat Problem, Chicago, American Veterinary Medical Association, May 21–23, 1974.

Proceedings of the First Canadian Symposium on Pets and Society, Toronto, Canadian Veterinary Medical Association, June 23–25, 1976.

Proceedings of the Second Canadian Symposium on Pets and Society, Vancouver, Canadian Veterinary Medical Association, May 30–June 1, 1979.

Proceedings of the Third Canadian Symposium on Pets and Society, Toronto, Canadian Veterinary Medical Association, April 28–30, 1982.

Rabelais, François. *Gargantua and Pantagruel.* New York: Norton, 1991.

Sarton, May. *The Fur Person.* New York: Signet, 1957.

Scott, John Paul; and John Fuller. *Genetics and the Social Behavior of the Dog.* Chicago, Ill.: University of Chicago Press, 1965.

Scott, M. D.; and K. Causey. "Ecology of Feral Dogs in Alabama." *Journal of Wildlife Management* 37, no. 3 (1973): 253–65.

Serpell, James. *The Domestic Dog: Its Evolution, Behaviour and Interactions with People.* New York: Cambridge University Press, 1995.

Thomas, Elizabeth Marshall. *The Hidden Life of Dogs.* Boston, Mass.: Houghton Mifflin Co., 1993.

Thoreau, Henry David. *Walden.* New York: Harper, 1950.

Wilson, James. *Law and Ethics of the Veterinary Profession.* Yardley, Pa.: Priority Press, 1988.

Wolforth, Morgan G. *Family Guide to Dog Care and Training.* New York: Good Housekeeping Books, 1977.

Woolpy, Jerome H.; and Benson E. Ginsburg. "Wolf Socialization: A Study of Temperament in a Wild Species." *American Zoologist* 7 (1967): 357–63.

Young, Stanley Paul. *The Wolf in North American History.* Caldwell, Idaho: The Caxton Printers, 1946.

Young, Stanley Paul; and Edward A. Goldman. *The Wolves of North America.* New York: Dover Publications, 1944.

Zebrowitz, Leslie A. *Social Perception.* Pacific Grove, Calif.: Brooks/ Cole, 1990.

Zeuner, Frederick E. *A History of Domesticated Animals.* New York: Harper and Row, 1963.

SAMPLE OF RESOURCES ON THE INTERNET

Pets in Therapy

AAPA? . Based in Tucson, Arizona, TAAPA offers alternatives to traditional therapy which promote health and well being through human-animal bonds. "Equestrian psychotherapy", as it is clinically known, is just one of the animal-assisted therapies ... —[54] http://www.horseweb.com/client/anoasis/taapa.htm (5к)

Animal Outreach—Hugs to Share What is Animal Outreach? A group of dedicated individuals that are involved in animal-assisted therapy or animal visitation programs, including, but not limited to: school children, geriatric facilities, autistic and learning challenged children and...http://www.ipt.com/groups/bvas/outreach.htm - size 4к - 5 Dec 95

Bide-A-Wee Home Association Bide-A-Wee Is A Not-For-Profit 501(c)3 Charitable Organization That Has Operated No-Kill Animal Shelters Continuously Since 1903. Table of Contents. Bide-A-Wee Services. Introduction. Animal Shelters. Pet Adoptions . Pet ... — [69] http://www.inch.com/~bideawee/index. html (10к)

Canine Companions for Independence (CCI) Meet Don and Racer| . Canine Companions for Independence (CCI) is a nonprofit organization dedicated to serving people with disabilities by providing trained service, hearing and social dogs, and by providing con-

tinuing support to ensure the success ... http://www.tag
online.com/Ads/CCI/ (Score: 61, Size: 2к)

Canine Companions for Independence (CCI) is a nonprofit organization whose mission is to serve the needs of people with disabilities
by providing trained service, hearing, and social dogs, and by providing continuing support to ensure the success of the working
team. . CCI dogs are ..http://grunt.berkeley.edu/cci/cci.html
(Score: 64, Size: 5к)

Concern for Helping Animals in Israel (CHAI) Homepage
Concern for Helping Animals in Israel . CHAI is a nonprofit organization devoted to the support of pioneering efforts in Israel to
improve the quality of life for all living beings. HELPING ANI-
MALS HELPS PEOPLE . With companionship and ... — [53]
http://envirolink.org/arrs/chai/chaihome.html (7к)

Delta Society Texas Coastal Group Delta Society Texas Coastal
Group. Susan A. Zapf, President 5905 Heather Dr. League City,
Texas 77573 (713) 338-5095 Purpose Statement To promote pos-
itive interactions between people, animals, and the environment.
Publications Quarterly newsletter; Animal... http://space.rice.
edu/~cec/groups/alpha/delta.html - size 2к - 14 Nov 95

Delta Society Delta Society. Back to the Health Organizations Page.
Back to the Good Health Web. Information Services Director
Century Building, Suite 303 321 Burnett Avenue, South Renton,
WA 98055-2569. (206) 226-7357 (Voice) Abstract. The Delta
Society,...http://www.social.com/health/nhic/data/hr2300/hr23
75.html - size 2к - 18 Sep 95

No Title General. The Delta Society. Dogs for the Deaf. American
Humane Association. American Pet Society. Canine Companions
for Independence. National Animal Poison Control Center Information Page. Vet Genetics Lab. Agility home page. Flyball home
page. Purdue... http://www.familyinternet.com/pet/7-2.htm -
size 4к - 31 Oct 95

The Delta Society THE DELTA SOCIETY: BRIEF HISTORY, AC-
COMPLISHMENTS, OVERVIEW OF PROGRAMS. HIS-
TORY. The Delta Foundation was established in 1977 in
Portland, Oregon, under the leadership of Michael McCulloch,
MD. Delta's first president was Leo K. Bustad, DVM, PhD, dean
of... http://rampages.onramp.net/~drjim/delta.html - size 13к -
12 Jul 95

No Title Therapy Dog Associations and Programs. contributed by
Jennifer Alexander E-mail: jalexand@falcon.dallas.isd.tenet.edu.
Delta Society Pet Partners Programs 321 Burnett Ave. S. 3rd
Floor Renton, WA 98055-2569 Phone (206) 226-7357. A non-

profit organization...http://www.rahul.net/hredlus/therapy.html
- size 3к - 25 Jul 95

Dr. Dolphin Why does swimming with dolphins help humans heal? A
computer-wielding "neurohacker" may have found the answer. by
Richard Blow . For more resources on dolphin-human interaction,
see our resource guide. . David Cole knows that people consider ...
— [51] http://www.mojones.com/MOTHER_JONES/JF95/
blow.html (16к)

The Dolphin Circle HomepageWelcome to the Dolphin Circle! . "The
dolphins nurture our capacity for surrender and trust, for love and
serenity, and facilitate a level of consciousness . that has an un-
tapped therapeutic potential for humankind.". — [50]
http://www.premier1.net/~iamdavid/ (39к)

FAQS PETS AND HIV— http://www.sonic.net/~pals/ptfaqs.html
(Score 59, Size 11к)PETS AND HIV . - EVERYTHING YOU
ALWAYS WANTED TO KNOW, BUT WERE NOT ABLE TO
FIND - . Holding On to Your Best Friend Is Just the Right
Medicine . People with serious medical conditions often are led to
believe that they should give ... (See also Similar Pages)

Green Chimneys Home PageGreen Chimneys . Putnam Lake Rd. .
Caller Box 719 . Brewster, New York 10509. Tel: 914-279-2995
Fax: 914-279-2714 . Tel: 718-892-6810 . Green Chimneys oper-
ates a 150 acre farm 60 miles north of New York City. Over 100
emotionally ... — [54] http://www.riverhope.org/gchimney/
(2к)

Greyhounds as Therapy Dogs A Breed Apart © Greyhounds as
Therapy Dogs. by marg mccarthy. ay I begin by saying that of all
the things I is, a writer I ain't. We adopted our first greyhound,
Miss Lily, through the Greyhounds as Pets program in Colorado.
She had been found by the... http://www2.pcix.com/~gryhnd/
abap/mirror/therapy.html - size 8к - 29 Aug 95

LIFESTYLE LIFESTYLE. ANIMALS & US. The Therapeutic
Application of Animals for People with Disabilities. This ABILI-
TIES five-part series will explore the relationship we have devel-
oped with animals—and, in particular, the therapeutic application
of animals for...http://www.utirc.utoronto.ca/AdTech/ABILI-
TIES/Articles/LFS_THEHUMAN_F95.html -size 8к - 19 Sep 9

Pet Pets Pets Are Pets Are Pets Are Loving Pets Are Loving Pets Are
Loving Support Pets Are Loving Support Pets Are Loving Supp
Pets Are Loving This site is a service of Pets Are Loving Support
in Sonoma County, California (USA). It will always be ... — [53]
http://www.sonic.net/~pals/ (5к)

PENINSULA HUMANE SOCIETY OF SAN MATEO COUNTY

PENINSULA HUMANE SOCIETY . 12 AIRPORT BOULE-VARD . SAN MATEO, CA 94401 . (415) 340-8200 . Fax (415) 348-7891 . VOLUNTEER OPPORTUNITIES AT THE PENINSULA HUMANE SOCIETY . Volunteers are a critical component of the Peninsula Humane Society. Each ... — [53] http://www.meer.net/users/taylor/penhumso.htm (9к)

PET ASSISTED THERAPY (PAT)PET ASSISTED THERAPY (PAT) This is a very rewarding experience! It is essentially, taking a dog that has the right temperament and training, to shut-ins, re-tirement homes, or to special needs patients. You and your K-9 buddy can make a real hit, and...http://spicerack.unh.edu/~tg/pat.html - size 1к - 30 Nov 95

Pets Are Wonderful Support 615 Congress Street . PO Box 5305 . Portland, Maine 04101 . (207) 775-PAWS . Why Are Pets So Important to People with AIDS? . All of us know the peace and pleasure we get from our animals. Pets are indeed very important for health and ... — [63] http://www.mainelink.net/PAWS/ (5к)

Raising a CCI puppy The puppy raising program provides a unique op-portunity for volunteers to help create a meaningful change in someone's life. Born of carefully selected pedigreed stock, CCI puppies are reared in private homes from eight weeks of age until ...http://grunt.berkeley.edu/cci/puppy_raising.html (Score: 59, Size: 6к)

Service Dogs Author. Cindy Tittle Moore, Copyright 1995 . Table of Contents . Dogs for the Blind. Hearing and Signal Dogs . Canine Companions for Independence . Assistance Dog International (ADI) . Therapy Dogs . More Information . Please note that ... - [52] http://www.zmall.com/pet_talk/tittle/pets/dog-faqs/service.html (23к)

NIH Technology Assessment - Pets 3. THE HEALTH BENEFITS OF PETS. National Institutes of Health OMAR Workshop. September 10–11, 1987. This statement was originally published as:The health benefits of pets. Workshop summary; 1987 Sep 10–11. Bethesda (MD): National Institutes of Health,... http://text.nlm.nih.gov/nih/ta/www/03.html - size 42к - 16 Nov 94

No Title 1. EVALUATING THE ELDERLY PATIENT: THE CASE FOR ASSESSMENT TECHNOLOGY National Institutes of Health NIH Technology Assessment Conference Summary June 29–30, 1983 This statement was originally published as: Evaluating the elderly patient: The case for... http://text.nlm.nih. gov/nih/ta/ftrs/rebuild/ta.db - size 570к - 31 May 95

Zoonoses ZOONOSES. pronounced (ZO-e-NO-zes) Extensive Page

Please, use navigation. HOME. Birds/Zoonoses. Cats/ Taxoplasmosis. Dogs/Taxoplasmosis. Cats/Technical. Birds Question You May Have About ZOONOSES AND YOUR BIRD What is Zoonoses? No it is not what you find... http:// www.sonic.net/~pals/zoono.html - size 35K - 26 Jul 95

Pet Information

About the AAVI About the AAVI. The American Academy of Veterinary Informatics exists to: 1. Facilitate the dissemination and application of veterinary medical knowledge in teaching, research, and practice for the purpose of delivering better health care to animals,... http://netvet.wustl.edu/org/aavi/aavidesc.htm - size 1K - 12 Dec 95

AKC Mission The American Kennel Club Mission. The AKC's Mission: Maintain a registry for purebred dogs and preserve its integrity. Sanction dog events that promote interest in, and sustain the process of, breeding for type and function of purebred dogs. Take whatever... http://www.akc.org/akc/text/mission. htm - size 3K - 22 Sep 95

Baron & Nevar's Index of Small Dog Breeds Small Dog Breeds . I'm currently searching for a small dog to join my girlfriend's two little dogs, Baron and Nevar. I've found that it's really hard to track down information about the small breeds on the Web. There's a lot of useful ... — [78] http://www.coil.com/~steve/ small-dogs.html (10K)

Cyber-Pet [Home Page] [Mission List] . Cyber-Dog has successfully completed his mission. . The information you requested has been assembled into our . Finding a Pet page . The purpose of this page is to provide you with important information ... — [68] http://www.cyberpet.com/cyberdog/findpet/findpet.htm (2K)

Dog Journals Dogs. A M S C O P E Newsletter / American Miniature Schnauzer Club 302 Southwood Lancaster, Tx 75146 : m : $0 Breed Publication - Dogs n3 - Advocate (Old Brookville) / Owner Handler Association of Amer C/O Mildred Mesh Six Michaels Ln. Old Brookville, NY... http://www.rapidnet.com/~cldavies/ dogs.html - size 29K - 28 Nov 95

Dogs, Breed Information, Breeders compiled by: Don & Gretchen Plemmons (cyberpet@ix.netcom.com) . Cyberpet. Version 1 - October 25, 1995 . The Clearinghouse is sponsored by Argus Associates and the University of Michigan . . — [81] http://www.lib.umich.edu/chouse/inter/561.html (1K)

Guinea Pig FAQ, Version 1.2.2 An informational document posted monthly to the usenet newsgroup rec.pets, about the care and maintenance of guinea pigs as pets. . A current version of this FAQ can be found: . In the newsgroups rec.pets, rec.answers, and news.answers (posted ... — ⌈62⌉ http://www.princeton.edu/ ~ecrocke/html/gpfaq.html (34к)

Informational Dog-Related Web Sites This compilation is Copyright 1995 by Cindy Tittle Moore. . The posted version may be found on rtfm.mit.edu under pub/usenet/news.answers/dogs-faq/www-list; to get a copy by email, send a message to mailserver@rtfm.mit.edu with send ... —⌈56⌉ http://www. zmall.com/pet_talk/dog-faqs/lists/www-list.html (59к)

Internet Kid's Web-Animals Animals . Have fun with activities about Aussie Animals. Discover some unique Australian native animals and fun activities. These pages feature the work of some Australian school children in a creative and interesting way. . Animal ...⌈53⌉ http://psych.hanover.edu/kidsweb/animals.html (1к)

Misc. Animal Related Journals Aardvarks in the news / National Assn. for the Advancement of Aardvarks in... 947 Perkins Ave Waukesha, WI 53186-5247 : : $0 Breed publication - Aardvarks n287 - 11/22/95. Buffalo! / Natl. Buffalo Assn 10 Main St. Box 580 Ft. Pierre, SD 57532 605-223-2829... http://www.rapidnet. com/~cldavies/misc.html - size 16к - 28 Nov 95

National/International Index List of All the National/International Organizations. A B C D E F G H I J K L M N O P R S T U V W Y Z NUMBERS. —NUMBERS— 1631 100 Black Men of America 1521 4-H: The National 4-H Council 0406 52 Association for the Handicapped 1901 9 to 5 Working Women... http://www.red-stone.army.mil/cfc/n-index.html - size 41к - 5 Sep 95

Pet Surfing Menu Pet Surfing. The purpose of this public document is to inform, access individual pet pages, and most importantly...to have fun! Canine Page. Feline Page. Any Other Pet As soon as I start receiving more stuff regarding specific animal companions, I will... http://www.sonic.net/~pals/surfmen.html - size 2к - 9 Aug 95

Pet Index Homepage I've listed link indices below. Note that if at all possible I prefer to link to lists (I have enough work with dog and cat links without tracking ALL other pet links, I'll let others do that work :-). Hence, if you have, for example, a ferret ... — ⌈59⌉ http://www.zmall.com/pet_talk/pet-faqs/homepage.html (4к)

PetsForum Group — Pet Vendors Forums: Dog Products PET PROD-UCTS FORUM. DOG PRODUCTS. PetsForum Group has 2 forums on CompuServe just for pet products companies (Go

PFVenA & Go PFVenB). The following companies are all available on CompuServe's Pet Products Forum. You will find their catalogs, technical... http://www.petsforum.com/petsforum/pets/petvendors/dogvendors.html - size 4κ - 29 Nov 95

rec.pets.cats: Getting A Cat FAQ Getting a Cat FAQ From the rec.pets.cat newsgroup, answers to questions about getting a cat. — [51] http://www.cis.ohio-state.edu/hypertext/faq/usenet/cats-faq/getting-a-cat/faq.html (22κ)

rec.pets.dogs: Assorted Topics FAQ, Part II Archive-name: dogs-faq/misc2 Last-modified: 1 January 1993 This is one of the FAQ (Frequently Asked Questions) Lists for rec.pets.dogs. It is posted on a monthly basis: updates, additions, and corrections (including attributions) are always ... — [51] http://www.cis.ohio-state.edu/ hypertext/faq/usenet/dogs-faq/misc2/faq.html (38κ)

Animal Behavior

Applied-ethology an email discussion list . The APPLIED-ETHOL-OGY e-mail network was set up for the exchange of information, discussions, announcements, news items, etc. that are of interest to people working and studying in the field of applied animal ... — [82] http://res.agr.ca/PUB/CDRN/portfoli/private/jeff/a-e.html (5κ)

Applied Developmental Psychology Ph.D. Program . Professional Goals and Resources . In this doctoral program in the emerging field of applied developmental psychology at the University of Maryland Baltimore County, students acquire skills in analysis, research, and practical ... — [61] http://umbc2.umbc.edu /~mjohns7/adp.html (4κ)

APBC index— http://webzone1.co.uk/www/apbc/ (Score: 58, Size: 4κ) THE ASSOCIATION OF . PET BEHAVIOUR COUNSEL-LORS . ABOUT THE APBC MAIN SUBJECTS HOW TO CONTACT THE APBC LINKS TO RELATED ITEMS . About The Association of Pet Behaviour Counsellors . ...

Dog Owner's Guide: Dog Bites— http://www.canismajor.com/dog/bite1.html (Score 59, Size 8κ)Dog Owner's Guide [[Home Page]| [Topics]| [Index]|] . Dog Bites . An ounce of prevention protects kids from dog teeth . Introduction . Why dogs bite the hand that feeds them . An ounce of prevention . Be a Tree . I . Introduction . ... (See also Similar Pages)

Nebraska Behavioral Biology Group Home Page — http://cricket unl.edu/NBBG.html (Score: 59, Size: 12κ) NBBG Resources Internet Animal Behavior WWW Biology WWWMiscellaneous.

NEBRASKA BEHAVIORAL BIOLOGY GROUP . Pages served since June 1, 1995: 46278. The pages at this site look best when viewed with Netscape Navigator 1.1.

Pet Behavior & Training Seminars & Conferences . Chicago-land Area . Instructor's Workshop "How to Make Your Pet Classes User Friendly" . Lecturer: Terry Ryan. Terry is well known for her ability to be creative in all aspects of training. She is the author of ALPHAbetize ... — [62] http://users.aol.com/jemyers/nar_sem.htm (14к)

PSYCOLOQUY by topic base-rate, brain-rhythms, categorization, consciousness, data-archive, eeg-chaos, evolution-thinking, fodor-representation, frame-problem, frontal-cortex, human-animal-bond, language-comprehension, language-network, least-squares, ... — [70] http://cogsci.ecs.soton.ac.uk/~lac/topics.html (41к)

Socinsct Subscriptions NBBG Home . Applied Ethology Mailing List . How to subscribe . To subscribe to the Applied Ethology mailing list send the an e-mail message to: . applied-ethology-request @sask.usask.ca . Place the following in the text: . subscribe ... — [83] http://cricket.unl.edu/NBBG/Listservers/AppEth. html (1к)

Animal Care

Animals/Pets Cats | Dogs | Llamas | Veterinarians | Wildlife Rehabilitation. Cats . Cat Fanciers . Information on ca⁻ breeds, cat shows, feline medicine, animal welfare, and other cat topics..Dogs . Dogs! . Llamas . ... — [70] http://webvista.com/tlh/anml/ (1к)

Canine Web Welcome to Canine Web, maintained by Terri Watson http://snapple.cs.washington.edu:600/canine/canine.html (Score: 61, Size: 13к)

Complete List of Dog-Related Email Lists This compilation is Copyright 1995 by Cindy Tittle Moore. . The posted version may be found on rtfm.mit.edu under pub/usenet/news.answers/dogs-faq/email-lists; to get a copy by E-mail, send a message to mail-server@rtfm.mit.edu with send .. http://www.zmall.com/ pet_talk/dog-faqs/lists/email-list.html (Score: 54, Size: 48к)

Connections to Other Canine Related WEB Sites American Canine Association Inc. ACAcanines@AOL.com . Connections to Articles at Other Locations . The list below is a list of connections to other canine related WEB pages on the Internet. The appearance of names on this list does not .. http://www.eternin c.com/ aca/aca100.html (Score: 59, Size: 8к)

Cyberpet Veterinary Hospital, OSU Cyberpet Veterinary Hospital Waiting Room . The Ohio State University . College of Veterinary

Medicine . These exercises are intended for students in Veterinary Medicine. Welcome to the Cyberpet Veterinary Hospital. The faculty here at ... —[79] http://www.vet.ohio-state.edu/case/testpg.html (1к)

Dog Activity Directory Directory of Dog Activities. The following is a list of addresses where you can write for further information about "Wonderful Things You Can Do With Your Mixed Breed Dog". If you notice any errors or have any updates, contact me at rmm7e@virginia.edu....http://www.med.virginia.edu/~rmm7e/dogact.html - size 2к - 16 Aug 95

Dr. Jim's Virtual Veterinary Clinic Dr. Jim's Virtual Veterinary Clinic Dog and cat owners' alert: great tips on feline and canine pet care. The question-and-answer format in the Virtual Clinics is especially informative. -[58] http://rampages.onramp.net/~drjim/ (6к)

Getting A Pet A pet is for life, not just for Christmas . There are whole FAQs written on this subject including the Getting A Dog FAQ and the Getting A Cat FAQ. There is also a new site that contains similar info as below, but in *much* greater detail. ... — [56] http://www.tezcat.com/~ermiller/getapet.html (12к)

MERCY RESCUE NET: Useful Animal Tips USEFUL ANIMAL TIPS . Mercy Rescue Net . . — [58] http://www.aaarf.org/default/h4-tips.htm (1к)

NetVet - Cat Home Page Electronic Zoo/NetVet - Cats . Pet Cats . Big Cats . Other . Commercial . Pet Cats . Socks, the White House Cat . Cat Fanciers' Home Page . WWW Cat Map . Feline Information Page . rec.pets.cats . ... — [58] http://netvet.wustl.edu/cats.htm (14к)

NetVet - Dog Home Page Electronic Zoo/NetVet - Dogs . Pet Dogs . Other Canines . Commercial . Pet Dogs . Informational Dog-Related Web Sites (Cindy Tittle Moore) . Canine Web . Dogs WWW Page . The Canine Connection . Dog Care (4H Info) ... — [58] http://netvet.wustl.edu/dogs.htm (33к)

NetVet Web Searching Tools Web Searching Tools. Veterinary. General . Veterinary Searches . NetVet Gopher Search . World Wide Web Virtual Library - Veterinary Medicine . Yahoo WWW Guide - Veterinary Science . EINet Galaxy - Veterinary .. — [64] http://netvet.wustl.edu/search.htm (7к)

PetStation— http://petstation.com/ (Score 83, Size 5к)— Internet Home Base For Animal People — . The purity of a person's heart . Can be quickly measured . By how they regard animals. . SPONSOR OF THE WEEK: "Toys For Birds That Like To Screw Around" . Hey Look!! . ... (See also Similar Pages)

Safe Pet Guidelines Safe Pet Guidelines. SAFE PET GUIDELINES. Pets are wonderful! Anyone who has ever had a pet knows that the unconditional love and acceptance we receive is unlike what we generally experience within human relationships. This is especially important to us... http://www.sonic.net/~pals/sfptgid.html - size 19к - 28 Jul 95

USENET FAQs - rec.pets.dogs Subgroups . info . FAQs in this newsgroup . rec.pets.dogs: American Kennel Club FAQ . rec.pets.dogs: Behavior: Understanding and Modifying FAQ . rec.pets.dogs: Breeding Your Dog FAQ . rec.pets.dogs: Akitas Breed-FAQ . rec.pets.dogs:... http://www.cis.ohio-state.edu/hypertext/faq/bn-gusenet/rec/pets/dogs/top.html (Score: 54,Size: 8к)

What Is A Caregiver?Most of the volunteers who become involved with NMWR do so by accident. We are the person calling on the phone with an injured or "orphaned" animal or bird that needs help immediately!!! In my case it was a baby red squirrel that was so cold it ... — [61] http://aliens.com/business/nmwr/scaregiv.html (3к)

Pet Loss

EVERLASTING STONE PRODUCTS, the world's premier designers and makers of memorial stones, urns, and caskets for pets. . Gayle moved to Vermont about 15 years ago, and shortly afterward suffered the loss of the family dog. After her husband stayed up half the night ... — [59] http://plainfield.bypass.com/stone/ (5к)

Loss of ones' animal partner Loss of ones' animal partner by: Dogzoo. GRIEF AND PET LOSS. Just how deep are the feelings a zoo has for their animals? well, I know several who have become severely depressed and suicidal when they have lost or parted from their animals. The depth of... http://www.av.qnet.com/~stasya/loss.htm - size 10к - 23 Sep 95

Loss of ones' animal partner Loss of ones' animal partner. GRIEF AND PET LOSS. Just how deep are the feelings a zoo has for their animals? well, I know several who have become severely depressed and suicidal when they have lost or parted from their animals. The depth of feelings... http://www.c2.org/~doglover/loss.html - size 9к - 6 Nov 95

Pet Loss Pets are a part of one's family. The loss of a cherished pet is no less a source of grief than the loss of a child. Follows some materials that may help one come to grips with the loss of a furred child. These are plain text files that should be ... —[71] http://www.tapr.org/~n2wx/grief/ (1к)

srb9306 ISSN: 1052-5378. Animal Euthanasia. Provided by the Animal Welfare Information Center United States Department of Agriculture National Agricultural Library. United States Department of Agriculture National Agricultural Library 10301 Baltimore Blvd.... http://netvet.wustl.edu/org/awic/bib /srb9306.htm - size 84к - 13 Dec 95

Veterinary Education and Professional Services

Veterinary: AN ILLUSTRATED HISTORY OF VETERINARY MEDICINE: Culture. Dunlop, Williams AN ILLUSTRATED HISTORY OF VETERINARY MEDICINE: Animals in Culture Robert H. Dunlop, DVM, Univ. of Minnesota, College of Veterinary Medicine, St. Paul, MN and...http://www.mosby.com/ Mosby/Catalogs/Veterinary/LARGEANIMAL/0-8016-3209-9.html - size 3к - 9 Nov 95

A list of veterinary and Medical Services Links to Other Veterinary and Medical Servers . Links to other lists . NetVet's list of Colleges of Veterinary Medicine . NetVet's list of Veterinary and Animal Organizations. Michigan State's List. Veterinary Colleges . Auburn ... — [62] http://www.vet.ksu.edu/othersrv.htm (5к)

About Tufts University Tufts University . Chartered as a liberal arts college in 1852, Tufts today is a small, complex, private university offering highly diversified programs in engineering and applied sciences, liberal arts, law and diplomacy, medicine, ... — [60] http://www.eotc.tufts.edu/Documents/Tufts-Des.html (2к)

Animal Shelters Shelters and All-Breed Rescue Organizations . This is a list of on-line shelter and rescue organization information that I've compiled from posts to rec.pets.dogs.rescue and from submissions from Erin Miller. Please do not treat this list as ... — [59] http://pasture.ecn.purdue.edu/~laird/Dogs/Rescue/shelters.ht ml (12к)

Breed Rescue Organizations Rescue Organizations . This is a list of on-line rescue organization information that I've compiled from posts to rec.pets.dogs.rescue and from submissions from Erin Miller. Please do not treat this list as complete. If you need to contact a ... — [56]http://pasture.ecn.purdue.edu/~laird/Dogs/Rescue/bro.html (21к)

Center to Study Human-Animal Relationships and Environments. Center to Study Human-Animal Relationships and Environments. Back to the Health Organizations Page. Back to the Good Health Web. Director P.O. Box 734, Mayo Memorial Building 420 Delaware Street, SE Minneapolis, , MN 55455. (612)624-5909 (Voice) Abstract....http://www.social.com/health/nhic/data/ hr2000/hr2057.html - size 1к - 18 Sep 95

Chicago Shelters Chicago-area Shelters . If you work with a shelter (or breed rescue organization) and are interested in having a web page created for free for your organization send an email to Erin Miller. . Note: this is not an endorsement for any of ... — [56] http://www.tezcat.com/~ermiller/shelters.html (5к)

College of Veterinary Medicine Homepage The College of Veterinary Medicine . The University of Tennessee . Welcome to The University of Tennessee College of Veterinary Medicine World Wide Web Server. This server provides information about a wide range of acitivies ... — [61] http://funnelweb.utcc.utk.edu/vet/ (4к)

Cornell's College of Veterinary Medicine Cornell Vet Web Resource . Welcome to the Cornell University College of Veterinary Medicine Web Server. . Here is some general information about the Vet College and the Diagnostic Lab. . Check out the following local services: . ... — [59] http://zoo.vet.cornell.edu/ (3к)

Introduction to the School of Veterinary Medicine School of Veterinary Medicine, University of California, Davis . Office of the Dean: . Telephone:(916)-752-1360 . Fax:(916)-752-2801 . E-Mail:webmaster@vmdean.ucdavis.edu . VETERINARY MEDICINE IN DYNAMIC CHANGE TO MEET THE NEEDS OF ... —[55] http://www.vetnet.ucdavis.edu/svm.htm (15к)

NetVet Veterinary Resources Home PageNetVet . Veterinary Resources . featuring . The Electronic Zoo . Text and Non-Netscape Browsers, [Start Here] . NetVet &amp the Electronic Zoo originate from the vivid imagination and late night web-surfing of Dr. Ken Boschert, a ... — [73] http:// netvet.wustl.edu/ (5к)

No Title Animal Funds of America. 1801 American Humane Association (303-792-9900) Protecting children and animals from neglect, abuse, cruelty, and exploitation since 1877. Helping those who cannot help themselves by building an aware and caring society. 21.7%... ttp://agate.larc.nasa.gov/cfc/docs/CFC. Animal.html - size 6к - 21 Sep 95

Purdue University School of Veterinary Medicine Lynn Hall, West Lafayette, Indiana 47907 . What's New: Links to new pages on our server: . Medical Illustration opens its pages. Veterinary Medicine: An Illustrated History by Robert H. Dunlop and David J. Williams . Image ... — [74] http://vet.purdue.edu/ (5к)

Purdue University School of Veterinary Medicine summary As the 21st Century nears, Indiana's only School of Veterinary Medicine is closing-in on its goal of world leadership in veterinary medical teaching, service, and scientific investigation. As the SVM celebrates its 35th anniversary, its new ... — [61] http://vet.purdue.edu/info/about_svm.html(4к)

Special Hospital and Community Programs Special Hospital and Community Programs. The Veterinary Teaching Hospital at Colorado State University is an active participant in many local, regional, and statewide programs and concerns. We feel we have important roles to play and contributions to make... http://www.vth.colostate.edu/vth/special.html - size 2к - 19 Oct 95

The World-Wide Web Virtual Library: Veterinary Medicine (Biosciences) Veterinary Medicine (Biosciences) . What's New . Meetings and Conferences . Veterinary Images . Veterinary Publications. Veterinary Medical Degree Programs . Veterinary Laws and Regulations . World Wide Web sites . Gopher sites . Mailing Lists ... — [61] http://ss.niah.affrc.go.jp/NIAH/mirror/vetmed/vetmed.html (80к)

University of Pennsylvania School of Veterinary Medicine Welcome to the experimental World Wide Web server for the University of Pennsylvania School of Veterinary Medicine. The server is currently under construction - those items marked with (*) remain undeveloped. . The Office of the Dean (*) ... — [51] http://www.vet.upenn.edu/ (3к)

Veterinary Medicine Libraries Links, contact information and addresses for major veterinary medicine collections in Canada, United States, Europe, Africa and the Middle East. — [53] http://duke.usask.ca/~ladd/vet_libraries.html (11к)

Veterinary Medicine Resources - Schools Worldwide list of Schools of Veterinary Medicine plus the UPenn Vet School newsgroup. — [53] http://cahpwww.nbc.upenn.edu/vetmed/vetmed1.htm (7к)

Veterinary and Animal Organizations Veterinary & Animal Organizations . Science and Research Organizations . Animal Welfare and Rights Organizations . Commercial Animal Organizations . Caveat emptor!. Science and Research Organizations . WWW Virtual Library: ... —[63] http:// ss.niah.affrc.go.jp/NIAH/mirror/vetmed/org.html (49к)

Veterinary Reference Resources Animal Welfare Information Center (USDA-NAL) . Searching the Journal Literature for Animal Welfare Information (Johns Hopkins University) . Veterinary Medical Libraries Home Page . Veterinary Medical Libraries Section of Medical ... — [57] http://netvet.wustl.edu/vcp.htm (8к)

Veterinary and Animal LISTSERV Archives Veterinary & Animal LISTSERV Archives . Descriptions . All E-Mail Groups . Usenet Newsgroups . ABSNET (Animal Behaviour Society Newsletter) . AGDG (Animal Geneticists Discussion Group) . AGILITY-L (Dog Agility ... — [60] http://netvet.wustl.edu/vmla.htm (10к)

Wildlife Rehabilitation FAQ WLREHAB (Wildlife Rehabilitation)
Frequently Asked Questions (FAQ) . This FAQ is distributed on
the 15th of each month to the WLREHAB mailing list. To subscribe to that list, send an email message to: LISTSERV@
VM1.NODAK.EDU . with a blank ... —[81]http://www.tiac.net
/users/sbr/wlrehab.html (14к)

Zoological E-mail Directory This directory is an attempt to provide individuals who work with animals a means of locating colleagues
on the Internet. The following people are included: . Zoo and
aquarium employees . Administrators of animal-related associations and ... [62] http://www.aazk.ind.net/zoodir/ (1к)

Index

AAT (animal-assisted therapy), 102–4, 127, 129–34, 138, 142–43, 153–54; dolphins in, 138–39; guidelines for, 155–59; history of, 132–33. *See also* Delta Society; Pets, as therapy; Riding programs
Adelphi University, 82
ADHD (attention-deficit hyperactive disorder), 142–43. *See also* Devereux Foundation
AKC (American Kennel Club), 128
AMA (American Medical Association), 6
Ambivalence toward dogs, 235–38
American Veterinary Medical Association. *See* AVMA
Anderson, Robert, 130
Animal bites, 212. *See also* Dog bite
Animal collectors, 251–56
Animal control, 251 56. *See also* Dogs, stray; Euthanasia; Surplus dogs
Animal cruelty, 30–31, 52–53. *See also* Animal welfare; Humane societies
Animal Medical Center, 205
Animal shelters, 24
Animals in movies. *See* Movies and television
Animal welfare, 157–58. *See also* Humane societies
Aquarium, for relaxation, 7, 105–10
ASPCA (American Society for the Prevention of Cruelty to Animals), 247, 252

Assistance dogs, 147–49
Autism, 102, 136–38
AVMA (American Veterinary Medical Association), 45, 241
Avoiding bites, 218–19. *See also* Dog bite

Bachelard, Gaston, 118–19
Baltimore, 255. *See also* Dogs, stray
Beck, Alan, 33, 55–56, 74, 213–14, 217, 222, 228–29, 251
Benson, Herbert, 117–18
Berger, John, 208
Berzon, David, 215
Bestiality. *See* Sexual contact
Bieber, Natalie, 149
Birds, 84
Bite. *See* Dog bite
Blind people, and use of dogs. *See* Assistance dogs
Blood pressure, 79, 80–81, 105–9
Bond, Simon, 71
Borchelt, Peter, 222
Brickel, Clark, 135
Burch, Mary, 158
Bustad, Leo, 125, 151, 154

Cain, Ann, 41, 268
Campbell, Carol, 137
Camus, Albert, 15–16, 202
Cannibalism of pets, 22–23
Cat scratch disease, 246
CDC, 213, 218
Children, 272–76. *See also* Dog bite; Fatal dog bite
Christianity, 64–66, 75
Cohen, Susan, 205–6

Coleridge, Samuel, 124
Condoret, Ange, 102–3
Coppinger, Raymond, 168, 170. *See also* Domestication
Corson, Samuel and Elizabeth, 94, 125, 134–35, 150–51

Death of a pet, 20–25, 76, 195–208
Declawing, of cats, 246
De Hoff, John, 215
Delta Society, 156, 158–59, 206
Dental surgery, 7. *See also* Hypnosis
Devereux Foundation, 121, 142–47
Dog: behavior of, 171–81; body language of, 175; and dominance, 177–79, 278–79; feces of, 243–45, 247–50; heat, 189–90; packs, 176–79 (*see also* Domestication); pedigree, 188; population, 229–30, 241–42, 261–63; and play, 179–81
Dog bite, 183–84, 209–27. *See also* Avoiding bites; Fatal dog bite
Dogs: attack-trained, 250; disease from, 243–48 (*see also* Rabies; *Toxoplasmosis*; VLM); stray, 216–18, 227–35; urban stray, 231–34, 242–43, 247–50
Dog worms. See VLM
Dolphins, 138–39
Domestication, 60, 165–67
Dressing pets, 18–19
Dunn, Kathleen, 201, 205

Elderly. *See* Older adults
Euthanasia, 202–3, 207–8. *See also* Death of a pet
Evolution, 59
Exotic animals, 251–53. *See also* Animal control
Exotic pets, 77

Family membership. *See* Pets, as family

Famous pets, 41
Fatal dog bite, 219–27. *See also* Dog bite
Feeding animals, 16–18
Four-H (4-H), 13, 157
Fox, Michael, 90, 175
Frank, Harold, 236
Freud, Sigmund, 65, 127, 182, 204
Friedmann, Erika, 2–4, 80–82, 104

Gammonley, Judith, 129
Gershman, Kenneth, 218
Ginsberg, Benson, 173
Goodman, Joan, 137
Goodman, Laura, 80, 88
Goodman, Melissa, 80
Gould, Stephen Jay, 168. *See also* Domestication
Grandin, Temple, 136–37
Green, Leonard, 143. *See also* Devereux Foundation
Green Chimneys. *See* Ross, Sam
Guide dogs. *See* Assistance dogs

Hanna, Thomas, 214
Harlow, Harry, 68
Harris, David, 213–14
Harris, James, 200–201
Health departments, 258. *See also* New York City Department of Health
Heart disease, 2–8, 58
Hediger, Heini, 54
Helplessness, 58
Hollander, Mark, 239
Hopkins, Gerard Manley, 72
Humane societies, 258–63. *See also* ASPCA
Hutton, James, 52–53
Hypnosis, 112–16. *See also* Aquarium, for relaxation

Iannuzzi, Dorothy, 159
Igou, Sue, 136
Imperato, Pascal, 214

JAMA (*Journal of the American Medical Association*), 6, 221
Johnson, Virginia, 80

Jones, Barbara, 214

Katcher, Aaron, 2, 46, 74, 76, 78, 87, 101, 104, 113, 137, 142, 192, 201, 205–7, 236
Kennedy, Leslie, 219
Kennedy, Robert, 136
Kinsey, Alfred, 54

Lassie, 70, 209. *See also* Movies and television
Laws, 247, 257. *See also* Pet bans; Scoop laws
Leboyer, Frederick, 270–71
Lee, David, 152
Lee, Fran, 245
Levinson, Boris, 53, 61, 93–94, 133–34, 168
Lima State Hospital, 152–53
Lockwood, Randall, 53, 74, 213, 222. *See also* Dog bite; Fatal dog bite
Loney, Jan, 128
Looking at life, 101. *See also* Aquarium, for relaxation
Lorenz, Konrad, 119, 236–38
Lynch, James, 2, 78, 104

Macdonald, Alasdair, 14, 47
Mandelbrot, Benoit, 123
Masters, William, 80
McCulloch, Michael, 51, 140–42
Mech, David, 173
Melson, Gail, 61
Men and touch. *See* Pets, touching
Merton, Peter, 154
Messent, Peter, 73–74, 175
Money, John, 55
Mourning a pet, 200–207. *See also* Death of a pet
Movies and television, 168–70, 172–73, 183. *See also* Mythical animals
Multiple animal owners. *See* Animal collectors
Murie, Adolf, 173
Mythical animals, 64–65, 194

NARHA (North American Riding for the Handicapped Asso-

ciation). *See* Riding programs
Neoteny, 168–70. *See also* Domestication
New York City, 212–14, 228, 244, 247–63
New York City Department of Health, 55–56, 248
Nixon, Richard, 41
Nurturing, 58–60. *See also* Psychology of ownership

Older adults, 126, 130, 150–52, 256–58

Parenting. *See* Psychology of ownership
Patronek, Gary, 203, 261
Pennsylvania, University of. *See* University of Pennsylvania
People Pet Partnership Program. *See* Bustad, Leo
Pérez, Cynthia, 246
Perin, Constance, 68–69, 71
Pet bans, 256–58. *See also* Laws
Pet death. *See* Death of a pet
Pet names, 11–13
Pets, 4; children with, 61–62, 93–94; intimacy with, 78, 83, 90–95; as family, 29, 40; perception of, 73; as self, 63; sleeping with, 19–20, 49, 70, 73; talking to, 14–15, 78, 80, 82, 95; as therapy, 125–59; touching, 43, 79, 83–86, 88–89.
Pinchney, Lee, 219
Pit bulls, 221
Play, 31–33
Predation. *See* Dog bite
Prisons, pets in, 152–54
Psychiatric settings, 136
Psychology of ownership, 184–94, 238–40, 267–80
Puppy mills, 24–25
Purdue University, 205
Purdy Correction Center, 154

Quackenbush, Jamie, 201

Rabies, 215. *See also* Dog bite
Redefer, Laurel, 137
Riding programs, 149–50. *See also*
    AAT
Robin, Michael, 47–48, 201
Rogers, Carl, 91–92
Roosevelt, Franklin, 41
Rosenberg, Marc, 76, 203
Ross, Sam, 142–43
Rowan, Andrew, 159
Rubin, Hildy, 228
Ruby, Jay, 13

Sacks, Jeffrey, 218
Sacks, Oliver, 136–37
Schenkel, Rudolph, 174
Scoop laws, 247–50. *See also*
    Laws; Pet bans
Sexual conflicts, 49–50
Sexual contact, with pets, 54–57
Sexuality, of pets, 191–94
Sleeping with pets. *See* Pets,
    sleeping with
Smith, Betsy, 138–39
Snakes, 77
Social celebrations, 18
Spaying/neutering of pets, 246,
    262
Stewart, Mary, 201–2
Stray dogs. *See* Dogs, stray
Strimple, Earl, 153
Stuffed animals, 66–68
Surplus dogs, 261–63. *See also*
    Animal control

Talking to pets. *See* Pets, talking
    to
Therapeutic horseback riding. *See*
    Riding programs
Thompson, Mary, 136
Thoreau, Henry David, 121–23
Touch. *See* Pets, touching
Toxocara canis. See VLM
Toxoplasmosis, 245–46
Type A, 9–10. *See also* Heart dis-
    ease

Ulrich, Roger, 116
University of California at Davis,
    205
University of Pennsylvania,
    20–21, 110, 137, 201, 205–6,
    223

Vampires. *See* Mythical animals
Van de Castle, Robert, 72
VLM (*visceral larval migrans*),
    244–46. *See also* Dogs, dis-
    ease from
Voith, Victoria, 51, 222, 223–25

Walsh, Paul, 154
Walthner-Toews, David, 130
Washington State University. *See*
    Bustad, Leo
Werewolves. *See* Mythical ani-
    mals
White House Conference on
    Aging, 257. *See also* Older
    adults
Widmer, Pat, 193
Wilkins, Gregory, 143
Wilson, E. O., 123
Wolf, 166–67, 170, 173–75. *See
    also* Domestication
Wolf boy. *See* Mythical animals
Women and touch. *See* Pets,
    touching
Woodhouse, Barbara, 178
Woolpy, Jerome, 173. *See also*
    Wolf
Worth, Dooley, 251–52
Wright, John, 218

Yates, Judy, 129
Young, Stanley, 173

Zasloff, Ruth, 74
Zee, Alysia, 147–48
Zoophilia. *See* Sexual contact